Nuclear Winter™

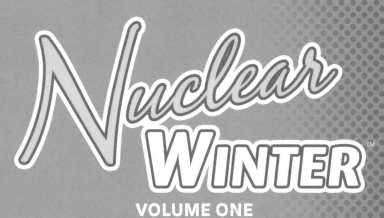

VOLUME ONE

BOOM! BOX™

Ross Richie CEO & Founder
Matt Gagnon Editor-In-Chief
Filip Sablik President of Publishing & Marketing
Stephen Christy President of Development
Lance Kreiter VP of Licensing & Merchandising
Phil Barbaro VP of Finance
Arune Singh VP of Marketing
Bryce Carlson Managing Editor
Scott Newman Production Design Manager
Kate Henning Operations Manager
Sierra Hahn Senior Editor
Dafna Pleban Editor, Talent Development
Shannon Watters Editor
Eric Harburn Editor
Whitney Leopard Editor
Cameron Chittock Editor
Chris Rosa Associate Editor
Matthew Levine Associate Editor
Sophie Philips-Roberts Assistant Editor

Amanda LaFranco Executive Assistant
Katalina Holland Editorial Administrative Assistant
Jillian Crab Production Designer
Michelle Ankley Production Designer
Kara Leopard Production Designer
Marie Krupina Production Designer
Grace Park Production Design Assistant
Chelsea Roberts Production Design Assistant
Elizabeth Loughridge Accounting Coordinator
Stephanie Hocutt Social Media Coordinator
José Meza Event Coordinator
Holly Aitchison Operations Coordinator
Megan Christopher Operations Assistant
Rodrigo Hernandez Mailroom Assistant
Morgan Perry Direct Market Representative
Cat O'Grady Marketing Assistant
Liz Almendarez Accounting Administrative Assistant
Cornelia Tzana Administrative Assistant

NUCLEAR WINTER Volume One, May 2018. Published by BOOM! Box, a division of Boom Entertainment, Inc. Nuclear Winter is ™ & © 2018 Caroline Breault. All rights reserved. BOOM! Box™ and the BOOM! Box logo are trademarks of Boom Entertainment, Inc., registered in various countries and categories. All characters, events, and institutions depicted herein are fictional. Any similarity between any of the names, characters, persons, events, and/or institutions in this publication to actual names, characters, and persons, whether living or dead, events, and/or institutions is unintended and purely coincidental. BOOM! Box does not read or accept unsolicited submissions of ideas, stories, or artwork.

BOOM! Studios, 5670 Wilshire Boulevard, Suite 400, Los Angeles, CA 90036-5679. Printed in China. First Printing.

ISBN: 978-1-68415-163-9, eISBN: 978-1-61398-948-7

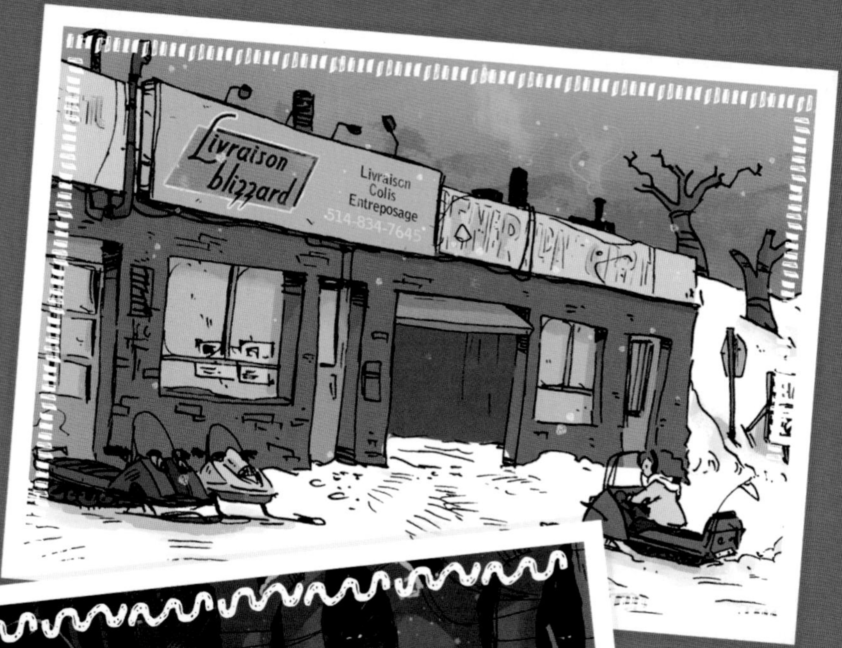
Livraison blizzard
Livraison
Colis
Entreposage
514-834-7645
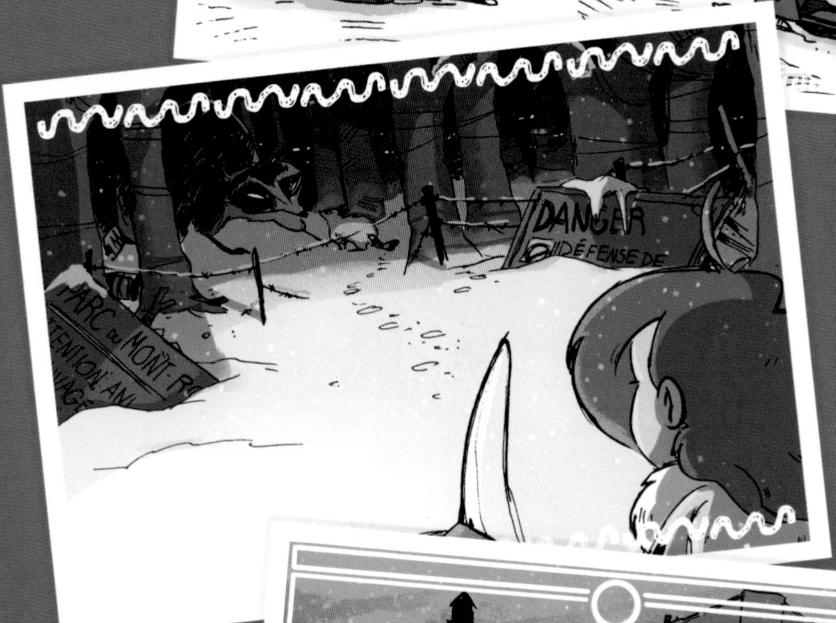
DANGER
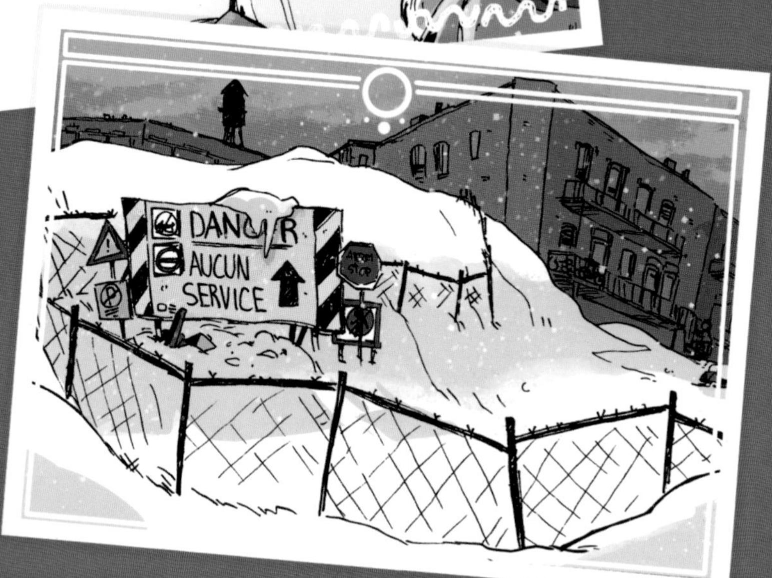
AUCUN
SERVICE

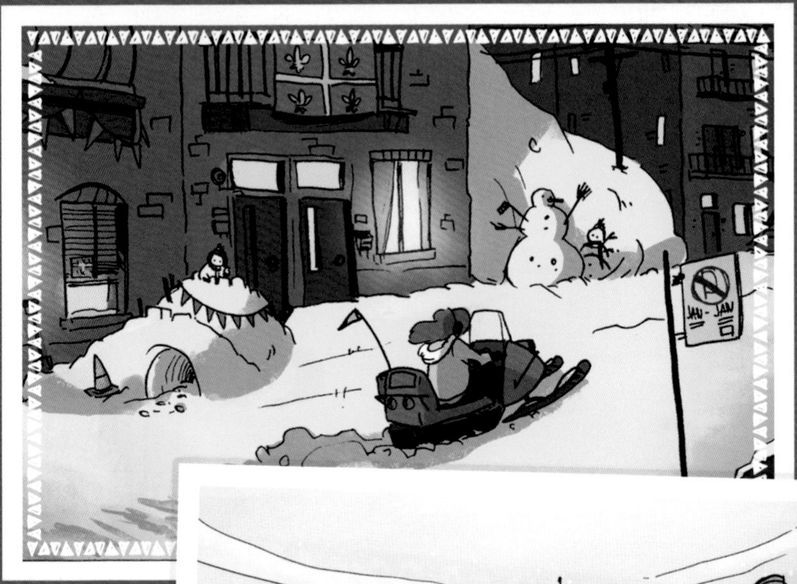

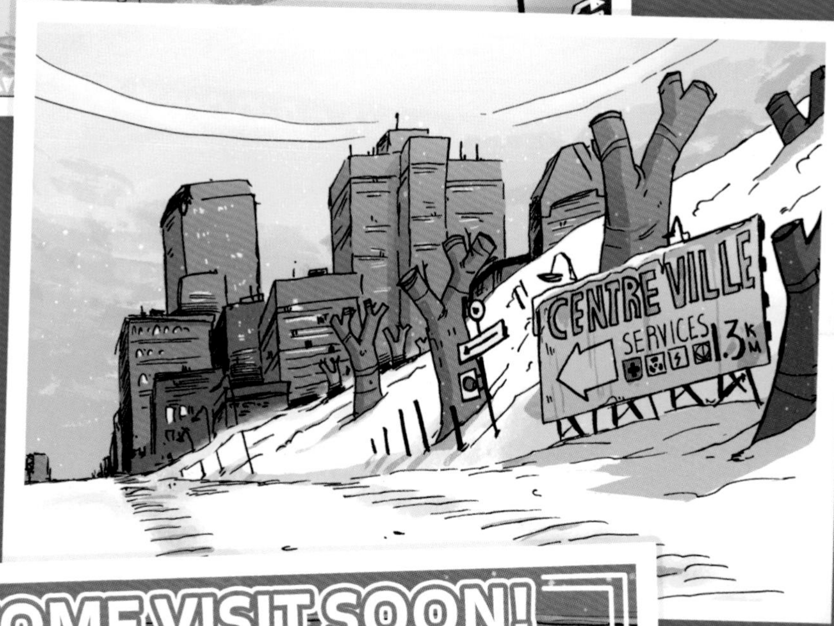
CENTRE VILLE
SERVICES
1.3 KM

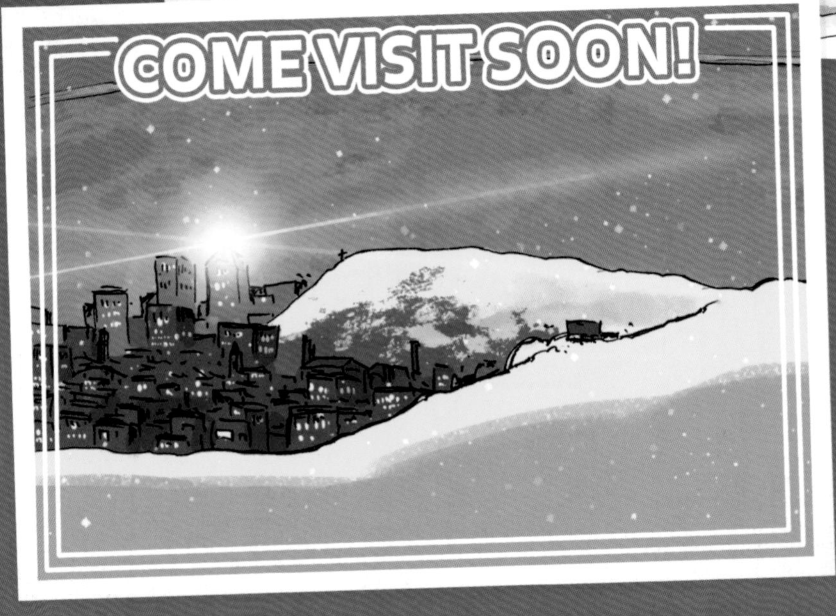
COME VISIT SOON!

Written & Illustrated by
Cab

Letters by
Jim Campbell

Designer
Kara Leopard

Assistant Editor
Sophie Philips-Roberts

Editor
Shannon Watters

Special thanks to Carolyn Yates for Canadian
consultation on the English translation.

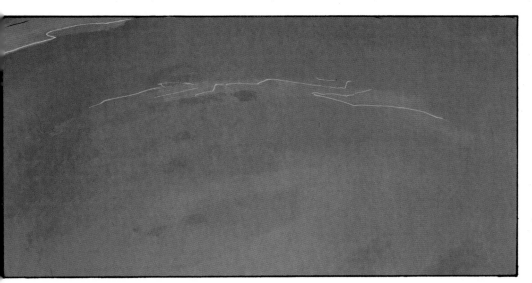

CHAPTER 1
THE ST-JEAN STORM

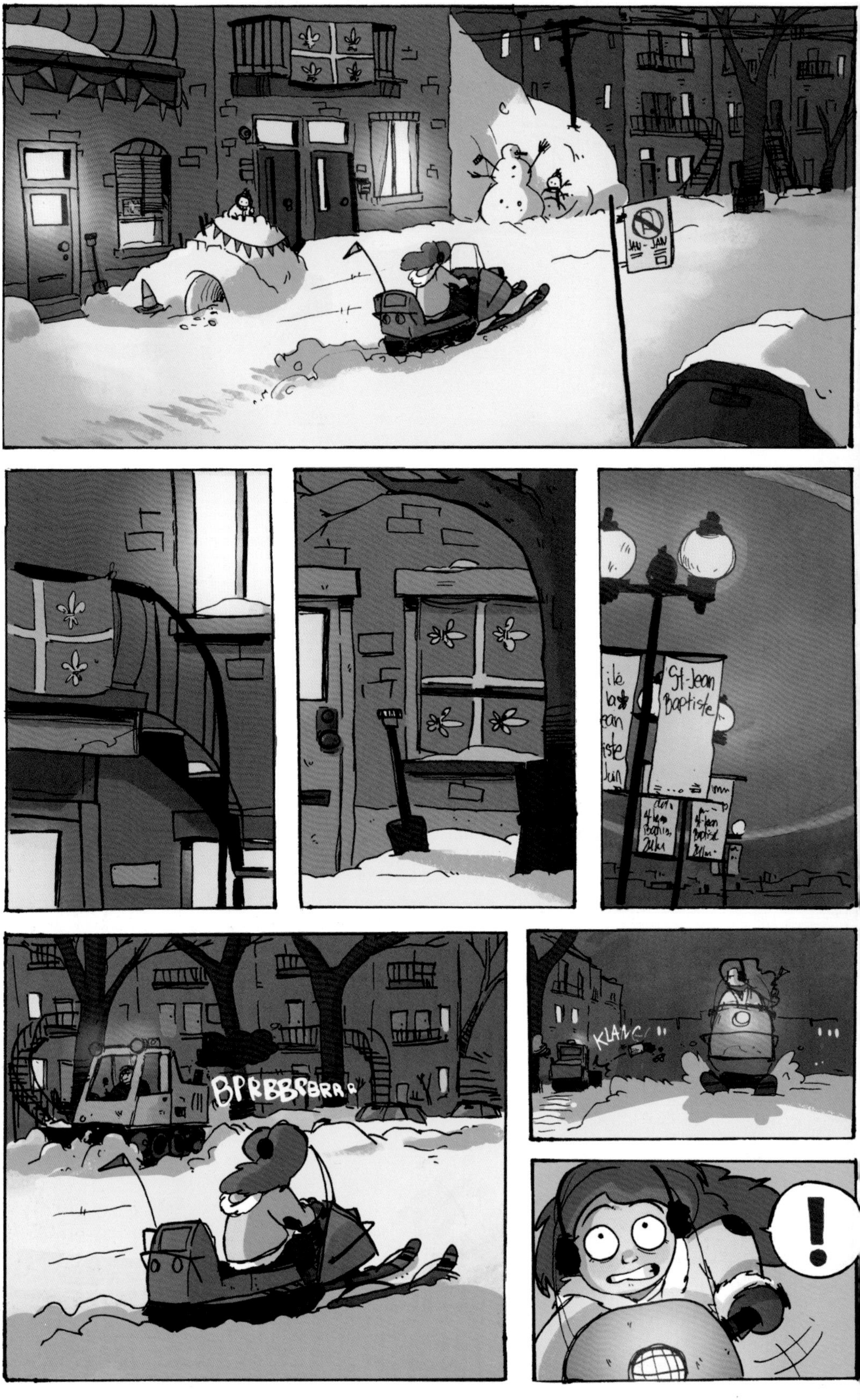

JAN - JAN
St-Jean Baptiste
BPRBBRBRRR
KLANG!
!

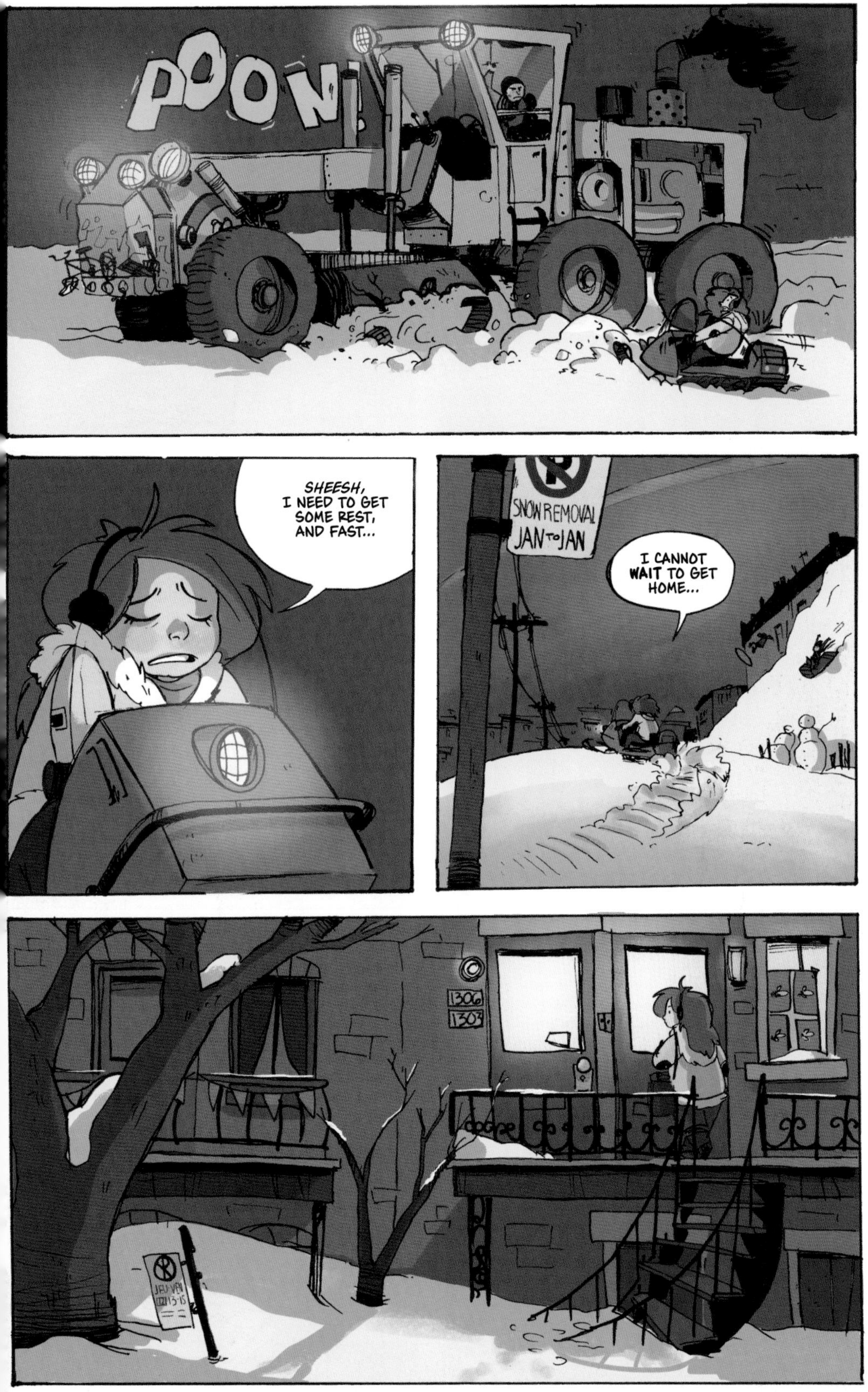
POON!
SHEESH, I NEED TO GET SOME REST, AND FAST...
SNOW REMOVAL JAN TO JAN
I CANNOT WAIT TO GET HOME...
1306
1303

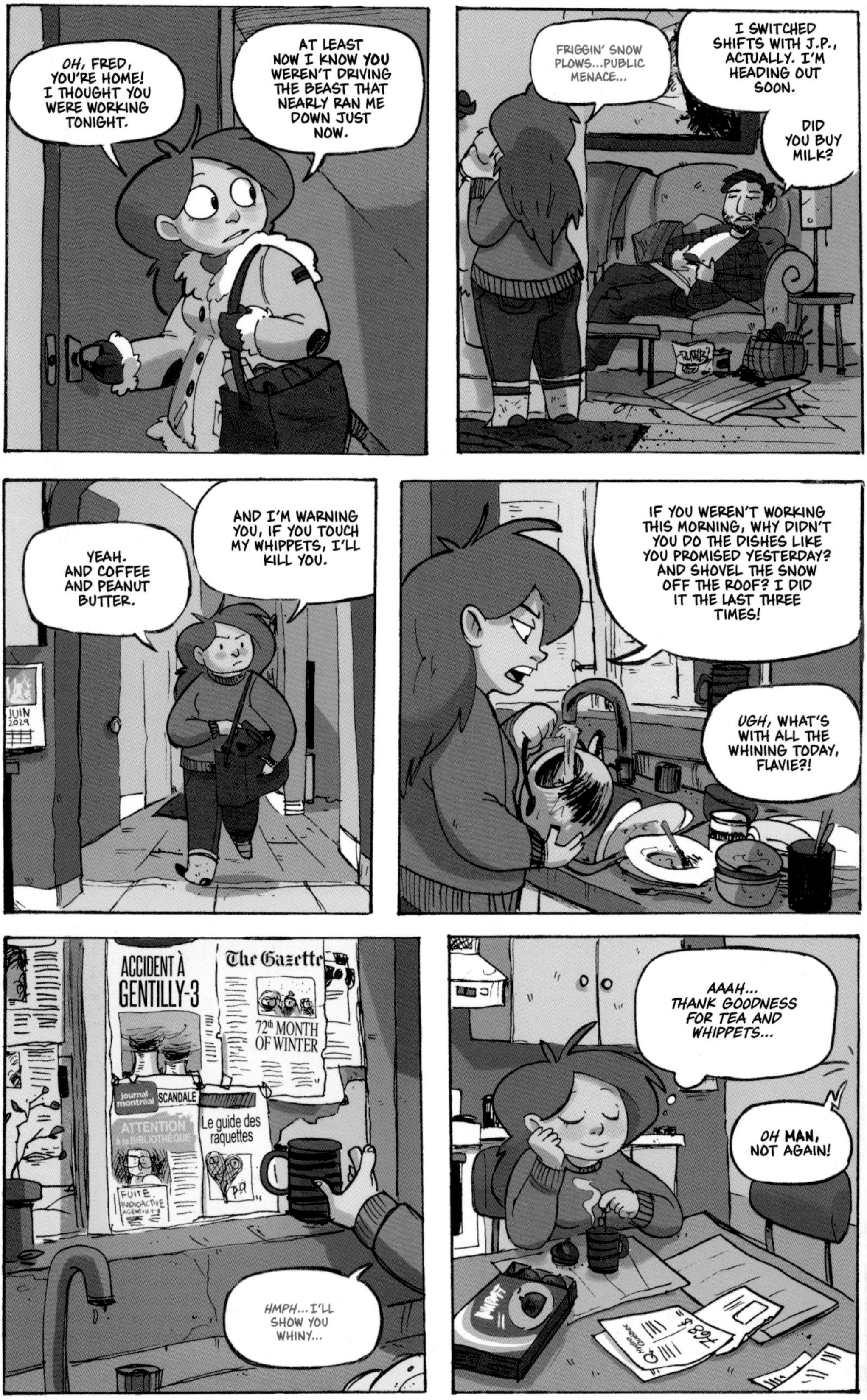

OH, FRED, YOU'RE HOME! I THOUGHT YOU WERE WORKING TONIGHT.
AT LEAST NOW I KNOW YOU WEREN'T DRIVING THE BEAST THAT NEARLY RAN ME DOWN JUST NOW.
FRIGGIN' SNOW PLOWS...PUBLIC MENACE...
I SWITCHED SHIFTS WITH J.P., ACTUALLY. I'M HEADING OUT SOON.
DID YOU BUY MILK?
YEAH. AND COFFEE AND PEANUT BUTTER.
AND I'M WARNING YOU, IF YOU TOUCH MY WHIPPETS, I'LL KILL YOU.
JUIN 2029
IF YOU WEREN'T WORKING THIS MORNING, WHY DIDN'T YOU DO THE DISHES LIKE YOU PROMISED YESTERDAY? AND SHOVEL THE SNOW OFF THE ROOF? I DID IT THE LAST THREE TIMES!
UGH, WHAT'S WITH ALL THE WHINING TODAY, FLAVIE?!
ACCIDENT À GENTILLY-3
The Gazette
72th MONTH OF WINTER
journal montréal
SCANDALE
ATTENTION à la BIBLIOTHÈQUE
Le guide des raquettes
HMPH...I'LL SHOW YOU WHINY...
AAAH... THANK GOODNESS FOR TEA AND WHIPPETS...
OH MAN, NOT AGAIN!

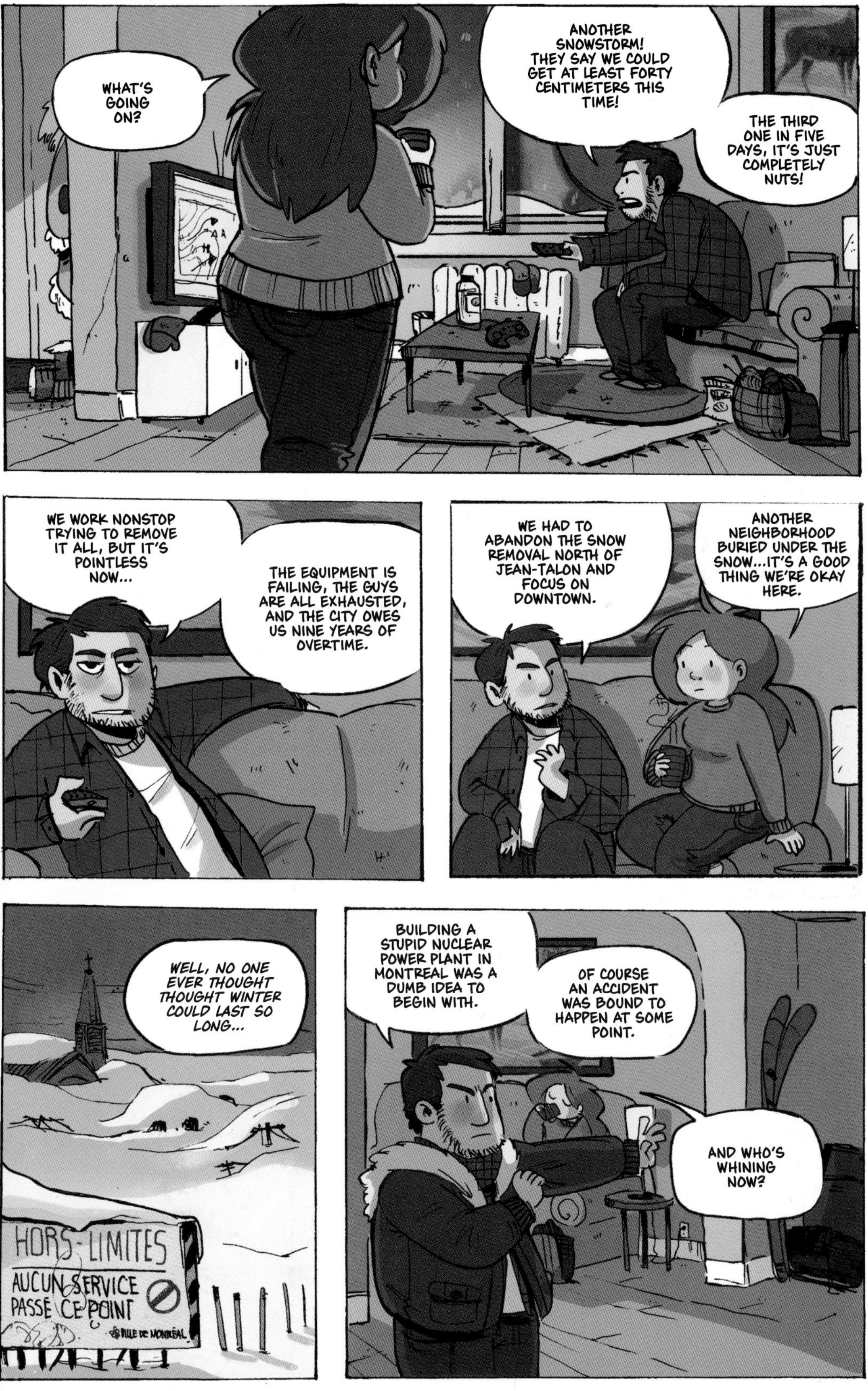
WHAT'S GOING ON?
ANOTHER SNOWSTORM! THEY SAY WE COULD GET AT LEAST FORTY CENTIMETERS THIS TIME!
THE THIRD ONE IN FIVE DAYS, IT'S JUST COMPLETELY NUTS!
WE WORK NONSTOP TRYING TO REMOVE IT ALL, BUT IT'S POINTLESS NOW...
THE EQUIPMENT IS FAILING, THE GUYS ARE ALL EXHAUSTED, AND THE CITY OWES US NINE YEARS OF OVERTIME.
WE HAD TO ABANDON THE SNOW REMOVAL NORTH OF JEAN-TALON AND FOCUS ON DOWNTOWN.
ANOTHER NEIGHBORHOOD BURIED UNDER THE SNOW...IT'S A GOOD THING WE'RE OKAY HERE.
WELL, NO ONE EVER THOUGHT THOUGHT WINTER COULD LAST SO LONG...
HORS-LIMITES
AUCUN SERVICE PASSÉ CE POINT
VILLE DE MONTRÉAL
BUILDING A STUPID NUCLEAR POWER PLANT IN MONTREAL WAS A DUMB IDEA TO BEGIN WITH.
OF COURSE AN ACCIDENT WAS BOUND TO HAPPEN AT SOME POINT.
AND WHO'S WHINING NOW?

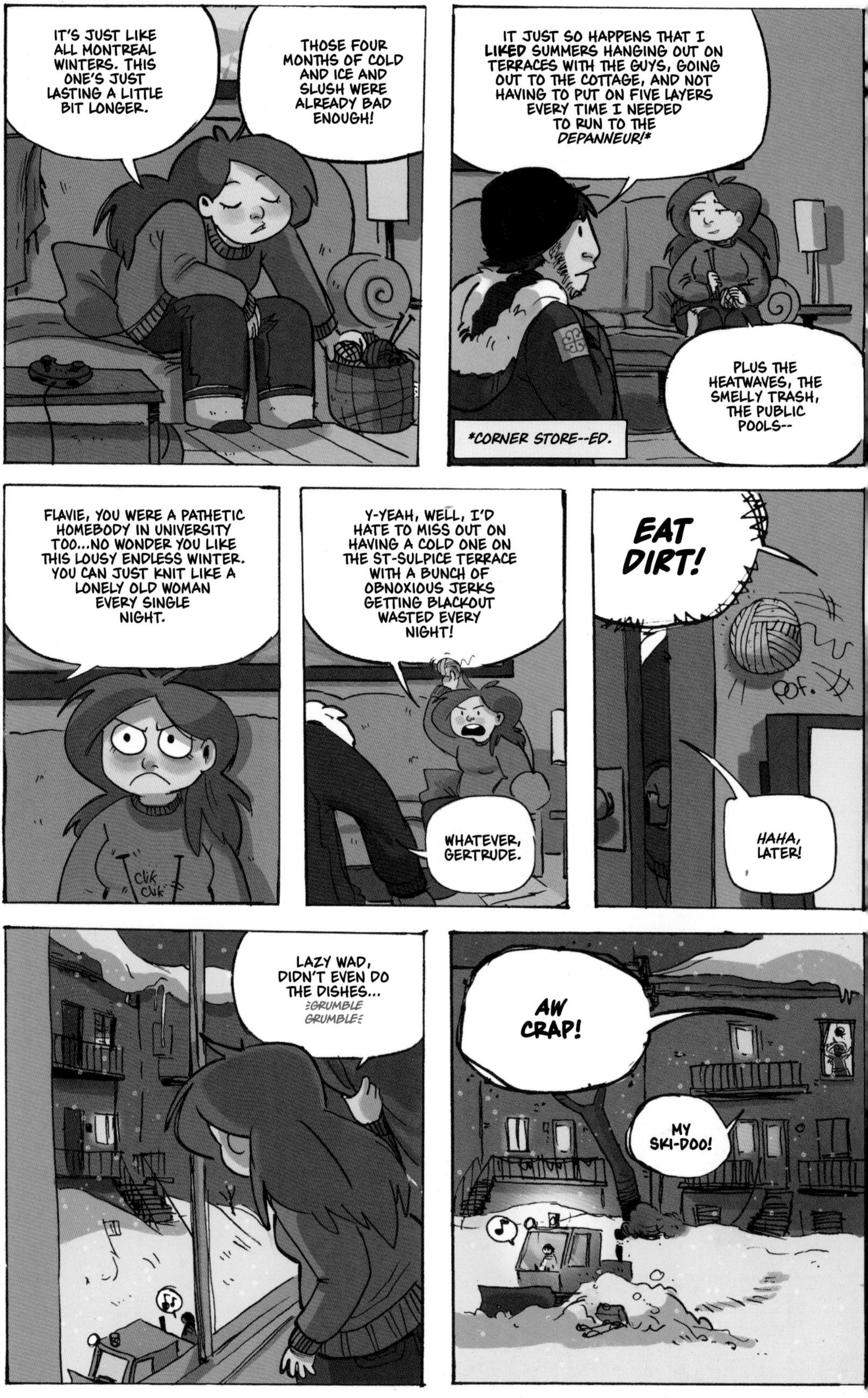
IT'S JUST LIKE ALL MONTREAL WINTERS. THIS ONE'S JUST LASTING A LITTLE BIT LONGER.
THOSE FOUR MONTHS OF COLD AND ICE AND SLUSH WERE ALREADY BAD ENOUGH!
IT JUST SO HAPPENS THAT I LIKED SUMMERS HANGING OUT ON TERRACES WITH THE GUYS, GOING OUT TO THE COTTAGE, AND NOT HAVING TO PUT ON FIVE LAYERS EVERY TIME I NEEDED TO RUN TO THE DEPANNEUR!*
PLUS THE HEATWAVES, THE SMELLY TRASH, THE PUBLIC POOLS--
*CORNER STORE--ED.
FLAVIE, YOU WERE A PATHETIC HOMEBODY IN UNIVERSITY TOO...NO WONDER YOU LIKE THIS LOUSY ENDLESS WINTER. YOU CAN JUST KNIT LIKE A LONELY OLD WOMAN EVERY SINGLE NIGHT.
CLIK CLIK
Y-YEAH, WELL, I'D HATE TO MISS OUT ON HAVING A COLD ONE ON THE ST-SULPICE TERRACE WITH A BUNCH OF OBNOXIOUS JERKS GETTING BLACKOUT WASTED EVERY NIGHT!
WHATEVER, GERTRUDE.
EAT DIRT!
POF.
HAHA, LATER!
LAZY WAD, DIDN'T EVEN DO THE DISHES...
GRUMBLE GRUMBLE
AW CRAP!
MY SKI-DOO!

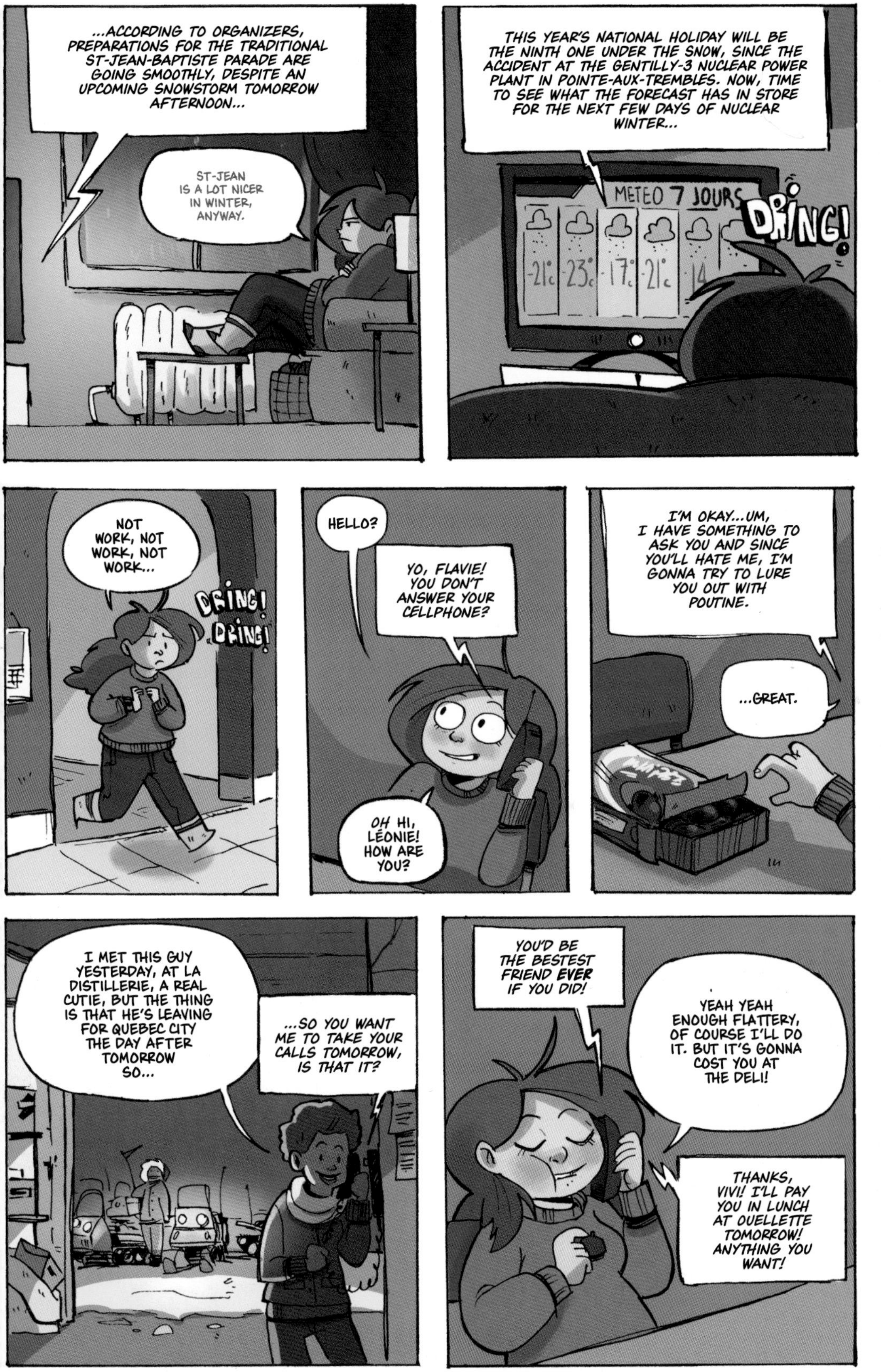
...ACCORDING TO ORGANIZERS, PREPARATIONS FOR THE TRADITIONAL ST-JEAN-BAPTISTE PARADE ARE GOING SMOOTHLY, DESPITE AN UPCOMING SNOWSTORM TOMORROW AFTERNOON...
ST-JEAN IS A LOT NICER IN WINTER, ANYWAY.
THIS YEAR'S NATIONAL HOLIDAY WILL BE THE NINTH ONE UNDER THE SNOW, SINCE THE ACCIDENT AT THE GENTILLY-3 NUCLEAR POWER PLANT IN POINTE-AUX-TREMBLES. NOW, TIME TO SEE WHAT THE FORECAST HAS IN STORE FOR THE NEXT FEW DAYS OF NUCLEAR WINTER...
METEO 7 JOURS
-21°c -23°c -17°c -21°c -14
DRING!
NOT WORK, NOT WORK, NOT WORK...
DRING!
DRING!
HELLO?
YO, FLAVIE! YOU DON'T ANSWER YOUR CELLPHONE?
OH HI, LÉONIE! HOW ARE YOU?
I'M OKAY...UM, I HAVE SOMETHING TO ASK YOU AND SINCE YOU'LL HATE ME, I'M GONNA TRY TO LURE YOU OUT WITH POUTINE.
...GREAT.
I MET THIS GUY YESTERDAY, AT LA DISTILLERIE, A REAL CUTIE, BUT THE THING IS THAT HE'S LEAVING FOR QUEBEC CITY THE DAY AFTER TOMORROW SO...
...SO YOU WANT ME TO TAKE YOUR CALLS TOMORROW, IS THAT IT?
YOU'D BE THE BESTEST FRIEND EVER IF YOU DID!
YEAH YEAH ENOUGH FLATTERY, OF COURSE I'LL DO IT. BUT IT'S GONNA COST YOU AT THE DELI!
THANKS, VIVI! I'LL PAY YOU IN LUNCH AT OUELLETTE TOMORROW! ANYTHING YOU WANT!

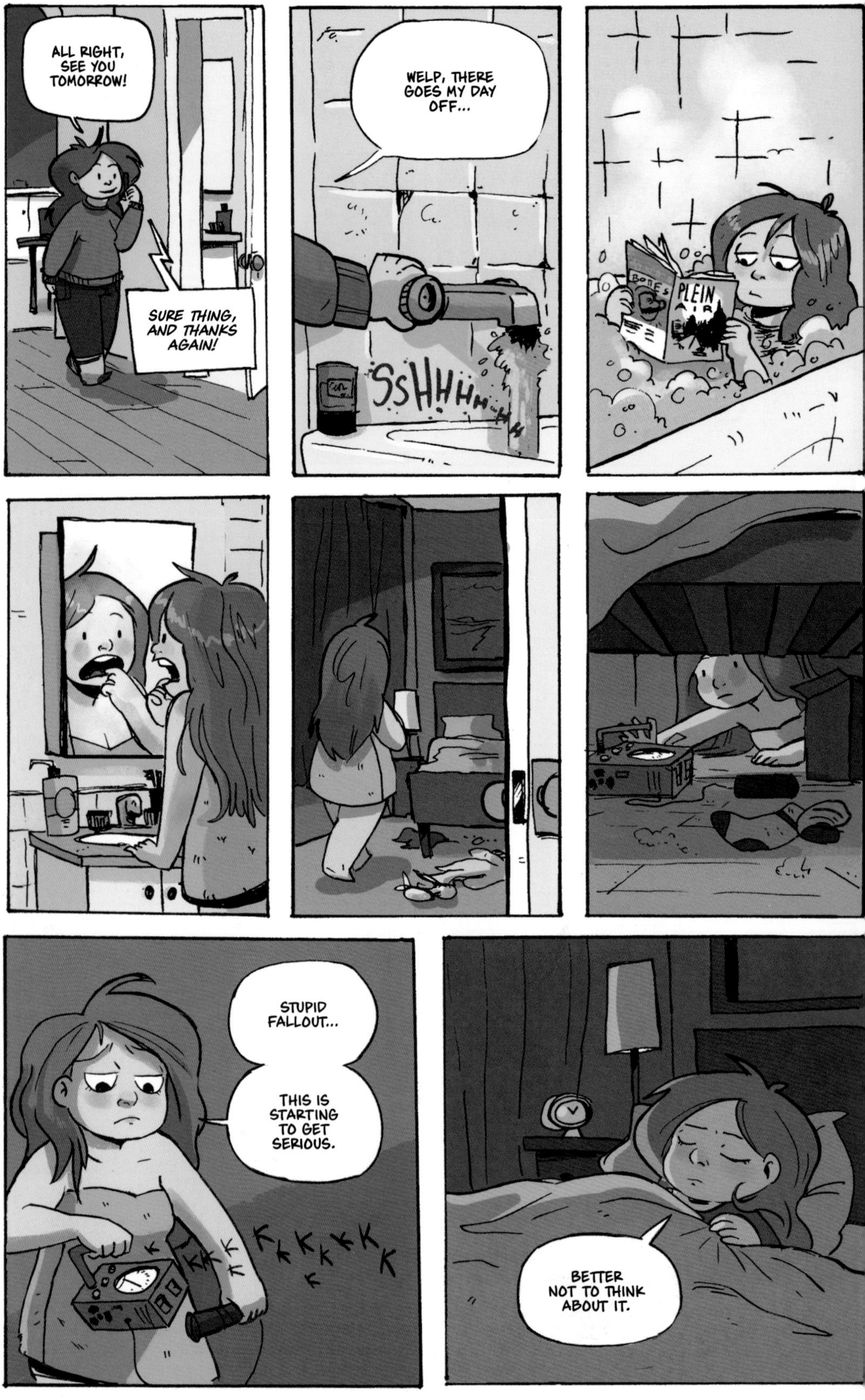
ALL RIGHT, SEE YOU TOMORROW!
SURE THING, AND THANKS AGAIN!
WELP, THERE GOES MY DAY OFF...
SsHHHHHH
PLEIN
STUPID FALLOUT...
THIS IS STARTING TO GET SERIOUS.
KKKKKKKK
BETTER NOT TO THINK ABOUT IT.

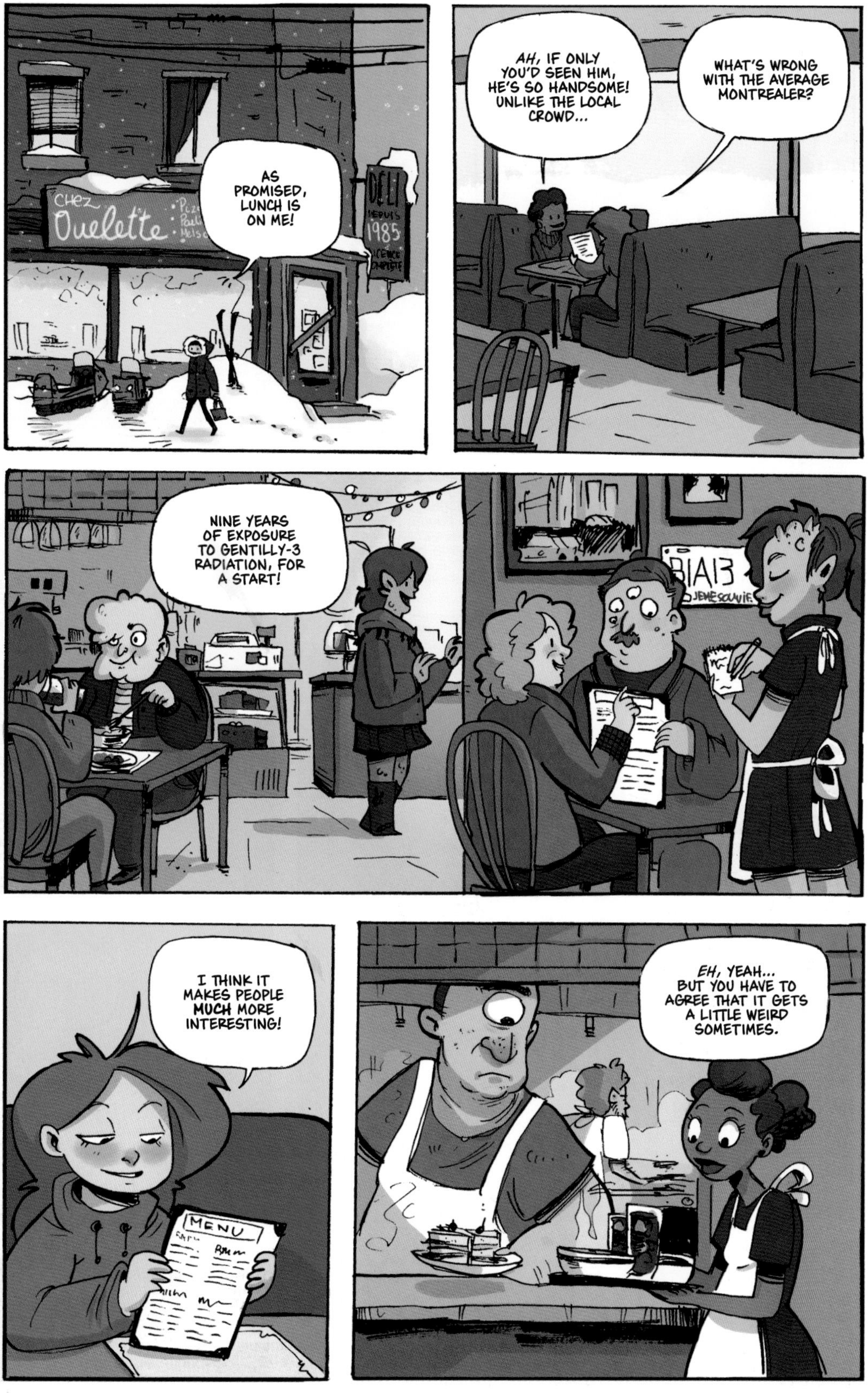
Chez Ouelette
DELI
1985
AS PROMISED, LUNCH IS ON ME!
AH, IF ONLY YOU'D SEEN HIM, HE'S SO HANDSOME! UNLIKE THE LOCAL CROWD...
WHAT'S WRONG WITH THE AVERAGE MONTREALER?
NINE YEARS OF EXPOSURE TO GENTILLY-3 RADIATION, FOR A START!
I THINK IT MAKES PEOPLE MUCH MORE INTERESTING!
MENU
EH, YEAH... BUT YOU HAVE TO AGREE THAT IT GETS A LITTLE WEIRD SOMETIMES.

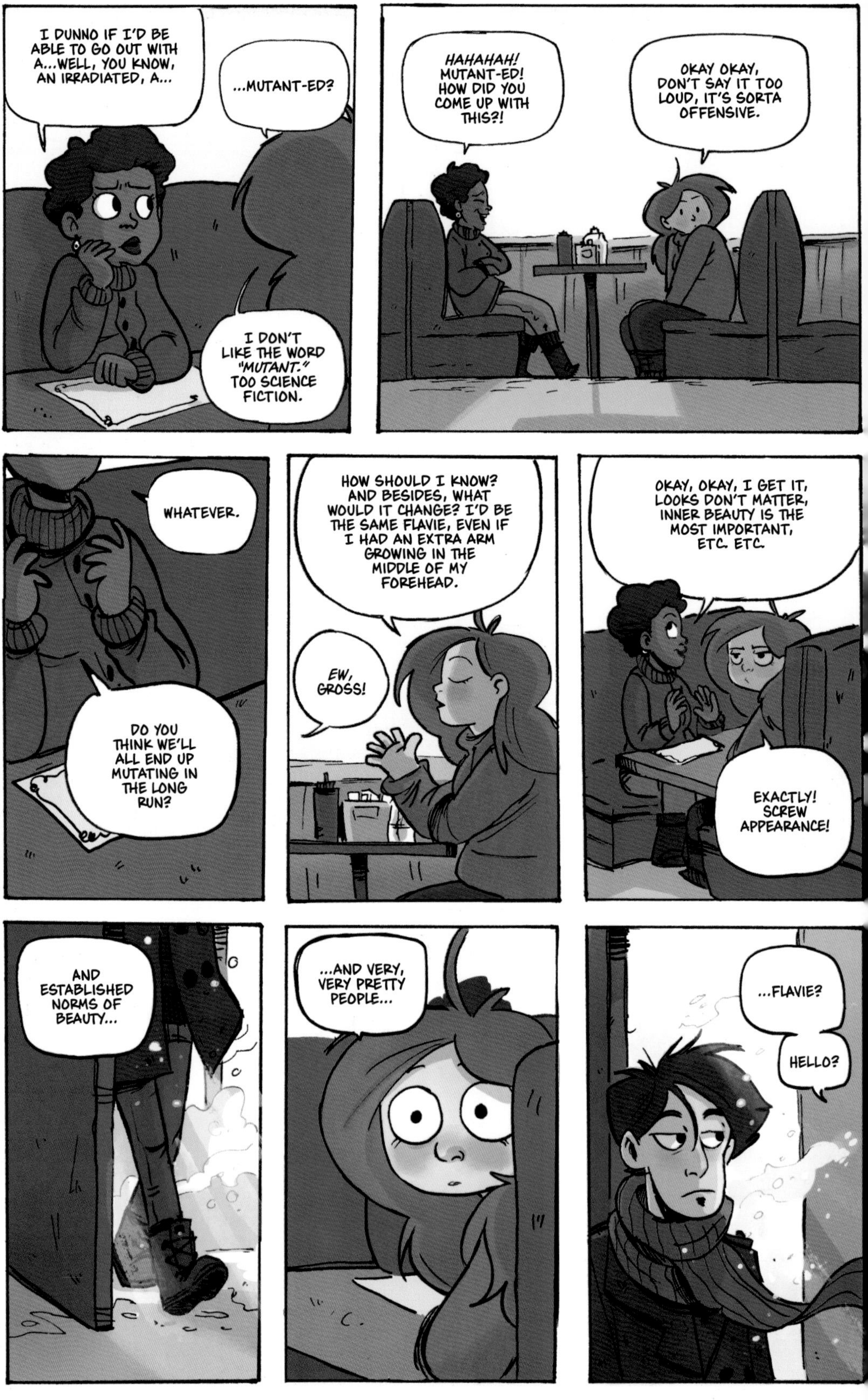
I DUNNO IF I'D BE ABLE TO GO OUT WITH A...WELL, YOU KNOW, AN IRRADIATED, A...
...MUTANT-ED?
I DON'T LIKE THE WORD "MUTANT." TOO SCIENCE FICTION.
HAHAHAH! MUTANT-ED! HOW DID YOU COME UP WITH THIS?!
OKAY OKAY, DON'T SAY IT TOO LOUD, IT'S SORTA OFFENSIVE.
WHATEVER.
DO YOU THINK WE'LL ALL END UP MUTATING IN THE LONG RUN?
HOW SHOULD I KNOW? AND BESIDES, WHAT WOULD IT CHANGE? I'D BE THE SAME FLAVIE, EVEN IF I HAD AN EXTRA ARM GROWING IN THE MIDDLE OF MY FOREHEAD.
EW, GROSS!
OKAY, OKAY, I GET IT, LOOKS DON'T MATTER, INNER BEAUTY IS THE MOST IMPORTANT, ETC. ETC.
EXACTLY! SCREW APPEARANCE!
AND ESTABLISHED NORMS OF BEAUTY...
...AND VERY, VERY PRETTY PEOPLE...
...FLAVIE?
HELLO?

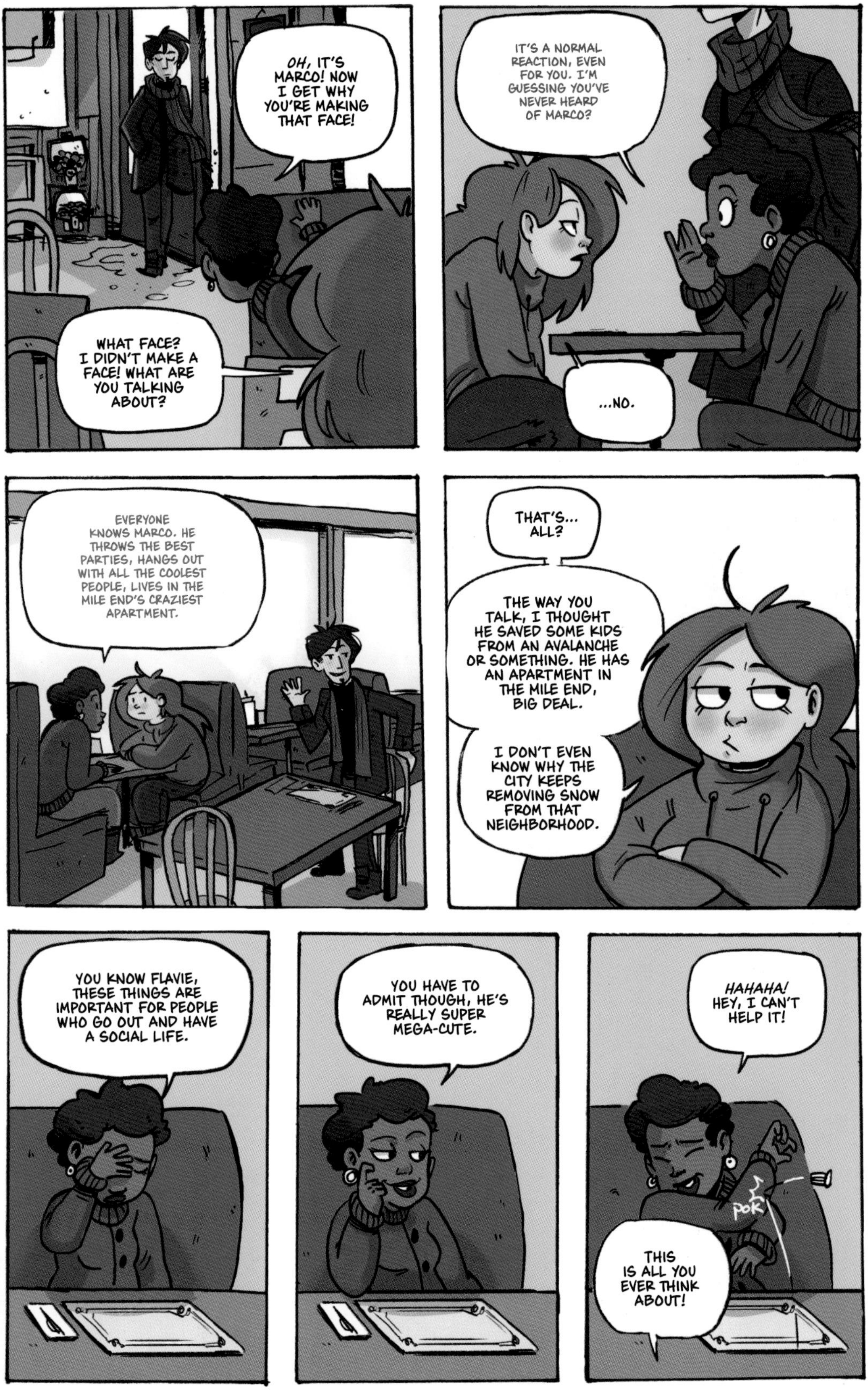
OH, IT'S MARCO! NOW I GET WHY YOU'RE MAKING THAT FACE!
WHAT FACE? I DIDN'T MAKE A FACE! WHAT ARE YOU TALKING ABOUT?
IT'S A NORMAL REACTION, EVEN FOR YOU. I'M GUESSING YOU'VE NEVER HEARD OF MARCO?
...NO.
EVERYONE KNOWS MARCO. HE THROWS THE BEST PARTIES, HANGS OUT WITH ALL THE COOLEST PEOPLE, LIVES IN THE MILE END'S CRAZIEST APARTMENT.
THAT'S... ALL?
THE WAY YOU TALK, I THOUGHT HE SAVED SOME KIDS FROM AN AVALANCHE OR SOMETHING. HE HAS AN APARTMENT IN THE MILE END, BIG DEAL.
I DON'T EVEN KNOW WHY THE CITY KEEPS REMOVING SNOW FROM THAT NEIGHBORHOOD.
YOU KNOW FLAVIE, THESE THINGS ARE IMPORTANT FOR PEOPLE WHO GO OUT AND HAVE A SOCIAL LIFE.
YOU HAVE TO ADMIT THOUGH, HE'S REALLY SUPER MEGA-CUTE.
HAHAHA! HEY, I CAN'T HELP IT!
POK
THIS IS ALL YOU EVER THINK ABOUT!

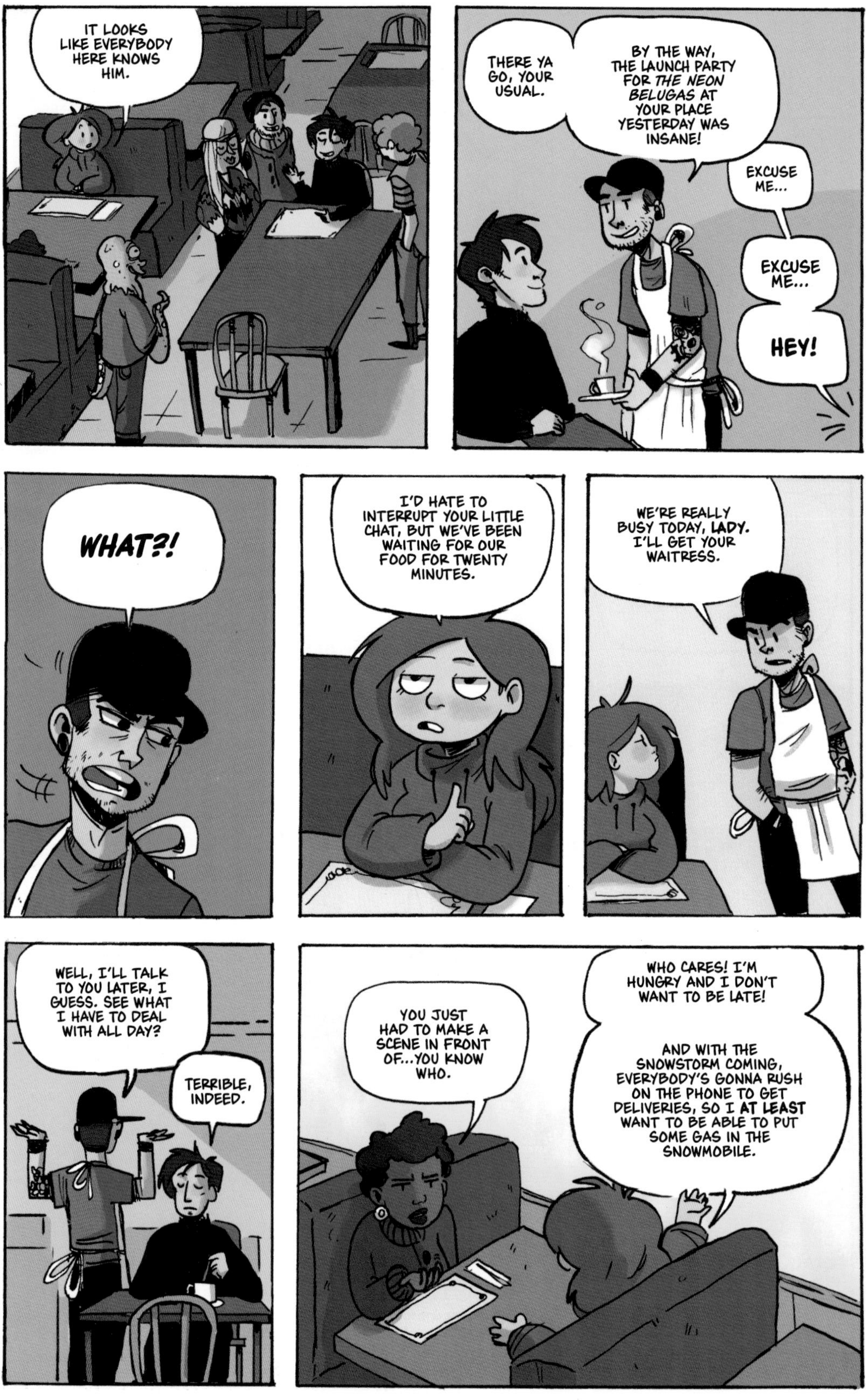
IT LOOKS LIKE EVERYBODY HERE KNOWS HIM.
THERE YA GO, YOUR USUAL.
BY THE WAY, THE LAUNCH PARTY FOR *THE NEON BELUGAS* AT YOUR PLACE YESTERDAY WAS INSANE!
EXCUSE ME...
EXCUSE ME...
HEY!
WHAT?!
I'D HATE TO INTERRUPT YOUR LITTLE CHAT, BUT WE'VE BEEN WAITING FOR OUR FOOD FOR TWENTY MINUTES.
WE'RE REALLY BUSY TODAY, **LADY.** I'LL GET YOUR WAITRESS.
WELL, I'LL TALK TO YOU LATER, I GUESS. SEE WHAT I HAVE TO DEAL WITH ALL DAY?
TERRIBLE, INDEED.
YOU JUST HAD TO MAKE A SCENE IN FRONT OF...YOU KNOW WHO.
WHO CARES! I'M HUNGRY AND I DON'T WANT TO BE LATE!
AND WITH THE SNOWSTORM COMING, EVERYBODY'S GONNA RUSH ON THE PHONE TO GET DELIVERIES, SO I **AT LEAST** WANT TO BE ABLE TO PUT SOME GAS IN THE SNOWMOBILE.

YOU'RE PRACTICAL, THAT'S FOR SURE! I WOULDN'T TRUST ANYONE ELSE WITH MY DELIVERIES.

AW, STOP IT.

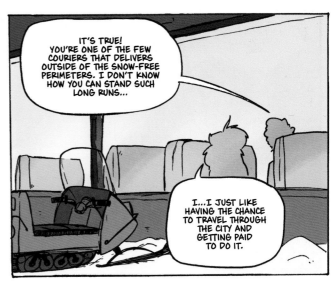

IT'S TRUE! YOU'RE ONE OF THE FEW COURIERS THAT DELIVERS OUTSIDE OF THE SNOW-FREE PERIMETERS. I DON'T KNOW HOW YOU CAN STAND SUCH LONG RUNS...

I...I JUST LIKE HAVING THE CHANCE TO TRAVEL THROUGH THE CITY AND GETTING PAID TO DO IT.

AND BEING ALONE IN THE MIDDLE OF ALL THIS SNOW IS VERY CALMING.

I THINK EVERYONE NEEDS SOME QUIET TIME ONCE IN AWHILE.

THERE YOU GO...

A DOUBLE CHEESEBURGER WITH EXTRA BACON, A BIG POUTINE WITH EXTRA CHEESE, A LARGE ROOT BEER AND...

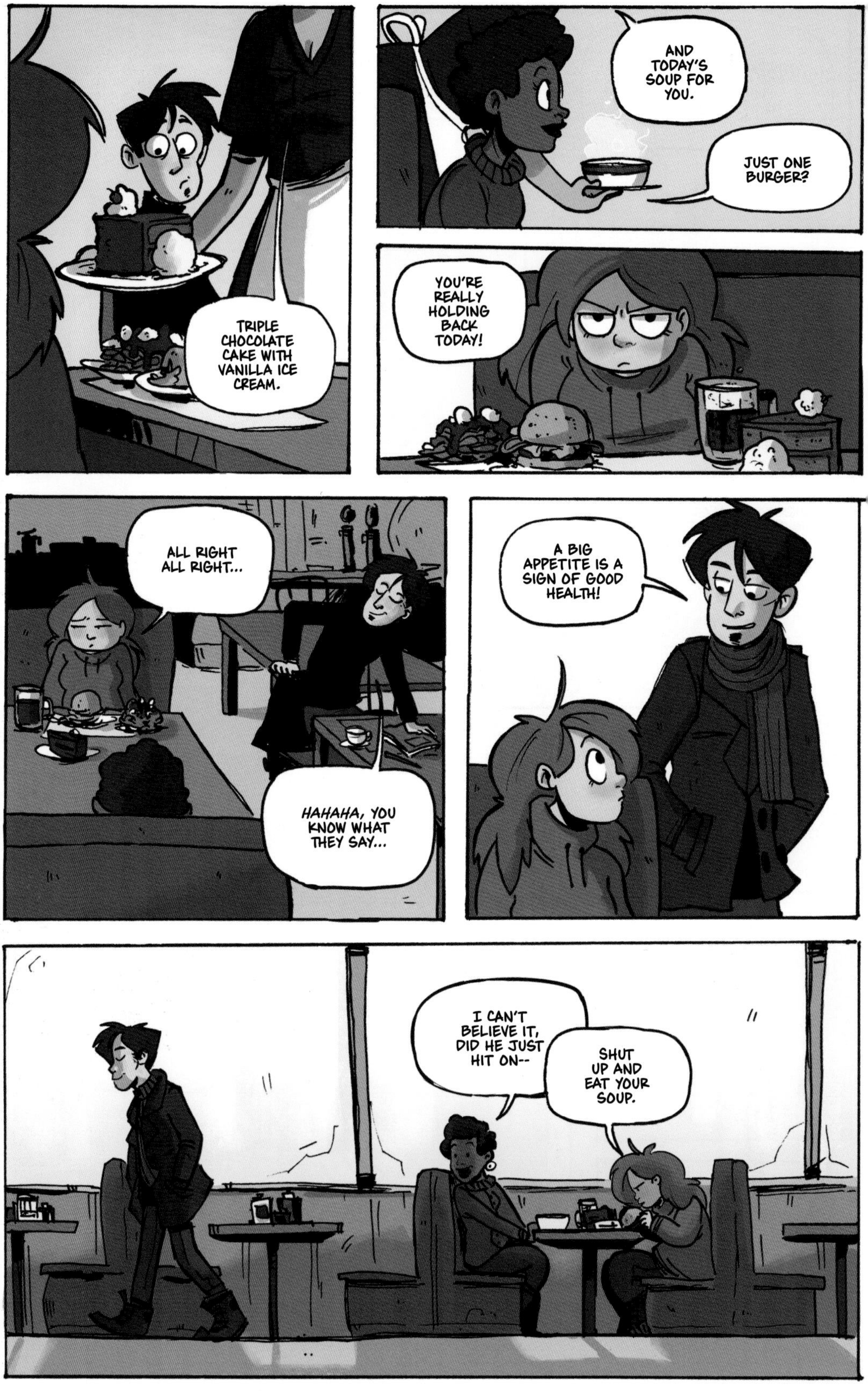
TRIPLE CHOCOLATE CAKE WITH VANILLA ICE CREAM.
AND TODAY'S SOUP FOR YOU.
JUST ONE BURGER?
YOU'RE REALLY HOLDING BACK TODAY!
ALL RIGHT ALL RIGHT...
HAHAHA, YOU KNOW WHAT THEY SAY...
A BIG APPETITE IS A SIGN OF GOOD HEALTH!
I CAN'T BELIEVE IT, DID HE JUST HIT ON--
SHUT UP AND EAT YOUR SOUP.

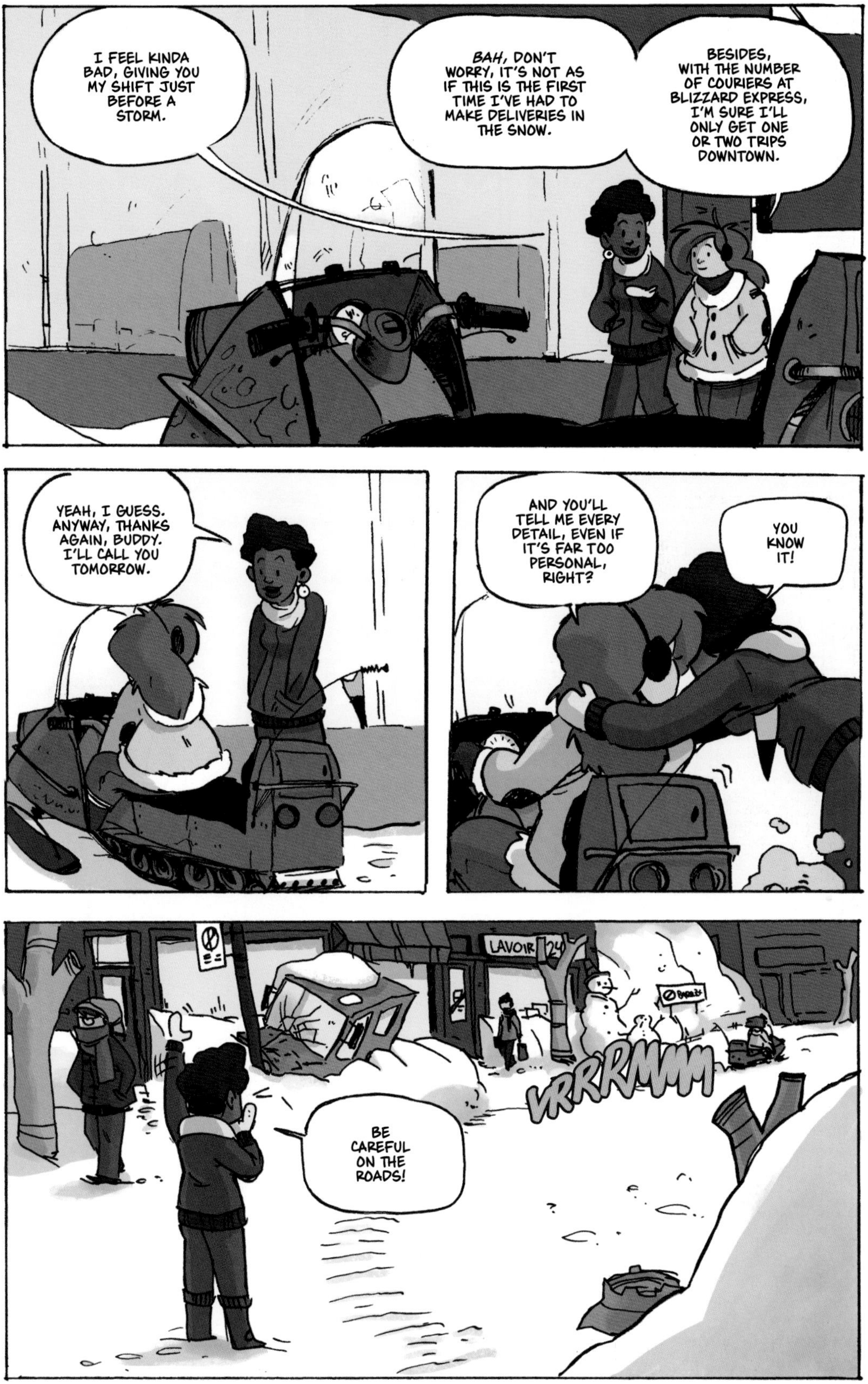
I FEEL KINDA BAD, GIVING YOU MY SHIFT JUST BEFORE A STORM.
BAH, DON'T WORRY, IT'S NOT AS IF THIS IS THE FIRST TIME I'VE HAD TO MAKE DELIVERIES IN THE SNOW.
BESIDES, WITH THE NUMBER OF COURIERS AT BLIZZARD EXPRESS, I'M SURE I'LL ONLY GET ONE OR TWO TRIPS DOWNTOWN.
YEAH, I GUESS. ANYWAY, THANKS AGAIN, BUDDY. I'LL CALL YOU TOMORROW.
AND YOU'LL TELL ME EVERY DETAIL, EVEN IF IT'S FAR TOO PERSONAL, RIGHT?
YOU KNOW IT!
LAVOIR 24
VRRRMMM
BE CAREFUL ON THE ROADS!

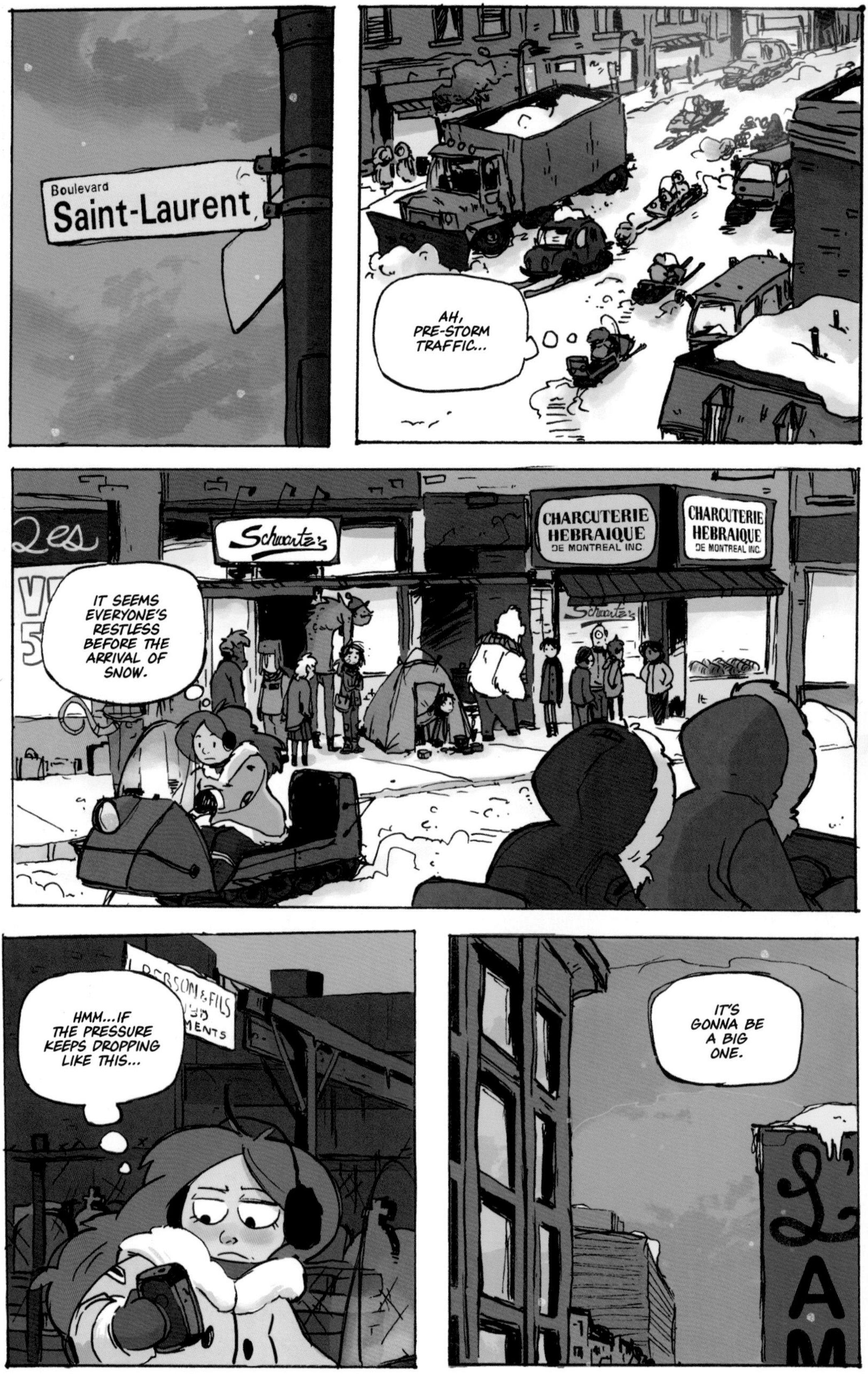
Boulevard Saint-Laurent
AH, PRE-STORM TRAFFIC...
Schwartz's
CHARCUTERIE HEBRAIQUE DE MONTREAL INC.
IT SEEMS EVERYONE'S RESTLESS BEFORE THE ARRIVAL OF SNOW.
HMM...IF THE PRESSURE KEEPS DROPPING LIKE THIS...
IT'S GONNA BE A BIG ONE.

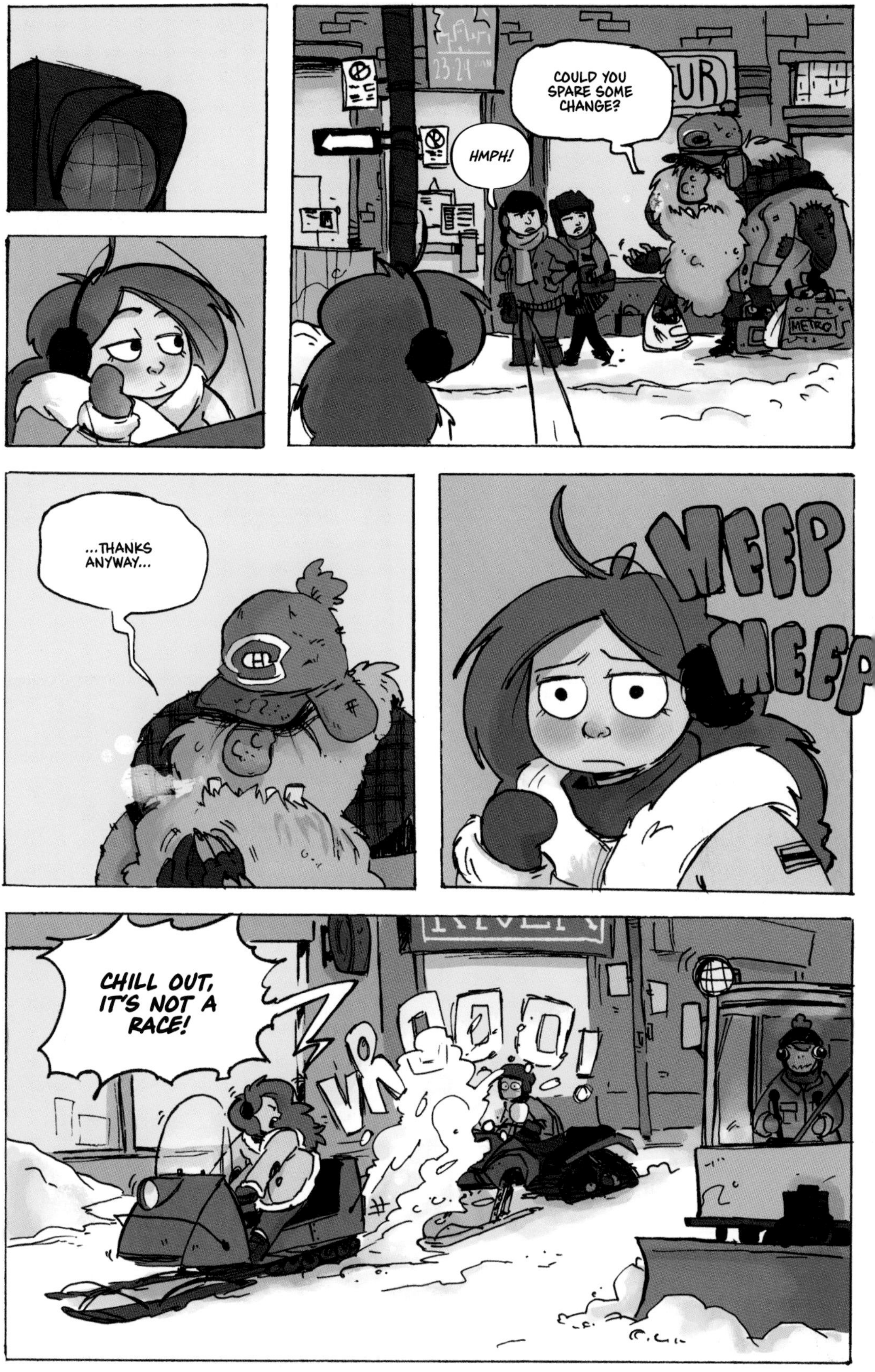
HMPH!
COULD YOU SPARE SOME CHANGE?
...THANKS ANYWAY...
MEEP MEEP
CHILL OUT, IT'S NOT A RACE!
VROOOOM!

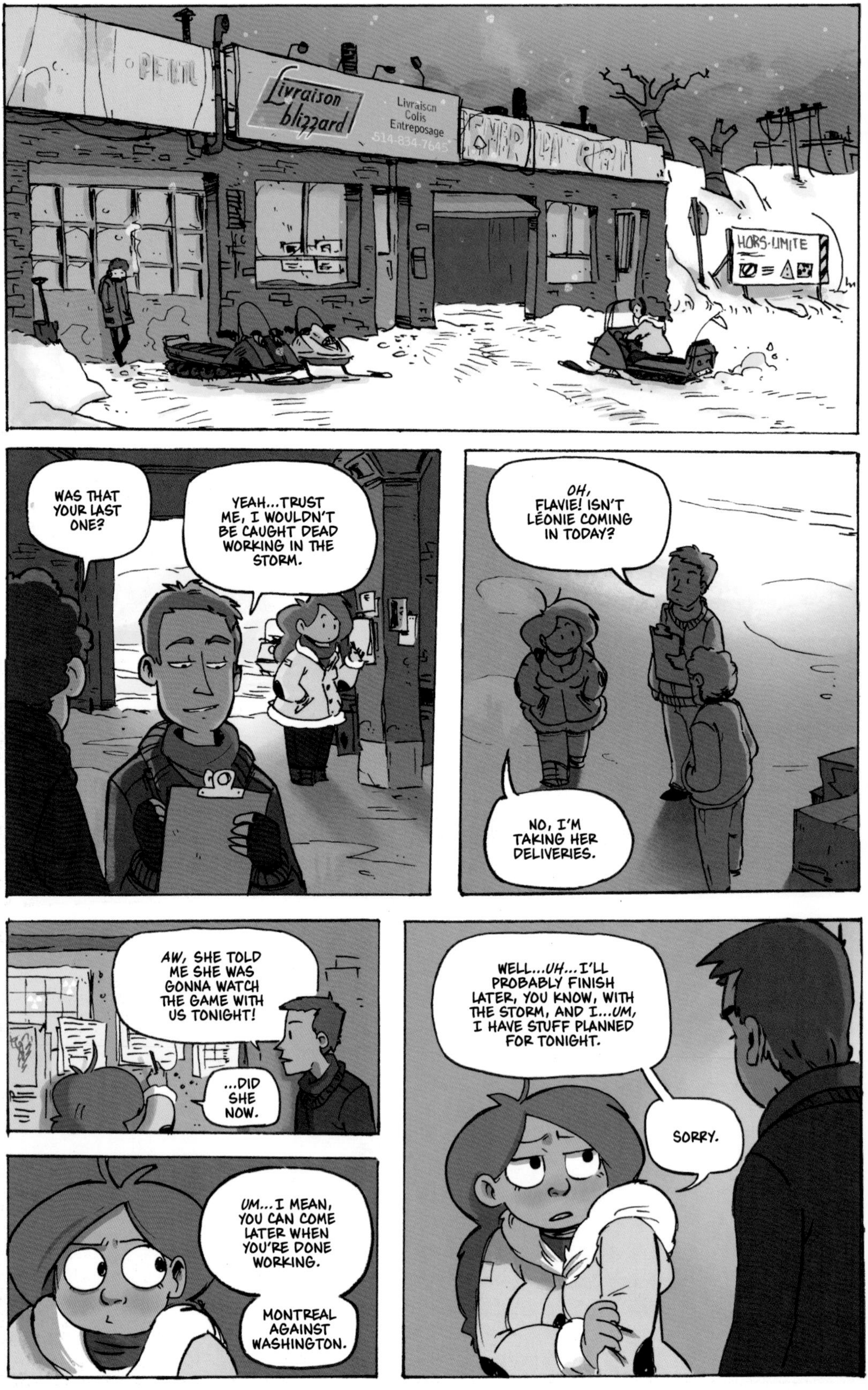
Livraison blizzard
Livraison
Colis
Entreposage
514-834-7645
HORS-LIMITE
WAS THAT YOUR LAST ONE?
YEAH...TRUST ME, I WOULDN'T BE CAUGHT DEAD WORKING IN THE STORM.
OH, FLAVIE! ISN'T LÉONIE COMING IN TODAY?
NO, I'M TAKING HER DELIVERIES.
AW, SHE TOLD ME SHE WAS GONNA WATCH THE GAME WITH US TONIGHT!
...DID SHE NOW.
UM... I MEAN, YOU CAN COME LATER WHEN YOU'RE DONE WORKING.
MONTREAL AGAINST WASHINGTON.
WELL...UH...I'LL PROBABLY FINISH LATER, YOU KNOW, WITH THE STORM, AND I...UM, I HAVE STUFF PLANNED FOR TONIGHT.
SORRY.

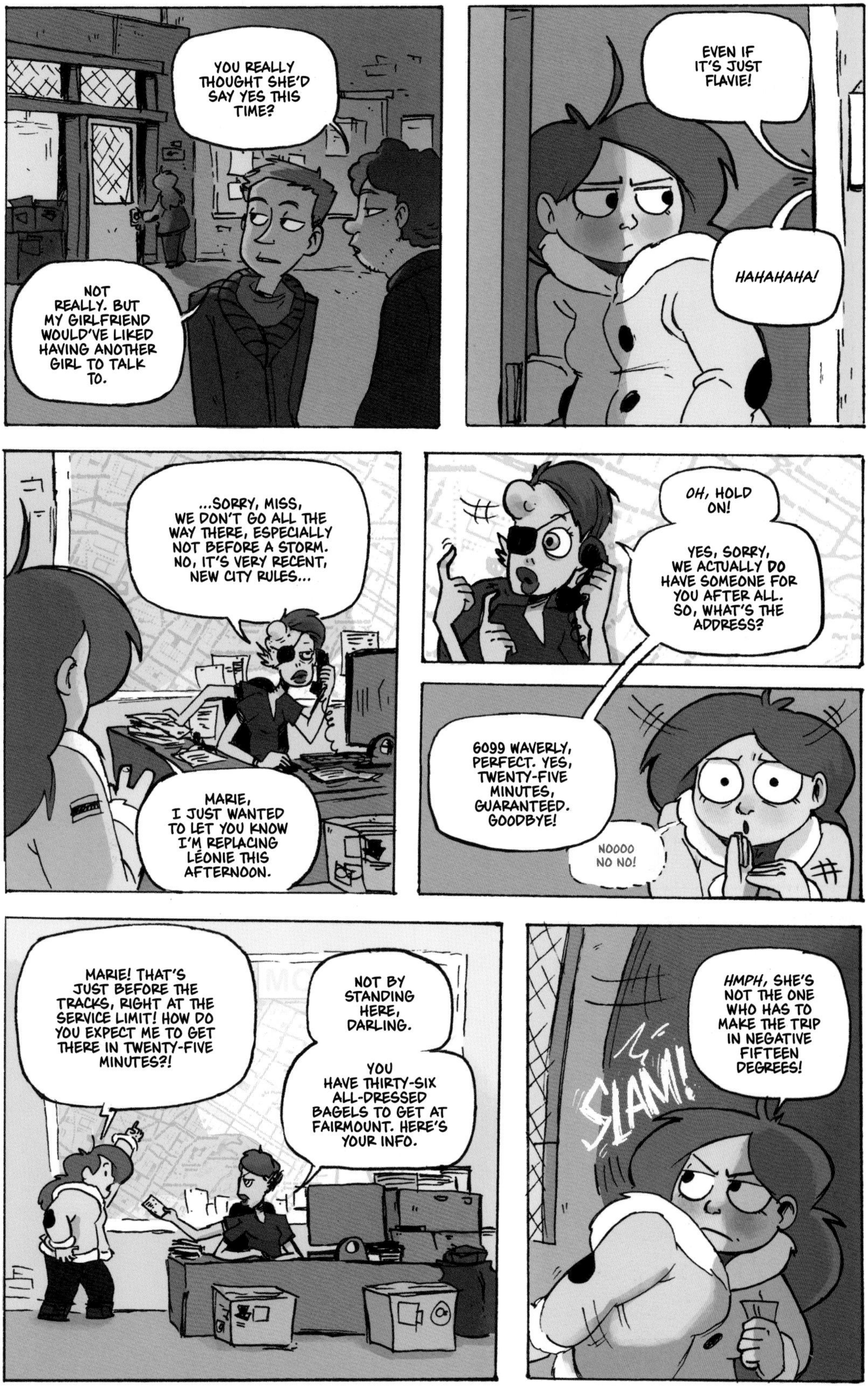
YOU REALLY THOUGHT SHE'D SAY YES THIS TIME?
NOT REALLY. BUT MY GIRLFRIEND WOULD'VE LIKED HAVING ANOTHER GIRL TO TALK TO.
EVEN IF IT'S JUST FLAVIE!
HAHAHAHA!
...SORRY, MISS, WE DON'T GO ALL THE WAY THERE, ESPECIALLY NOT BEFORE A STORM. NO, IT'S VERY RECENT, NEW CITY RULES...
MARIE, I JUST WANTED TO LET YOU KNOW I'M REPLACING LÉONIE THIS AFTERNOON.
OH, HOLD ON!
YES, SORRY, WE ACTUALLY DO HAVE SOMEONE FOR YOU AFTER ALL. SO, WHAT'S THE ADDRESS?
6099 WAVERLY, PERFECT. YES, TWENTY-FIVE MINUTES, GUARANTEED. GOODBYE!
NOOOO NO NO!
MARIE! THAT'S JUST BEFORE THE TRACKS, RIGHT AT THE SERVICE LIMIT! HOW DO YOU EXPECT ME TO GET THERE IN TWENTY-FIVE MINUTES?!
NOT BY STANDING HERE, DARLING.
YOU HAVE THIRTY-SIX ALL-DRESSED BAGELS TO GET AT FAIRMOUNT. HERE'S YOUR INFO.
SLAM!
HMPH, SHE'S NOT THE ONE WHO HAS TO MAKE THE TRIP IN NEGATIVE FIFTEEN DEGREES!

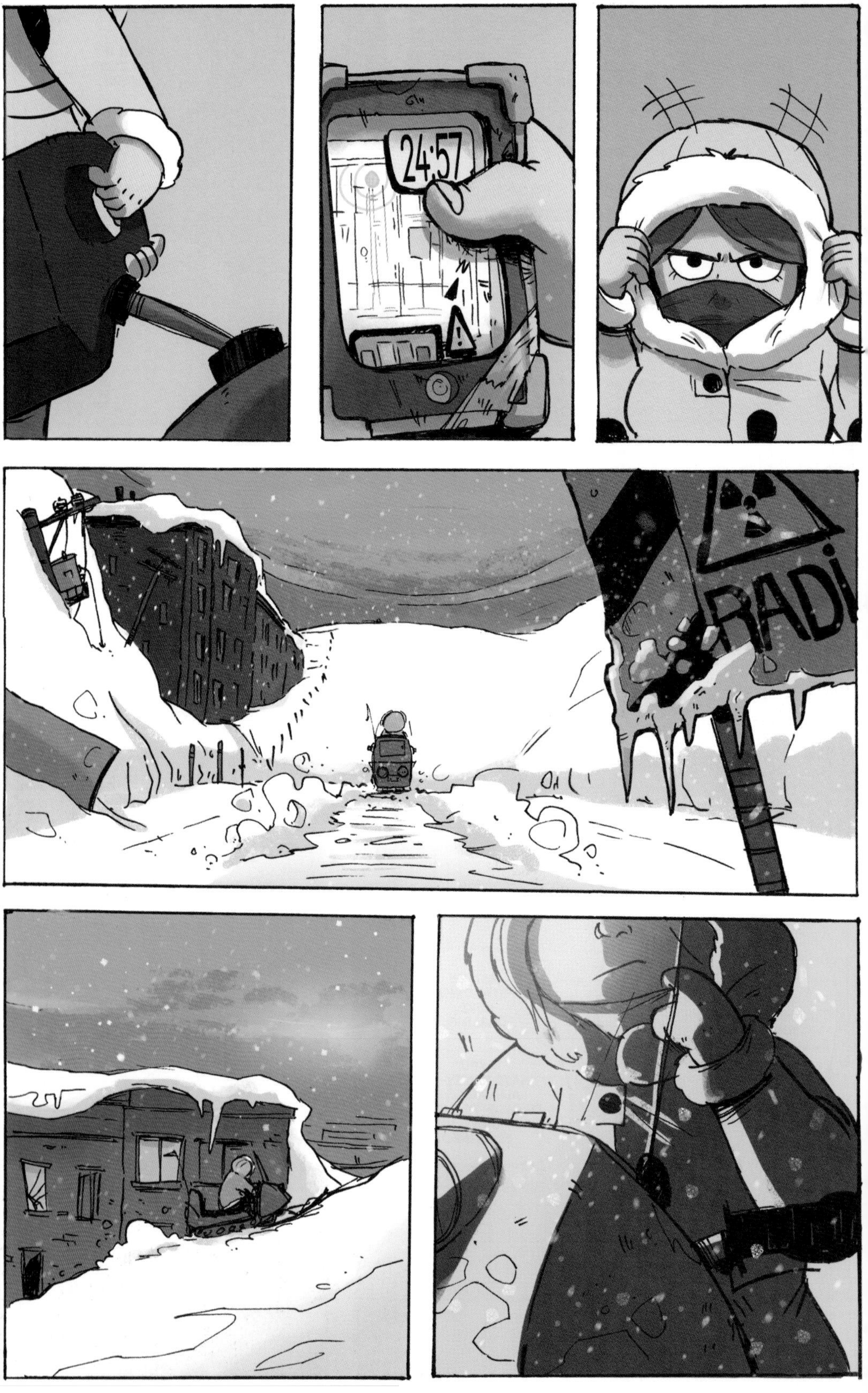
24:57
RADI

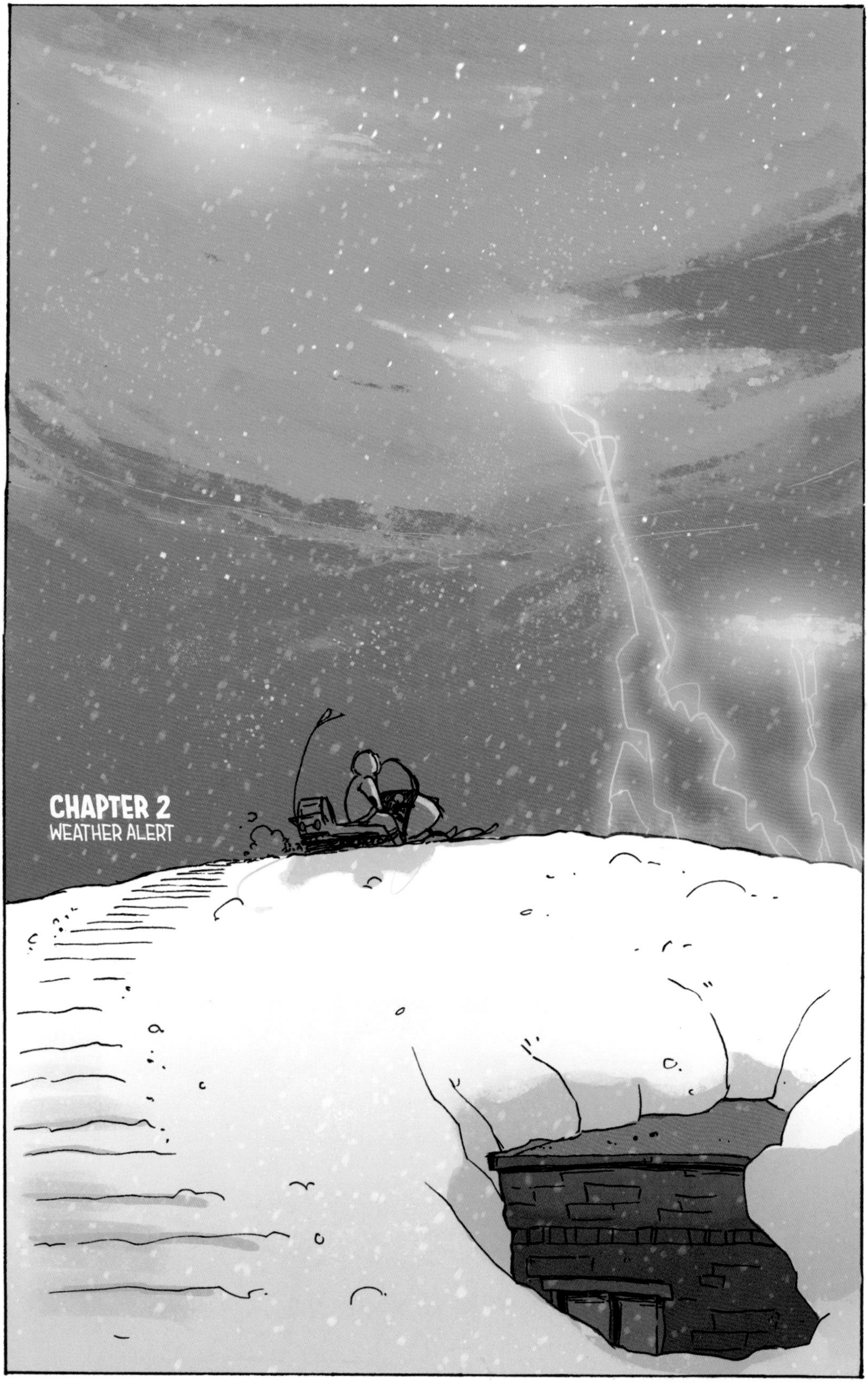
CHAPTER 2
WEATHER ALERT

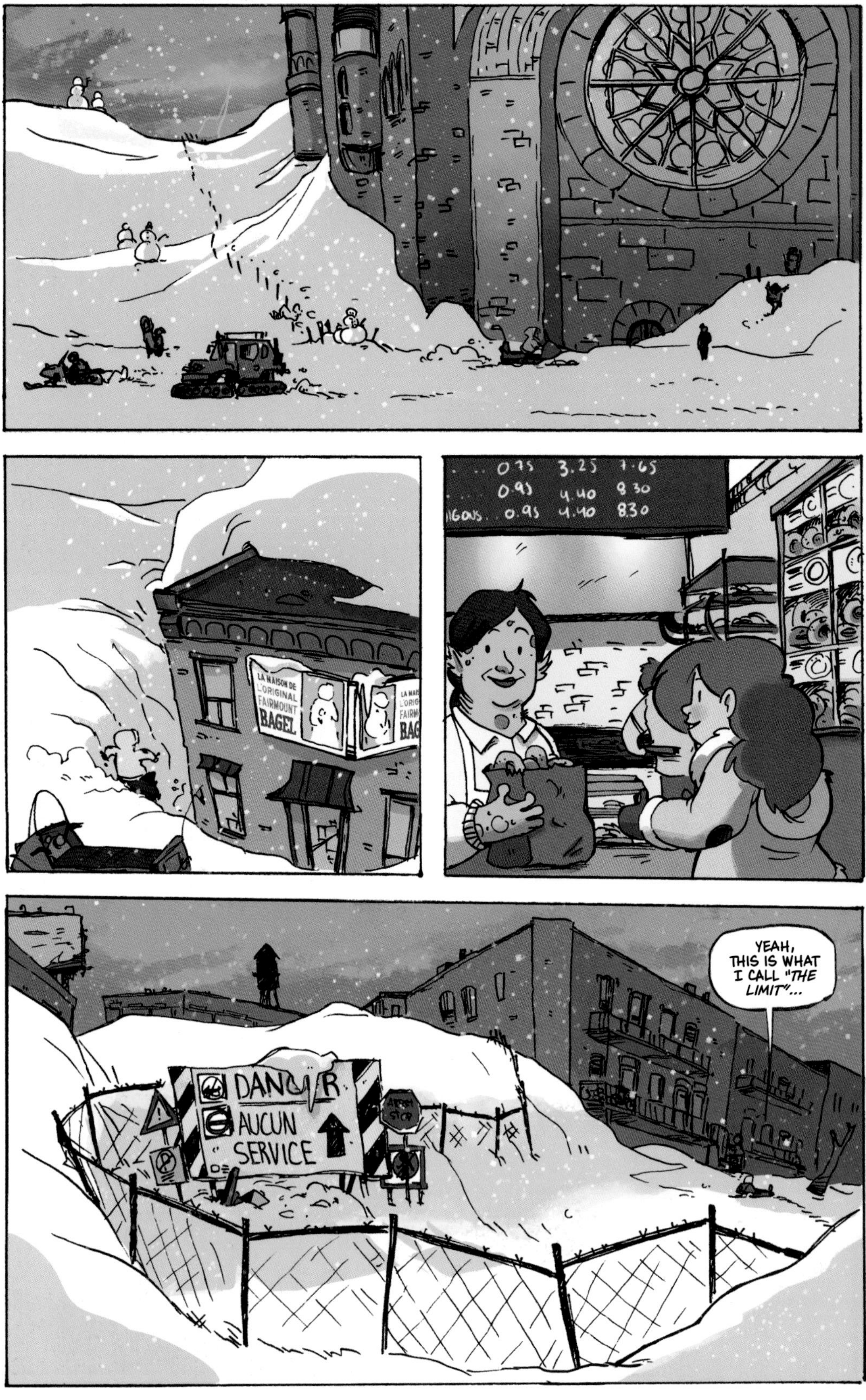
0.75 3.25 7.65
0.95 4.40 8.30
0.95 4.40 8.30
LA MAISON DE L'ORIGINAL FAIRMOUNT BAGEL
DANG R
AUCUN SERVICE
YEAH, THIS IS WHAT I CALL "THE LIMIT"...

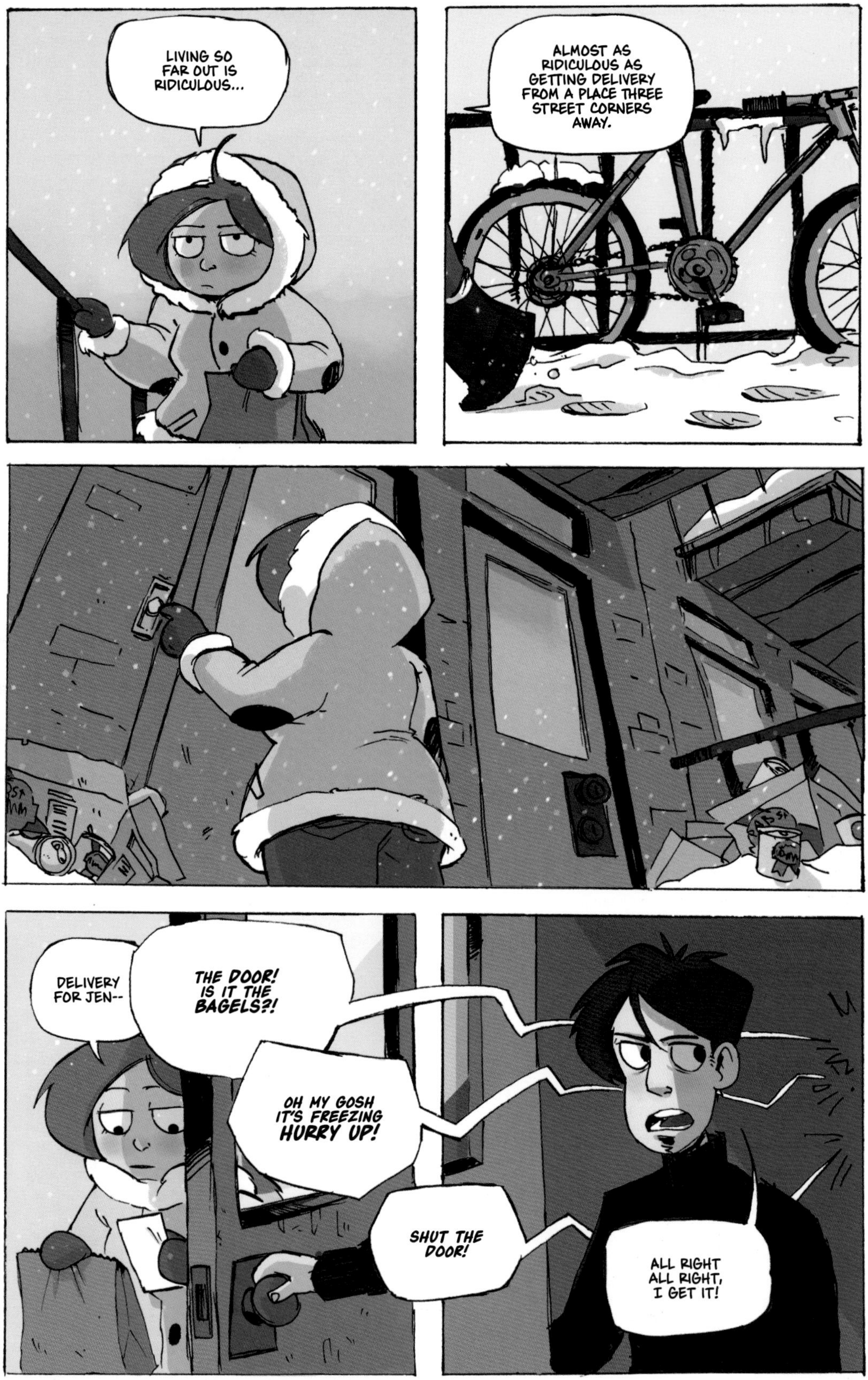
LIVING SO FAR OUT IS RIDICULOUS...
ALMOST AS RIDICULOUS AS GETTING DELIVERY FROM A PLACE THREE STREET CORNERS AWAY.
DELIVERY FOR JEN--
THE DOOR! IS IT THE BAGELS?!
OH MY GOSH IT'S FREEZING HURRY UP!
SHUT THE DOOR!
ALL RIGHT ALL RIGHT, I GET IT!

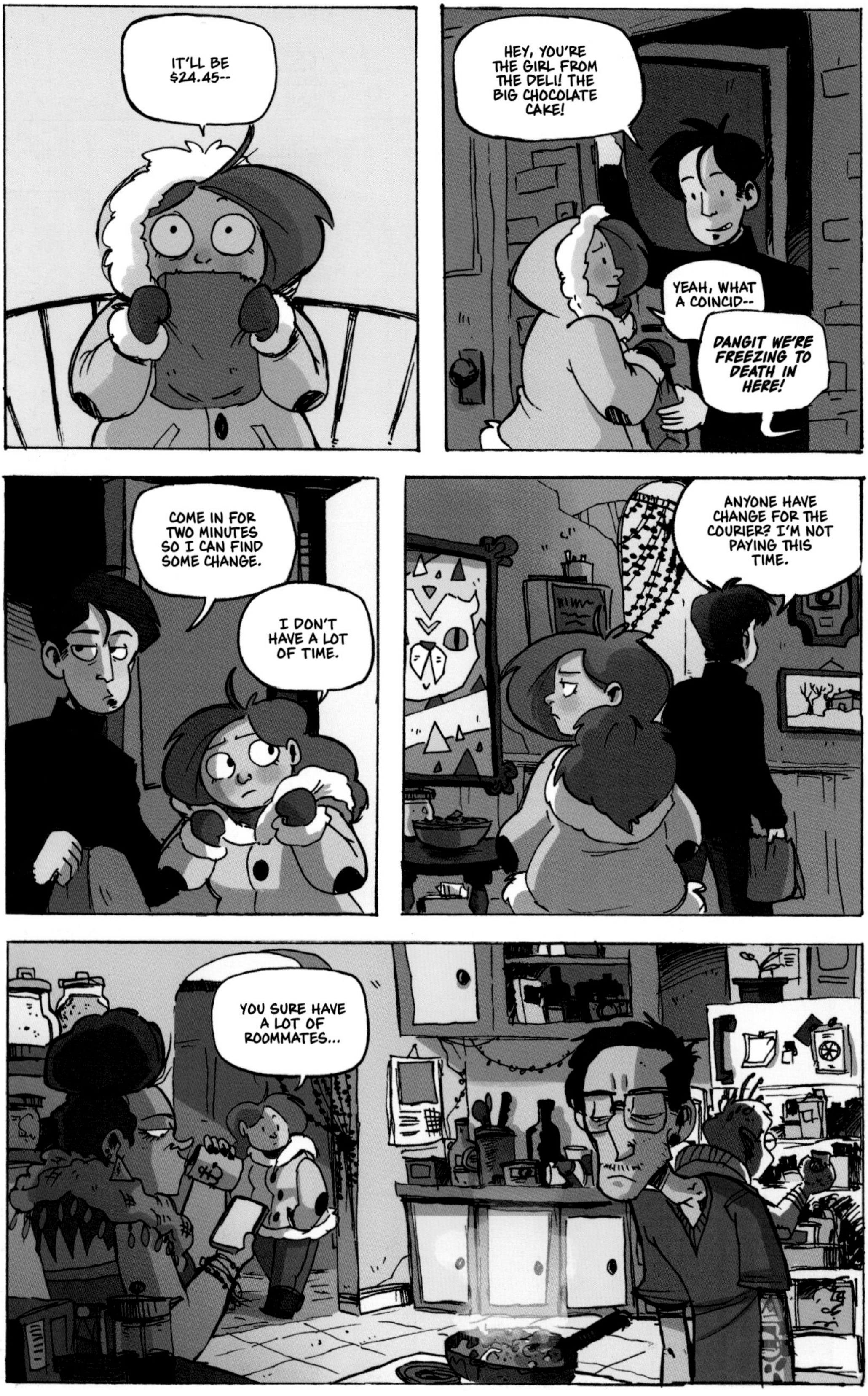
IT'LL BE $24.45--
HEY, YOU'RE THE GIRL FROM THE DELI! THE BIG CHOCOLATE CAKE!
YEAH, WHAT A COINCID--
DANGIT WE'RE FREEZING TO DEATH IN HERE!
COME IN FOR TWO MINUTES SO I CAN FIND SOME CHANGE.
I DON'T HAVE A LOT OF TIME.
ANYONE HAVE CHANGE FOR THE COURIER? I'M NOT PAYING THIS TIME.
YOU SURE HAVE A LOT OF ROOMMATES...

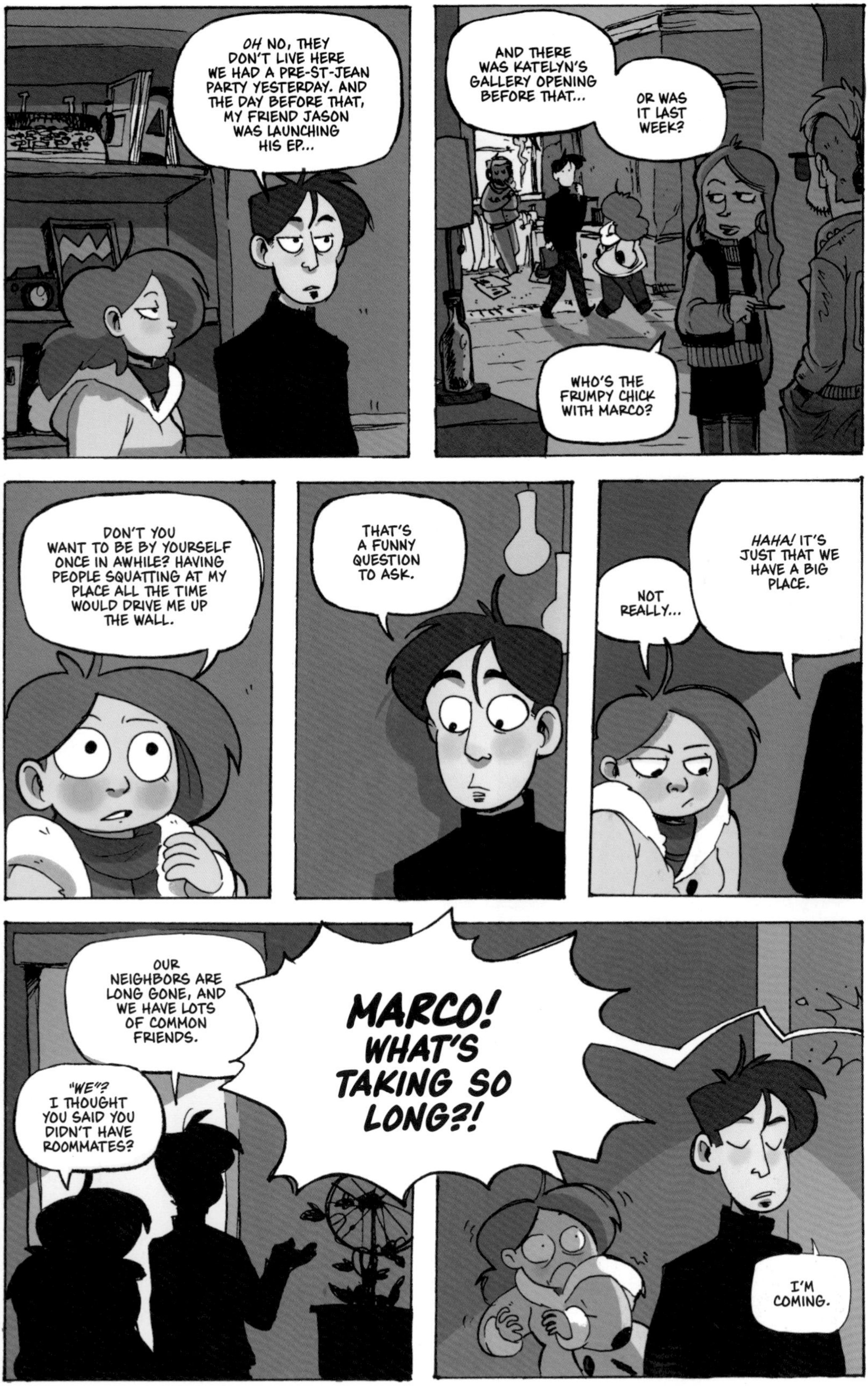
OH NO, THEY DON'T LIVE HERE WE HAD A PRE-ST-JEAN PARTY YESTERDAY. AND THE DAY BEFORE THAT, MY FRIEND JASON WAS LAUNCHING HIS EP...
AND THERE WAS KATELYN'S GALLERY OPENING BEFORE THAT...
OR WAS IT LAST WEEK?
WHO'S THE FRUMPY CHICK WITH MARCO?
DON'T YOU WANT TO BE BY YOURSELF ONCE IN AWHILE? HAVING PEOPLE SQUATTING AT MY PLACE ALL THE TIME WOULD DRIVE ME UP THE WALL.
THAT'S A FUNNY QUESTION TO ASK.
NOT REALLY...
HAHA! IT'S JUST THAT WE HAVE A BIG PLACE.
OUR NEIGHBORS ARE LONG GONE, AND WE HAVE LOTS OF COMMON FRIENDS.
"WE"? I THOUGHT YOU SAID YOU DIDN'T HAVE ROOMMATES?
MARCO! WHAT'S TAKING SO LONG?!
I'M COMING.

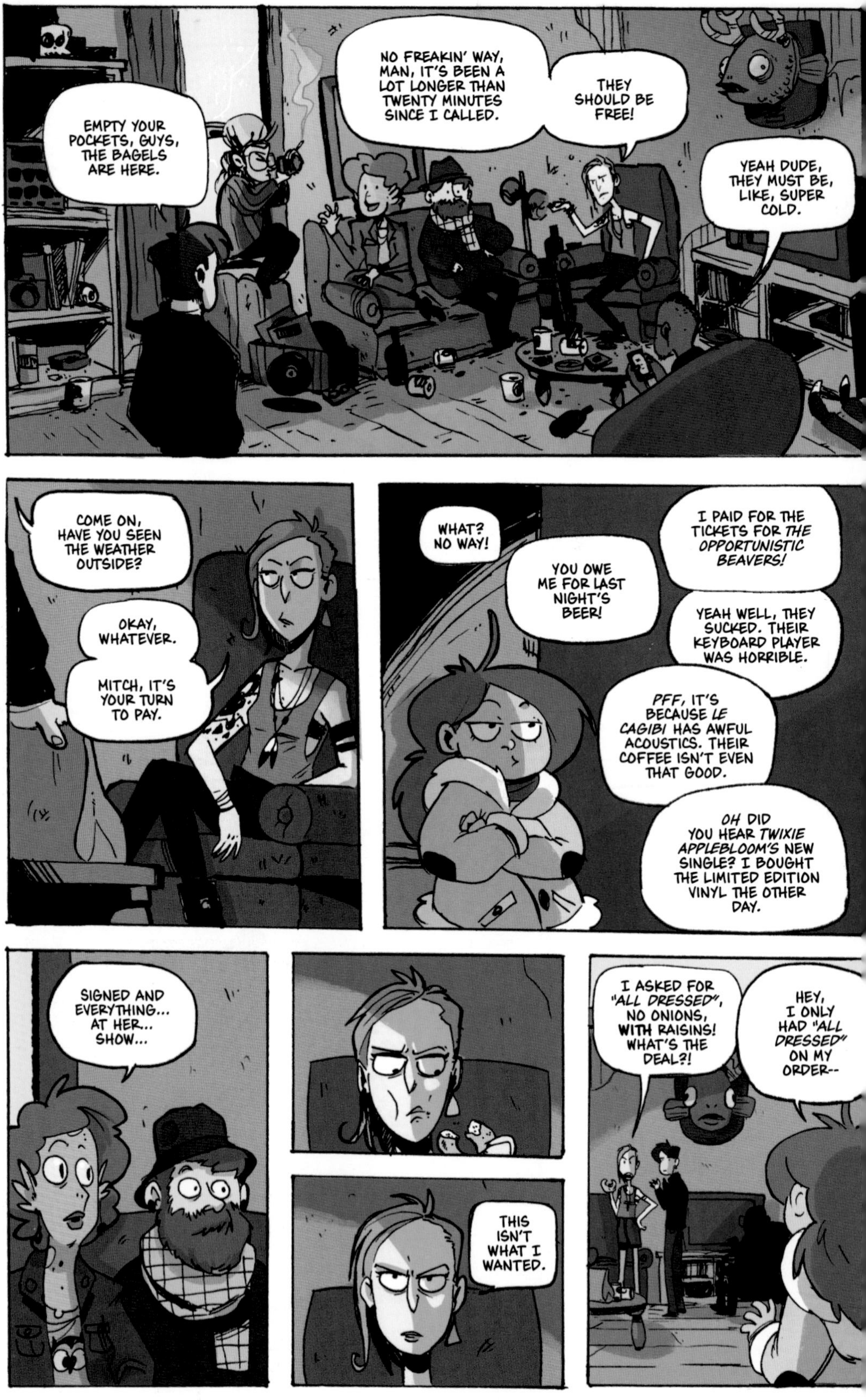

EMPTY YOUR POCKETS, GUYS, THE BAGELS ARE HERE.
NO FREAKIN' WAY, MAN, IT'S BEEN A LOT LONGER THAN TWENTY MINUTES SINCE I CALLED.
THEY SHOULD BE FREE!
YEAH DUDE, THEY MUST BE, LIKE, SUPER COLD.
COME ON, HAVE YOU SEEN THE WEATHER OUTSIDE?
OKAY, WHATEVER.
MITCH, IT'S YOUR TURN TO PAY.
WHAT? NO WAY!
YOU OWE ME FOR LAST NIGHT'S BEER!
I PAID FOR THE TICKETS FOR *THE OPPORTUNISTIC BEAVERS!*
YEAH WELL, THEY SUCKED. THEIR KEYBOARD PLAYER WAS HORRIBLE.
PFF, IT'S BECAUSE *LE CAGIBI* HAS AWFUL ACOUSTICS. THEIR COFFEE ISN'T EVEN THAT GOOD.
OH DID YOU HEAR *TWIXIE APPLEBLOOM'S* NEW SINGLE? I BOUGHT THE LIMITED EDITION VINYL THE OTHER DAY.
SIGNED AND EVERYTHING... AT HER... SHOW...
THIS ISN'T WHAT I WANTED.
I ASKED FOR *"ALL DRESSED"*, NO ONIONS, **WITH** RAISINS! WHAT'S THE DEAL?!
HEY, I ONLY HAD *"ALL DRESSED"* ON MY ORDER--

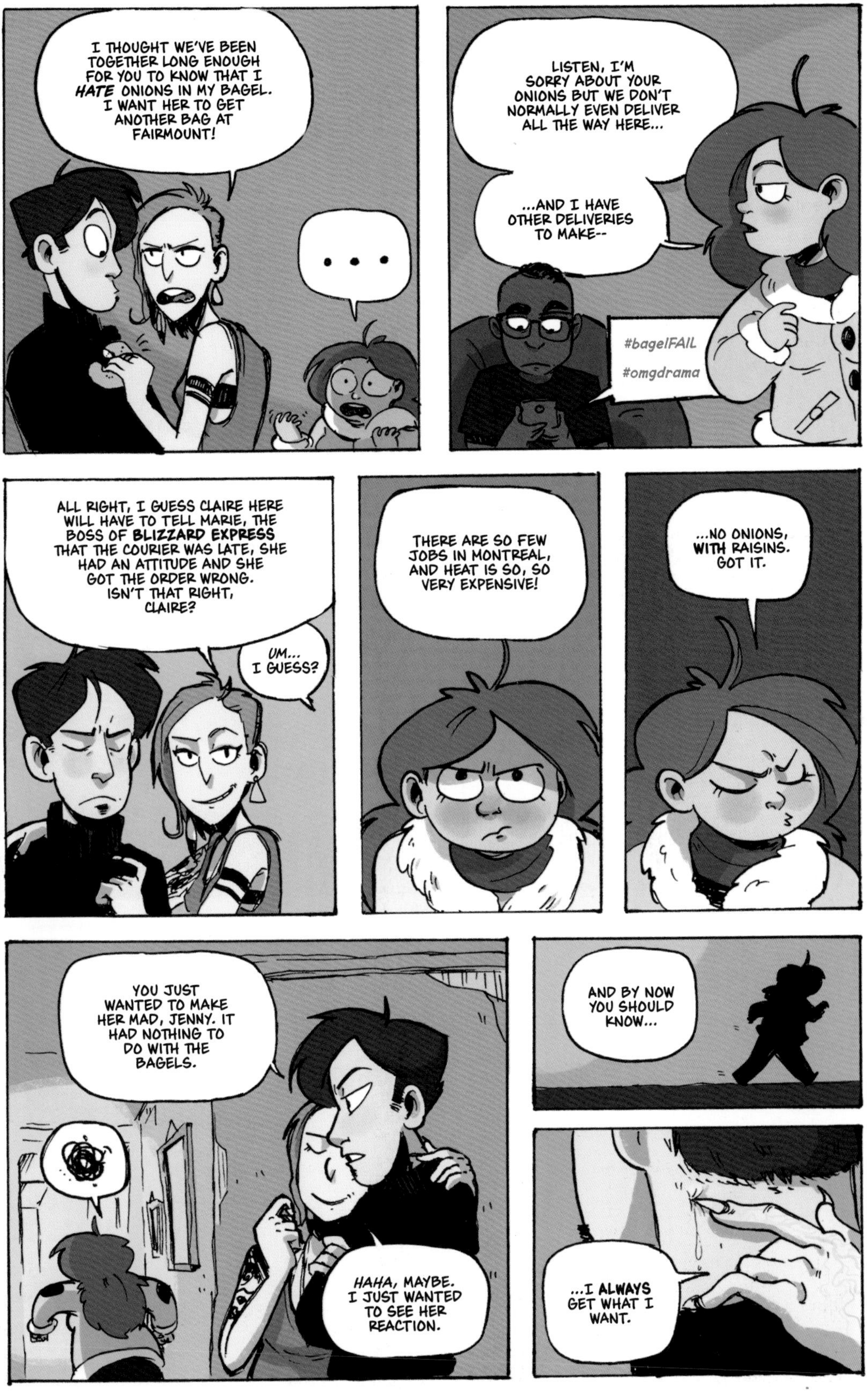
I THOUGHT WE'VE BEEN TOGETHER LONG ENOUGH FOR YOU TO KNOW THAT I *HATE* ONIONS IN MY BAGEL. I WANT HER TO GET ANOTHER BAG AT FAIRMOUNT!
. . .
LISTEN, I'M SORRY ABOUT YOUR ONIONS BUT WE DON'T NORMALLY EVEN DELIVER ALL THE WAY HERE...
...AND I HAVE OTHER DELIVERIES TO MAKE--
#bagelFAIL
#omgdrama
ALL RIGHT, I GUESS CLAIRE HERE WILL HAVE TO TELL MARIE, THE BOSS OF **BLIZZARD EXPRESS** THAT THE COURIER WAS LATE, SHE HAD AN ATTITUDE AND SHE GOT THE ORDER WRONG. ISN'T THAT RIGHT, CLAIRE?
UM... I GUESS?
THERE ARE SO FEW JOBS IN MONTREAL, AND HEAT IS SO, SO VERY EXPENSIVE!
...NO ONIONS, **WITH** RAISINS. GOT IT.
YOU JUST WANTED TO MAKE HER MAD, JENNY. IT HAD NOTHING TO DO WITH THE BAGELS.
HAHA, MAYBE. I JUST WANTED TO SEE HER REACTION.
AND BY NOW YOU SHOULD KNOW...
...I **ALWAYS** GET WHAT I WANT.

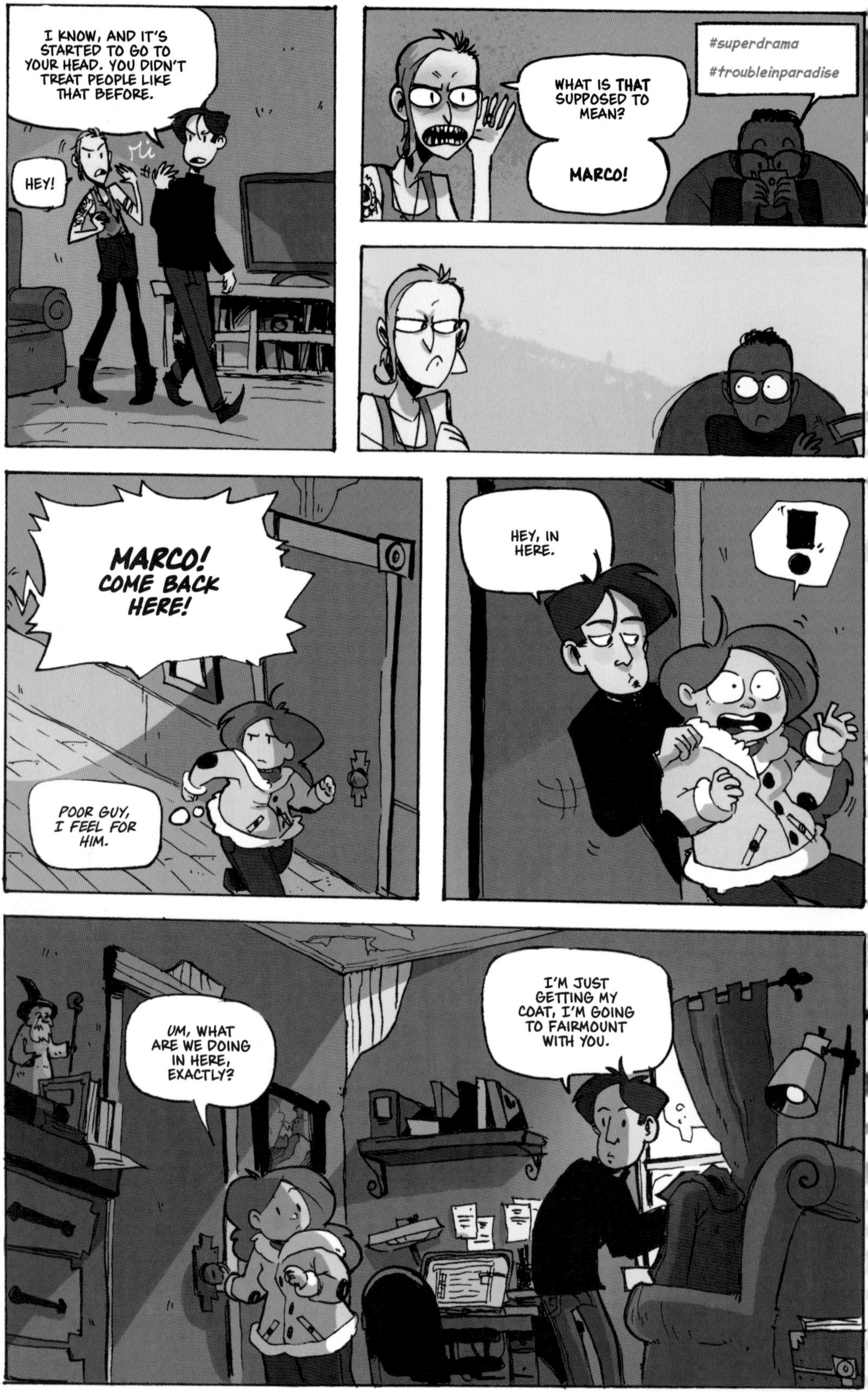
I KNOW, AND IT'S STARTED TO GO TO YOUR HEAD. YOU DIDN'T TREAT PEOPLE LIKE THAT BEFORE.
HEY!
WHAT IS THAT SUPPOSED TO MEAN?
MARCO!
#superdrama
#troubleinparadise
MARCO! COME BACK HERE!
POOR GUY, I FEEL FOR HIM.
HEY, IN HERE.
!
UM, WHAT ARE WE DOING IN HERE, EXACTLY?
I'M JUST GETTING MY COAT, I'M GOING TO FAIRMOUNT WITH YOU.

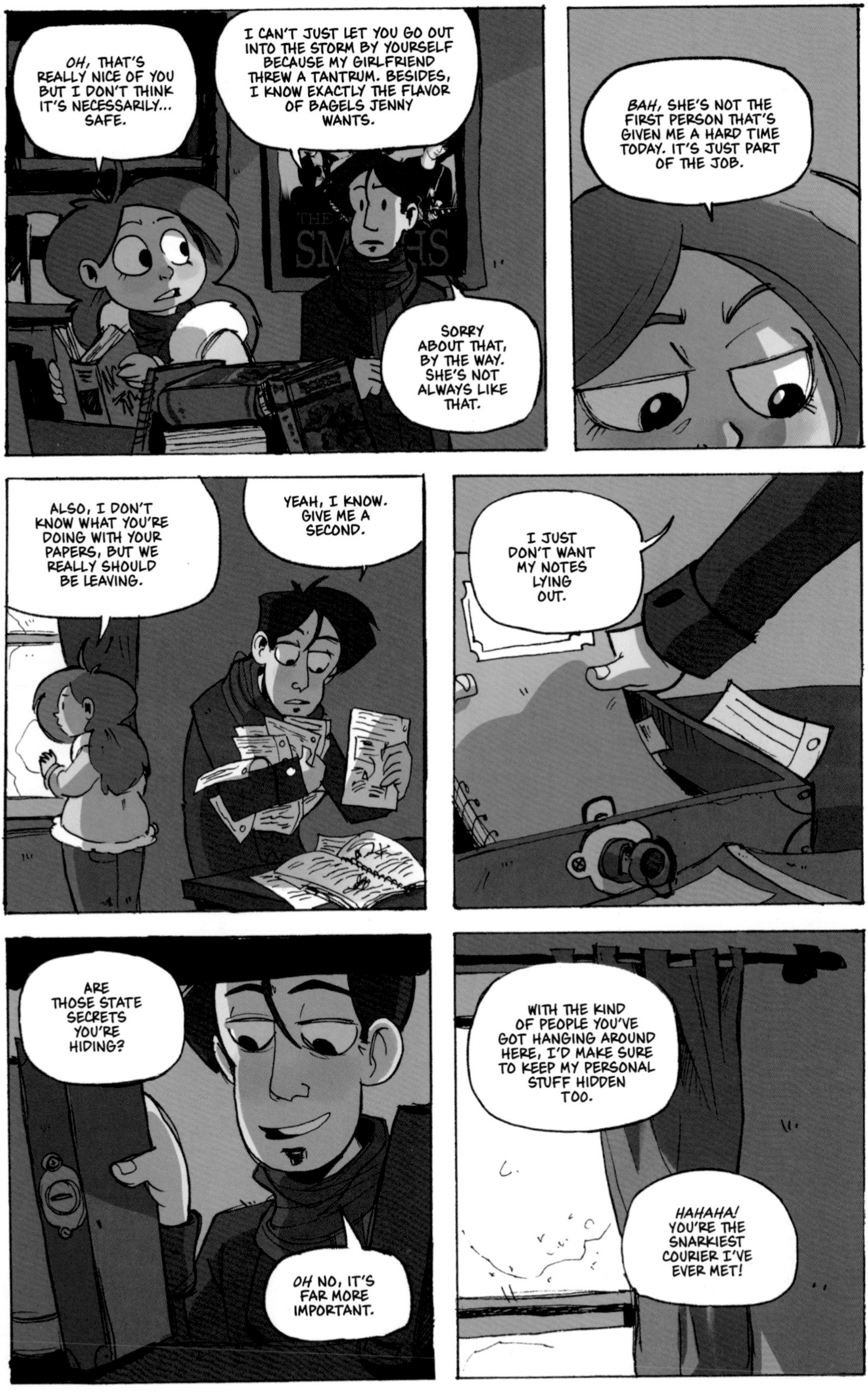
OH, THAT'S REALLY NICE OF YOU BUT I DON'T THINK IT'S NECESSARILY... SAFE.
I CAN'T JUST LET YOU GO OUT INTO THE STORM BY YOURSELF BECAUSE MY GIRLFRIEND THREW A TANTRUM. BESIDES, I KNOW EXACTLY THE FLAVOR OF BAGELS JENNY WANTS.
THE SMITHS
SORRY ABOUT THAT, BY THE WAY. SHE'S NOT ALWAYS LIKE THAT.
BAH, SHE'S NOT THE FIRST PERSON THAT'S GIVEN ME A HARD TIME TODAY. IT'S JUST PART OF THE JOB.
ALSO, I DON'T KNOW WHAT YOU'RE DOING WITH YOUR PAPERS, BUT WE REALLY SHOULD BE LEAVING.
YEAH, I KNOW. GIVE ME A SECOND.
I JUST DON'T WANT MY NOTES LYING OUT.
ARE THOSE STATE SECRETS YOU'RE HIDING?
OH NO, IT'S FAR MORE IMPORTANT.
WITH THE KIND OF PEOPLE YOU'VE GOT HANGING AROUND HERE, I'D MAKE SURE TO KEEP MY PERSONAL STUFF HIDDEN TOO.
HAHAHA! YOU'RE THE SNARKIEST COURIER I'VE EVER MET!

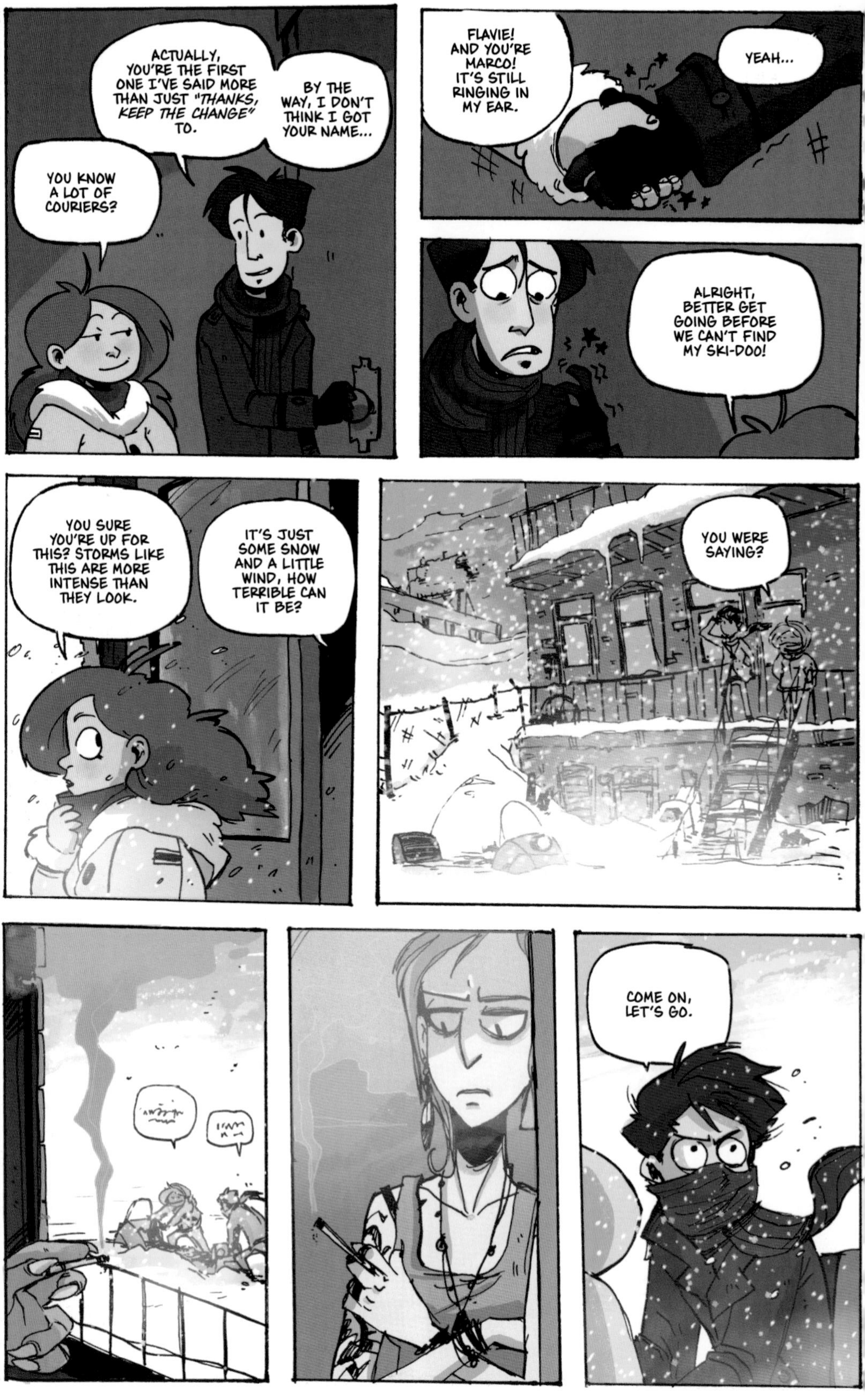

YOU KNOW A LOT OF COURIERS?
ACTUALLY, YOU'RE THE FIRST ONE I'VE SAID MORE THAN JUST "*THANKS, KEEP THE CHANGE*" TO.
BY THE WAY, I DON'T THINK I GOT YOUR NAME...
FLAVIE! AND YOU'RE MARCO! IT'S STILL RINGING IN MY EAR.
YEAH...
ALRIGHT, BETTER GET GOING BEFORE WE CAN'T FIND MY SKI-DOO!
YOU SURE YOU'RE UP FOR THIS? STORMS LIKE THIS ARE MORE INTENSE THAN THEY LOOK.
IT'S JUST SOME SNOW AND A LITTLE WIND, HOW TERRIBLE CAN IT BE?
YOU WERE SAYING?
COME ON, LET'S GO.

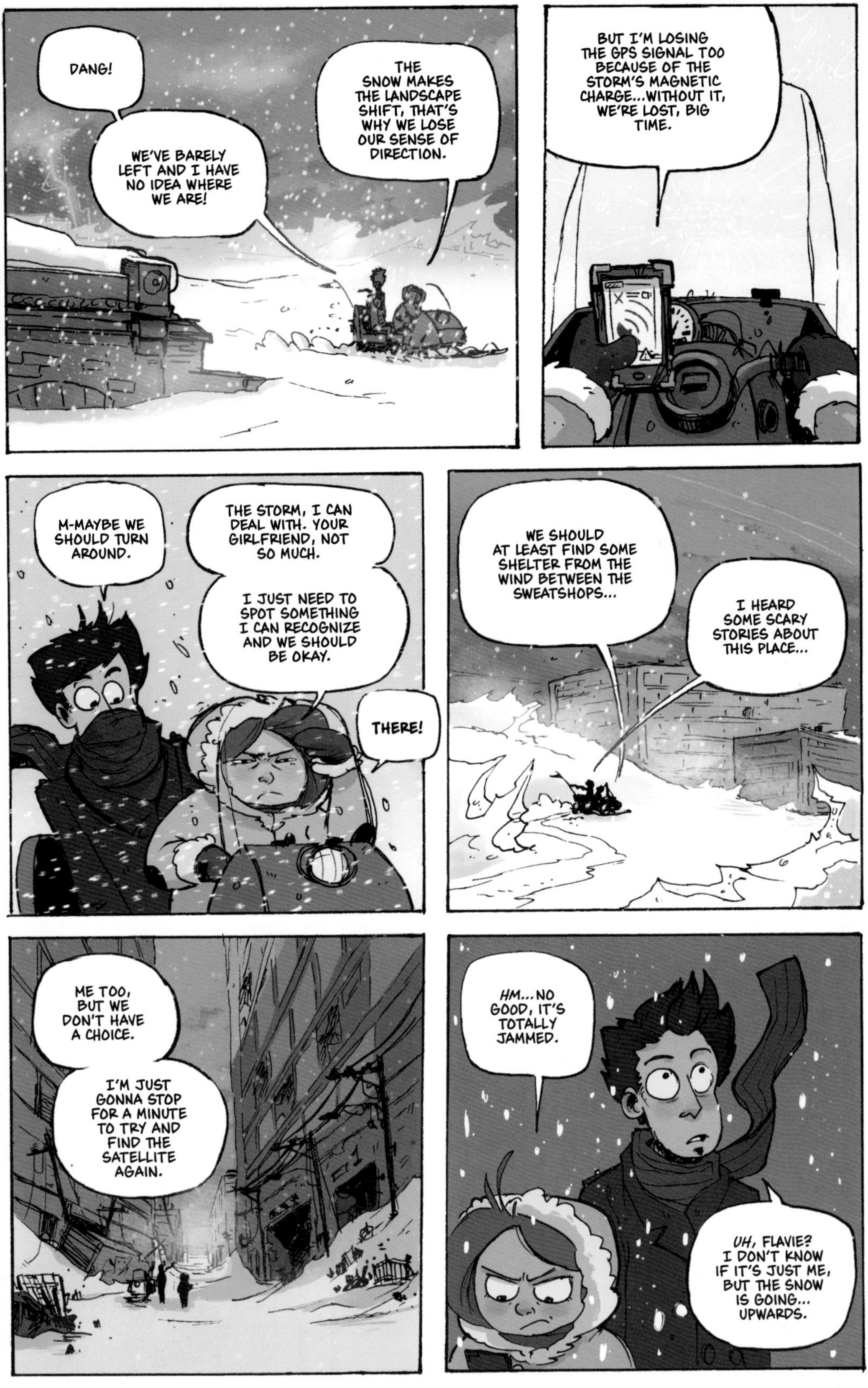
DANG!
WE'VE BARELY LEFT AND I HAVE NO IDEA WHERE WE ARE!
THE SNOW MAKES THE LANDSCAPE SHIFT, THAT'S WHY WE LOSE OUR SENSE OF DIRECTION.
BUT I'M LOSING THE GPS SIGNAL TOO BECAUSE OF THE STORM'S MAGNETIC CHARGE...WITHOUT IT, WE'RE LOST, BIG TIME.
M-MAYBE WE SHOULD TURN AROUND.
THE STORM, I CAN DEAL WITH. YOUR GIRLFRIEND, NOT SO MUCH.
I JUST NEED TO SPOT SOMETHING I CAN RECOGNIZE AND WE SHOULD BE OKAY.
THERE!
WE SHOULD AT LEAST FIND SOME SHELTER FROM THE WIND BETWEEN THE SWEATSHOPS...
I HEARD SOME SCARY STORIES ABOUT THIS PLACE...
ME TOO, BUT WE DON'T HAVE A CHOICE.
I'M JUST GONNA STOP FOR A MINUTE TO TRY AND FIND THE SATELLITE AGAIN.
HM...NO GOOD, IT'S TOTALLY JAMMED.
UH, FLAVIE? I DON'T KNOW IF IT'S JUST ME, BUT THE SNOW IS GOING... UPWARDS.

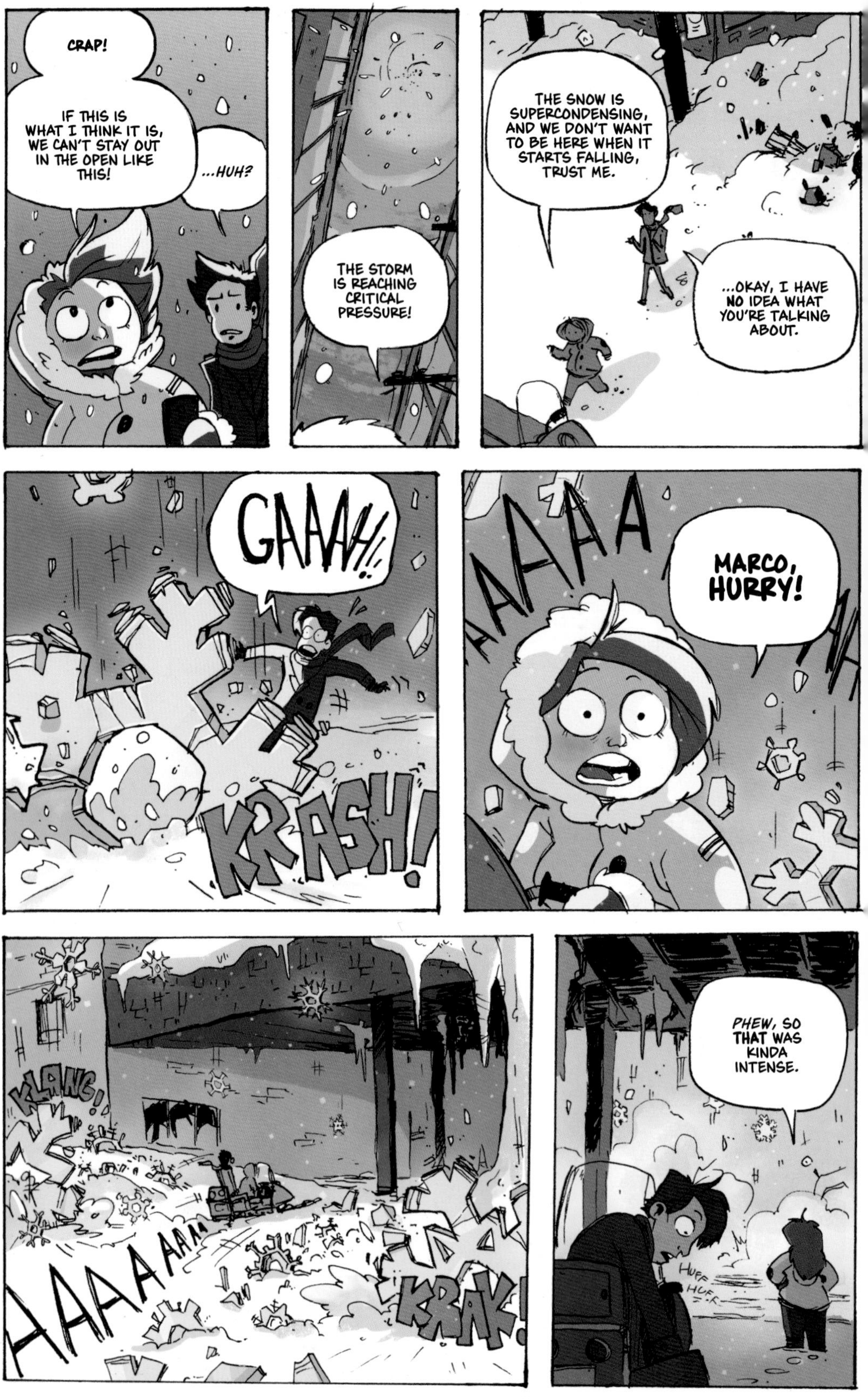
CRAP!
IF THIS IS WHAT I THINK IT IS, WE CAN'T STAY OUT IN THE OPEN LIKE THIS!
...HUH?
THE STORM IS REACHING CRITICAL PRESSURE!
THE SNOW IS SUPERCONDENSING, AND WE DON'T WANT TO BE HERE WHEN IT STARTS FALLING, TRUST ME.
...OKAY, I HAVE NO IDEA WHAT YOU'RE TALKING ABOUT.
GAAAH!!
KRASH!
AAAAA
MARCO, HURRY!
KLANG!
AAAAAAAA
KRAK!
PHEW, SO THAT WAS KINDA INTENSE.
HUFF HUFF

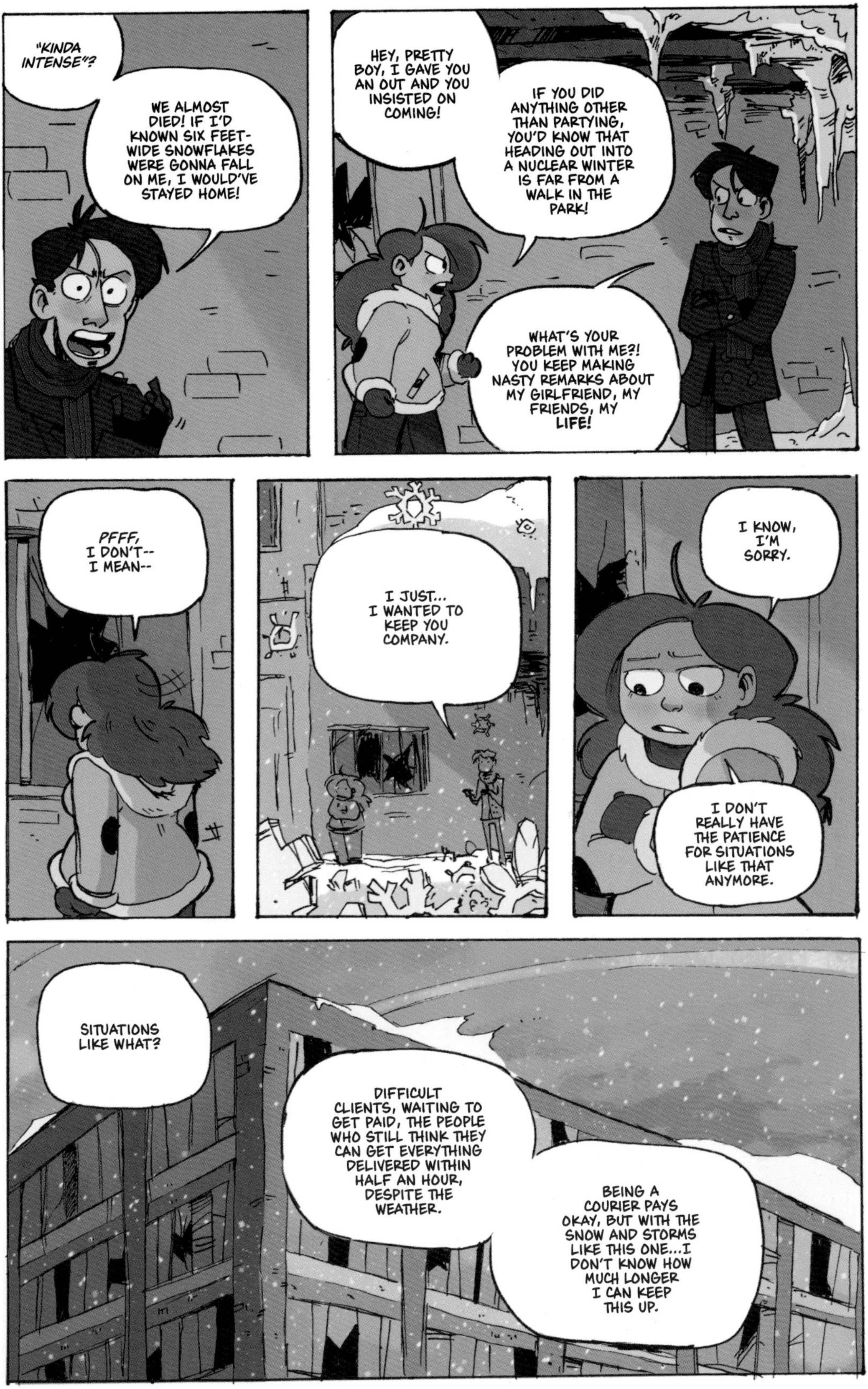
"KINDA INTENSE"?
WE ALMOST DIED! IF I'D KNOWN SIX FEET-WIDE SNOWFLAKES WERE GONNA FALL ON ME, I WOULD'VE STAYED HOME!
HEY, PRETTY BOY, I GAVE YOU AN OUT AND YOU INSISTED ON COMING!
IF YOU DID ANYTHING OTHER THAN PARTYING, YOU'D KNOW THAT HEADING OUT INTO A NUCLEAR WINTER IS FAR FROM A WALK IN THE PARK!
WHAT'S YOUR PROBLEM WITH ME?! YOU KEEP MAKING NASTY REMARKS ABOUT MY GIRLFRIEND, MY FRIENDS, MY LIFE!
PFFF, I DON'T-- I MEAN--
I JUST... I WANTED TO KEEP YOU COMPANY.
I KNOW, I'M SORRY.
I DON'T REALLY HAVE THE PATIENCE FOR SITUATIONS LIKE THAT ANYMORE.
SITUATIONS LIKE WHAT?
DIFFICULT CLIENTS, WAITING TO GET PAID, THE PEOPLE WHO STILL THINK THEY CAN GET EVERYTHING DELIVERED WITHIN HALF AN HOUR, DESPITE THE WEATHER.
BEING A COURIER PAYS OKAY, BUT WITH THE SNOW AND STORMS LIKE THIS ONE...I DON'T KNOW HOW MUCH LONGER I CAN KEEP THIS UP.

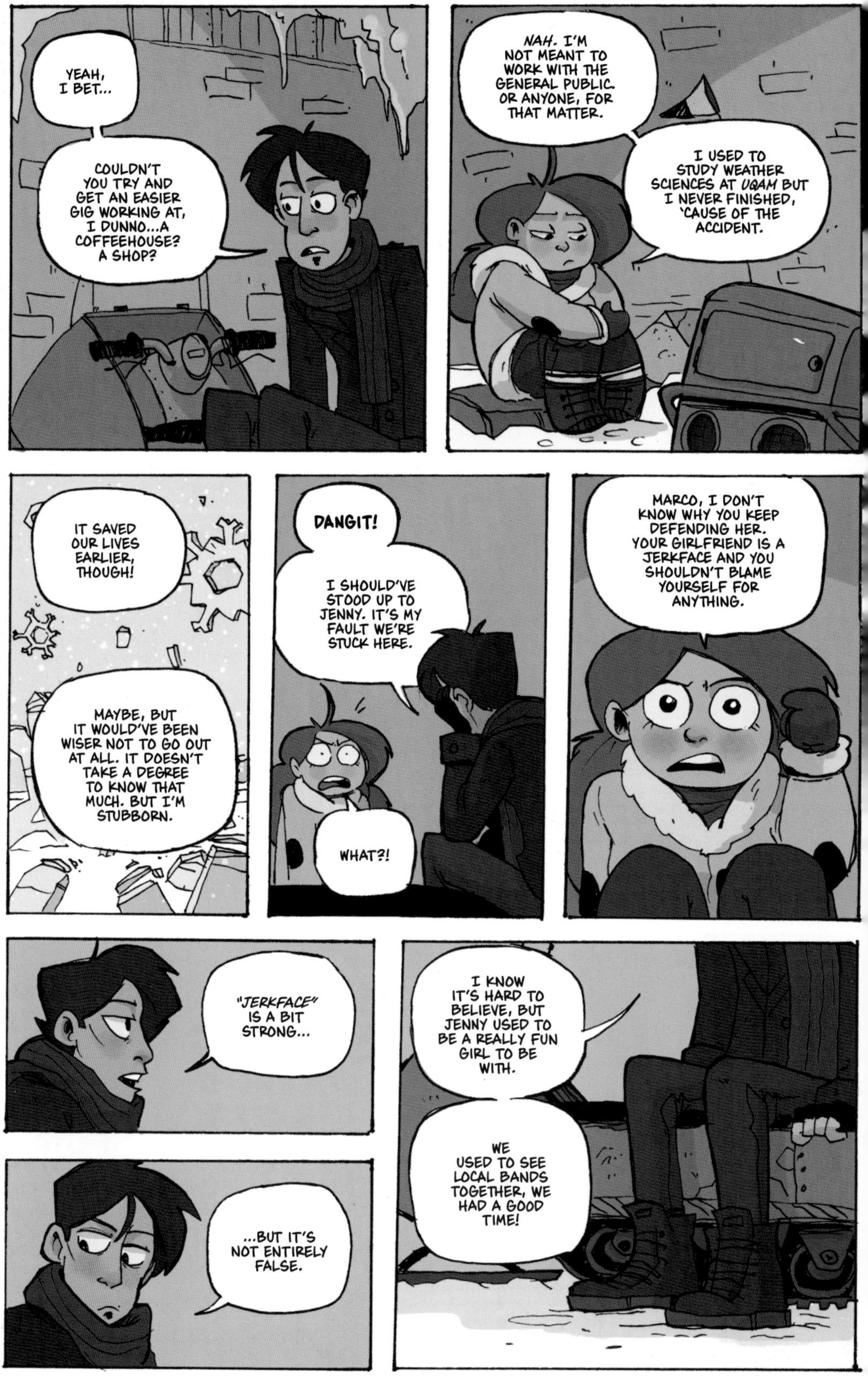
YEAH, I BET...
COULDN'T YOU TRY AND GET AN EASIER GIG WORKING AT, I DUNNO...A COFFEEHOUSE? A SHOP?
NAH. I'M NOT MEANT TO WORK WITH THE GENERAL PUBLIC. OR ANYONE, FOR THAT MATTER.
I USED TO STUDY WEATHER SCIENCES AT UQAM BUT I NEVER FINISHED, 'CAUSE OF THE ACCIDENT.
IT SAVED OUR LIVES EARLIER, THOUGH!
MAYBE, BUT IT WOULD'VE BEEN WISER NOT TO GO OUT AT ALL. IT DOESN'T TAKE A DEGREE TO KNOW THAT MUCH. BUT I'M STUBBORN.
DANGIT!
I SHOULD'VE STOOD UP TO JENNY. IT'S MY FAULT WE'RE STUCK HERE.
WHAT?!
MARCO, I DON'T KNOW WHY YOU KEEP DEFENDING HER. YOUR GIRLFRIEND IS A JERKFACE AND YOU SHOULDN'T BLAME YOURSELF FOR ANYTHING.
"JERKFACE" IS A BIT STRONG...
...BUT IT'S NOT ENTIRELY FALSE.
I KNOW IT'S HARD TO BELIEVE, BUT JENNY USED TO BE A REALLY FUN GIRL TO BE WITH.
WE USED TO SEE LOCAL BANDS TOGETHER, WE HAD A GOOD TIME!

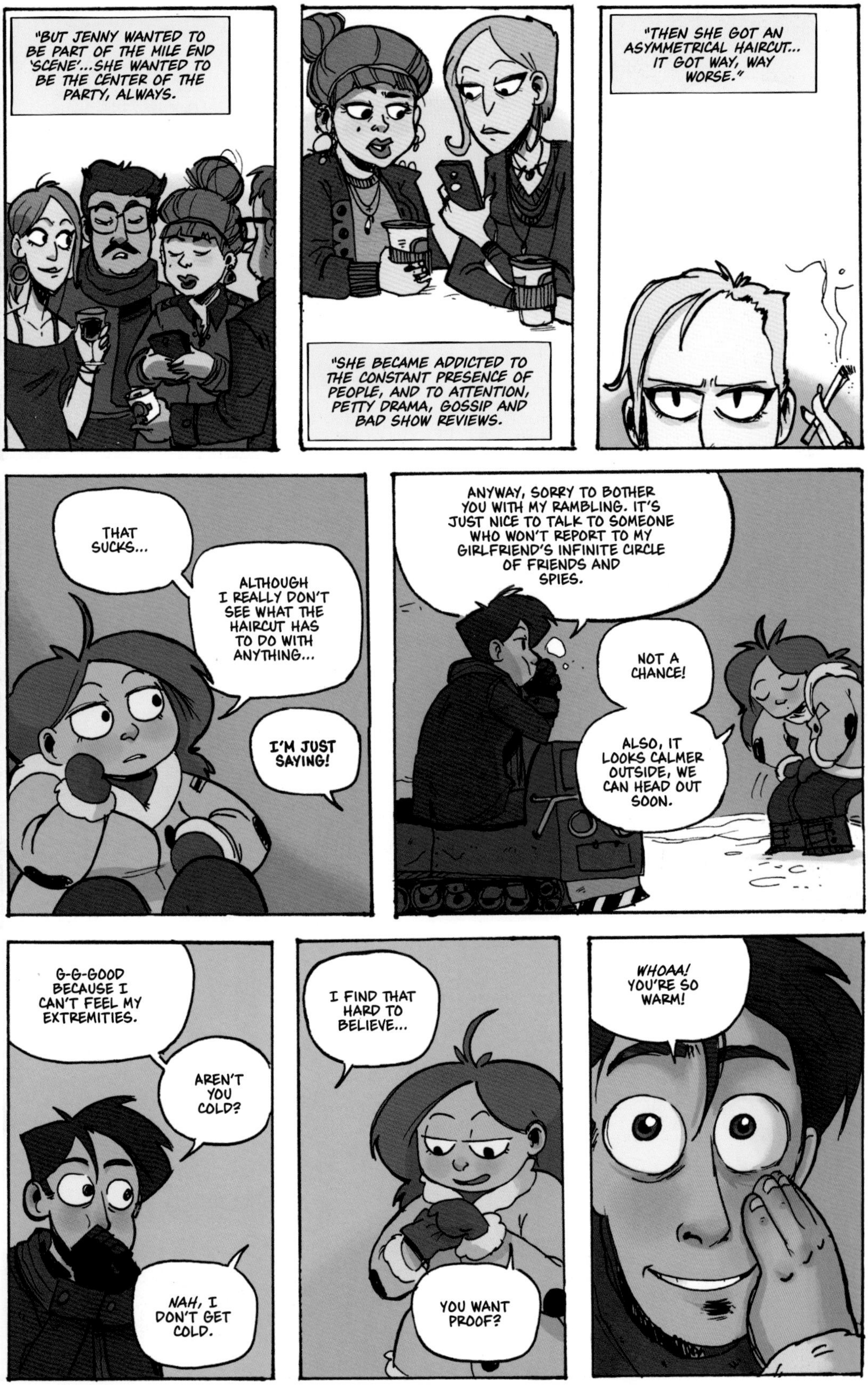
"BUT JENNY WANTED TO BE PART OF THE MILE END 'SCENE'...SHE WANTED TO BE THE CENTER OF THE PARTY, ALWAYS.
"SHE BECAME ADDICTED TO THE CONSTANT PRESENCE OF PEOPLE, AND TO ATTENTION, PETTY DRAMA, GOSSIP AND BAD SHOW REVIEWS.
"THEN SHE GOT AN ASYMMETRICAL HAIRCUT... IT GOT WAY, WAY WORSE."
THAT SUCKS...
ALTHOUGH I REALLY DON'T SEE WHAT THE HAIRCUT HAS TO DO WITH ANYTHING...
I'M JUST SAYING!
ANYWAY, SORRY TO BOTHER YOU WITH MY RAMBLING. IT'S JUST NICE TO TALK TO SOMEONE WHO WON'T REPORT TO MY GIRLFRIEND'S INFINITE CIRCLE OF FRIENDS AND SPIES.
NOT A CHANCE!
ALSO, IT LOOKS CALMER OUTSIDE, WE CAN HEAD OUT SOON.
G-G-GOOD BECAUSE I CAN'T FEEL MY EXTREMITIES.
AREN'T YOU COLD?
NAH, I DON'T GET COLD.
I FIND THAT HARD TO BELIEVE...
YOU WANT PROOF?
WHOAA! YOU'RE SO WARM!

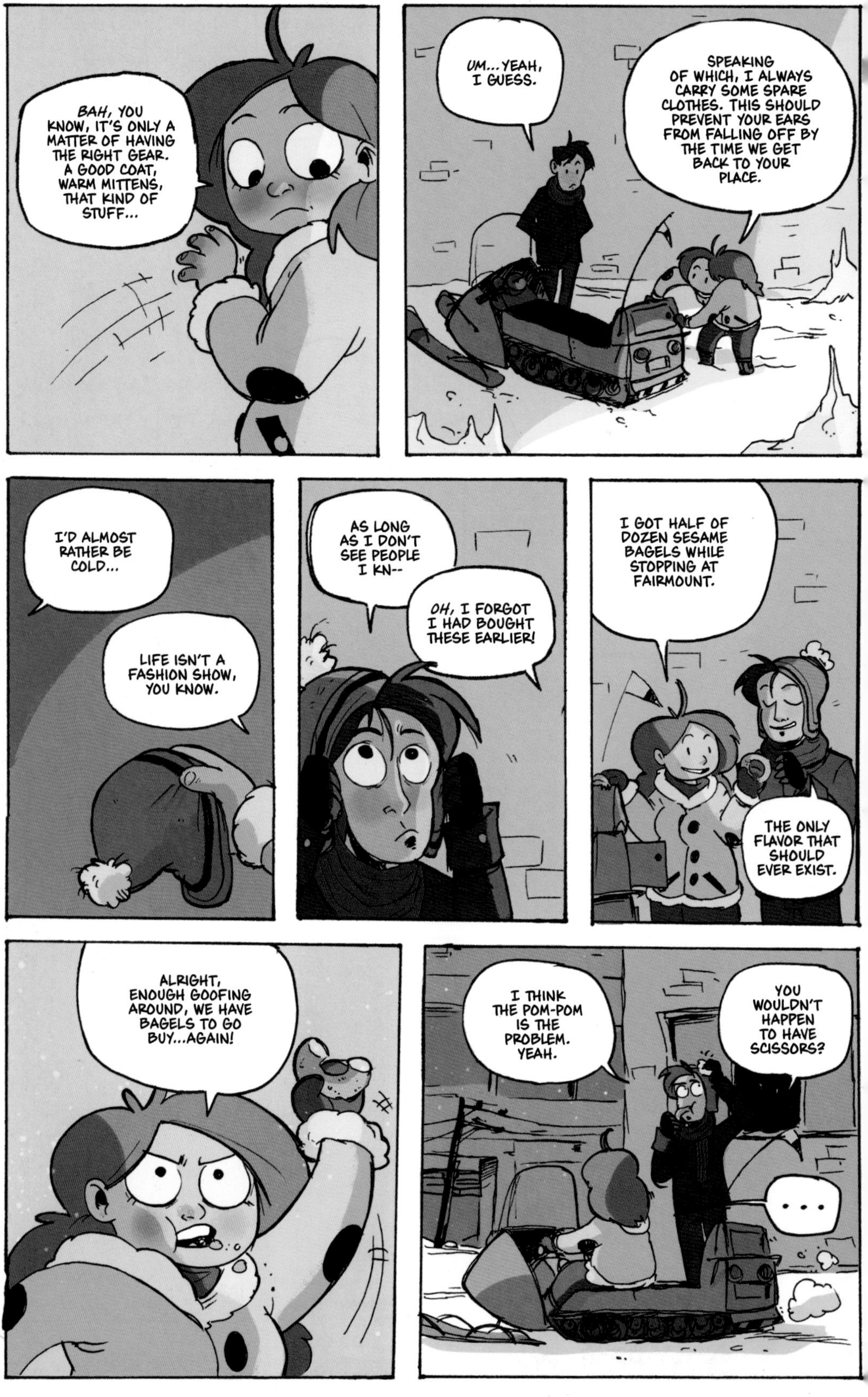
BAH, YOU KNOW, IT'S ONLY A MATTER OF HAVING THE RIGHT GEAR. A GOOD COAT, WARM MITTENS, THAT KIND OF STUFF...
UM... YEAH, I GUESS.
SPEAKING OF WHICH, I ALWAYS CARRY SOME SPARE CLOTHES. THIS SHOULD PREVENT YOUR EARS FROM FALLING OFF BY THE TIME WE GET BACK TO YOUR PLACE.
I'D ALMOST RATHER BE COLD...
LIFE ISN'T A FASHION SHOW, YOU KNOW.
AS LONG AS I DON'T SEE PEOPLE I KN--
OH, I FORGOT I HAD BOUGHT THESE EARLIER!
I GOT HALF OF DOZEN SESAME BAGELS WHILE STOPPING AT FAIRMOUNT.
THE ONLY FLAVOR THAT SHOULD EVER EXIST.
ALRIGHT, ENOUGH GOOFING AROUND, WE HAVE BAGELS TO GO BUY...AGAIN!
I THINK THE POM-POM IS THE PROBLEM. YEAH.
YOU WOULDN'T HAPPEN TO HAVE SCISSORS?
...

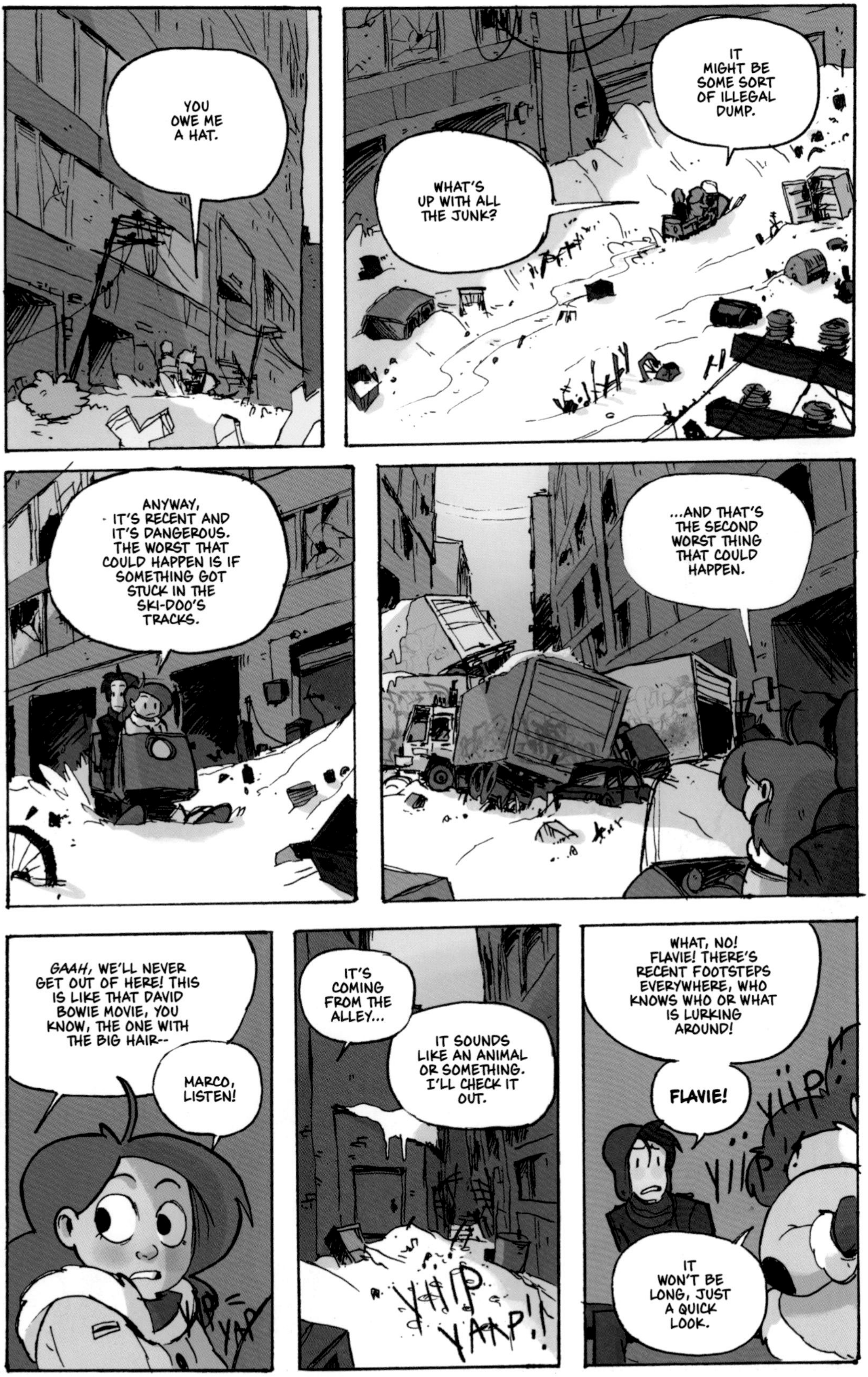
YOU OWE ME A HAT.
WHAT'S UP WITH ALL THE JUNK?
IT MIGHT BE SOME SORT OF ILLEGAL DUMP.
ANYWAY, IT'S RECENT AND IT'S DANGEROUS. THE WORST THAT COULD HAPPEN IS IF SOMETHING GOT STUCK IN THE SKI-DOO'S TRACKS.
...AND THAT'S THE SECOND WORST THING THAT COULD HAPPEN.
GAAH, WE'LL NEVER GET OUT OF HERE! THIS IS LIKE THAT DAVID BOWIE MOVIE, YOU KNOW, THE ONE WITH THE BIG HAIR--
MARCO, LISTEN!
YAP
YAP
IT'S COMING FROM THE ALLEY...
IT SOUNDS LIKE AN ANIMAL OR SOMETHING. I'LL CHECK IT OUT.
YIIP!
YAP!
WHAT, NO! FLAVIE! THERE'S RECENT FOOTSTEPS EVERYWHERE, WHO KNOWS WHO OR WHAT IS LURKING AROUND!
FLAVIE!
YIIP
YIIP
IT WON'T BE LONG, JUST A QUICK LOOK.

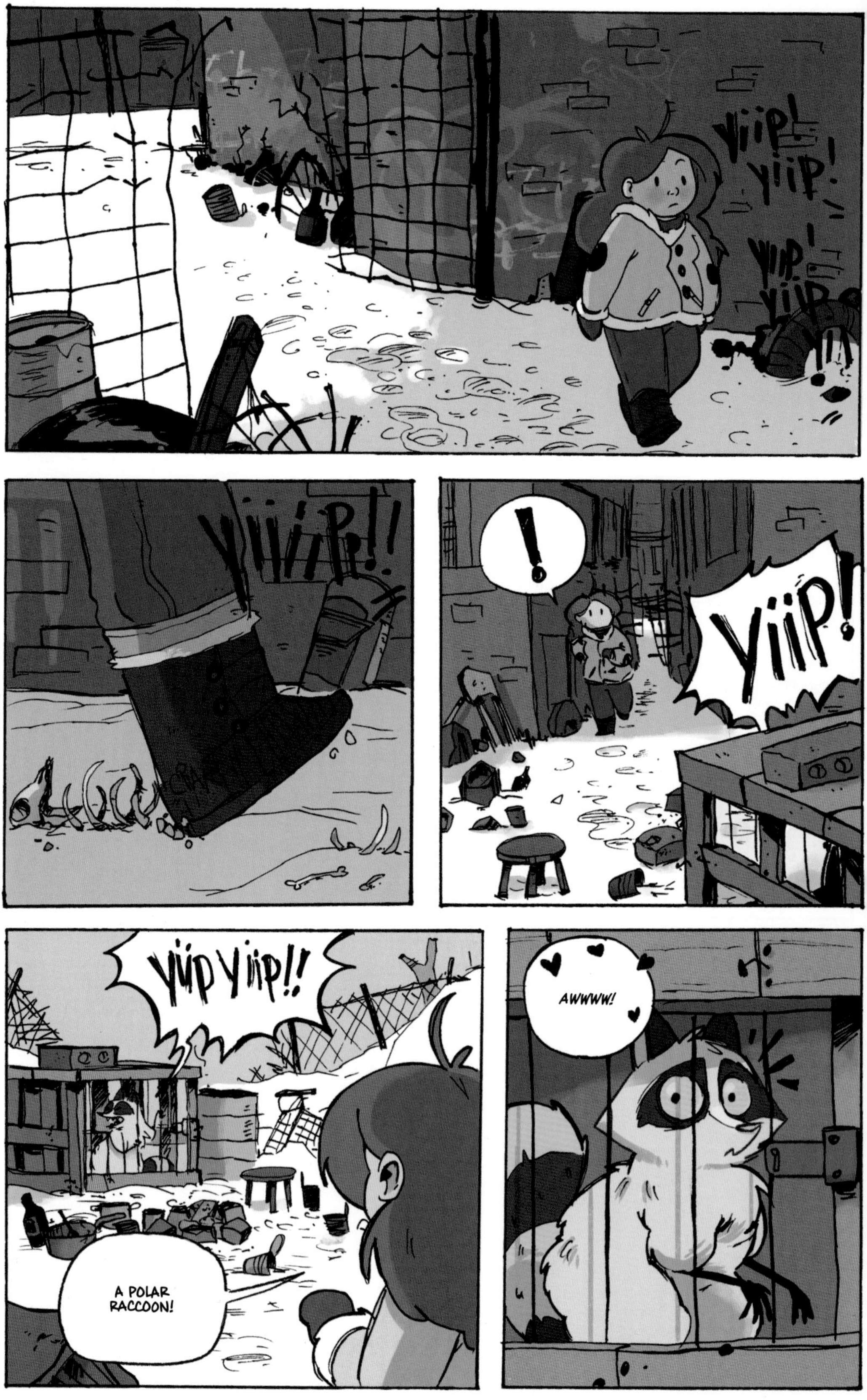
YIIP!
YIIP!
YIIP!
YIIP!
YIIIIP!!
!
YIIP!
YIIP YIIP!!
A POLAR RACCOON!
AWWWW!

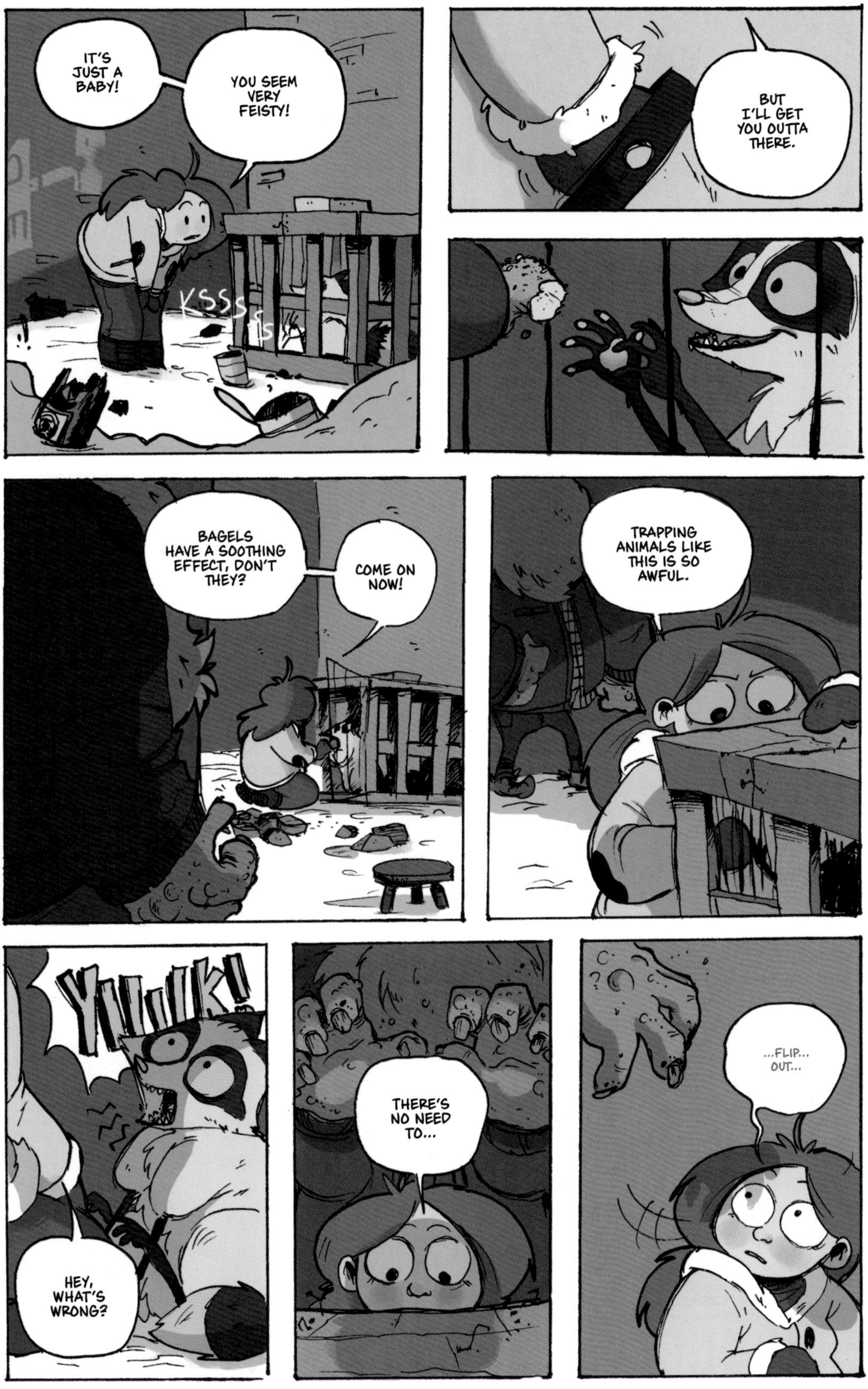
IT'S JUST A BABY!
YOU SEEM VERY FEISTY!
KSSSSS
BUT I'LL GET YOU OUTTA THERE.
BAGELS HAVE A SOOTHING EFFECT, DON'T THEY?
COME ON NOW!
TRAPPING ANIMALS LIKE THIS IS SO AWFUL.
YIIIIK!
HEY, WHAT'S WRONG?
THERE'S NO NEED TO...
...FLIP... OUT...

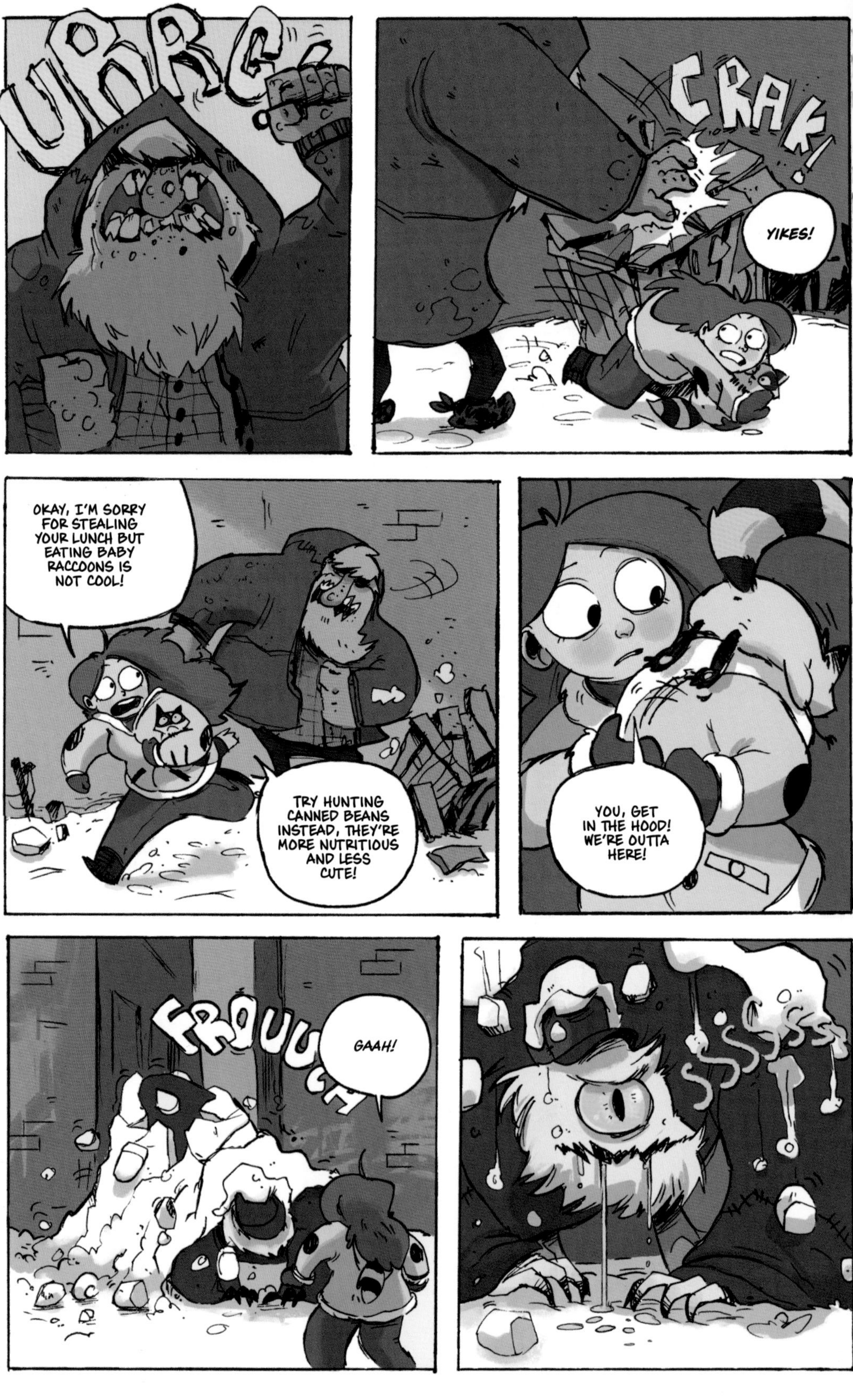
URRG!
CRAK!
YIKES!
OKAY, I'M SORRY FOR STEALING YOUR LUNCH BUT EATING BABY RACCOONS IS NOT COOL!
TRY HUNTING CANNED BEANS INSTEAD, THEY'RE MORE NUTRITIOUS AND LESS CUTE!
YOU, GET IN THE HOOD! WE'RE OUTTA HERE!
FROUUCH
GAAH!
SSSSSS

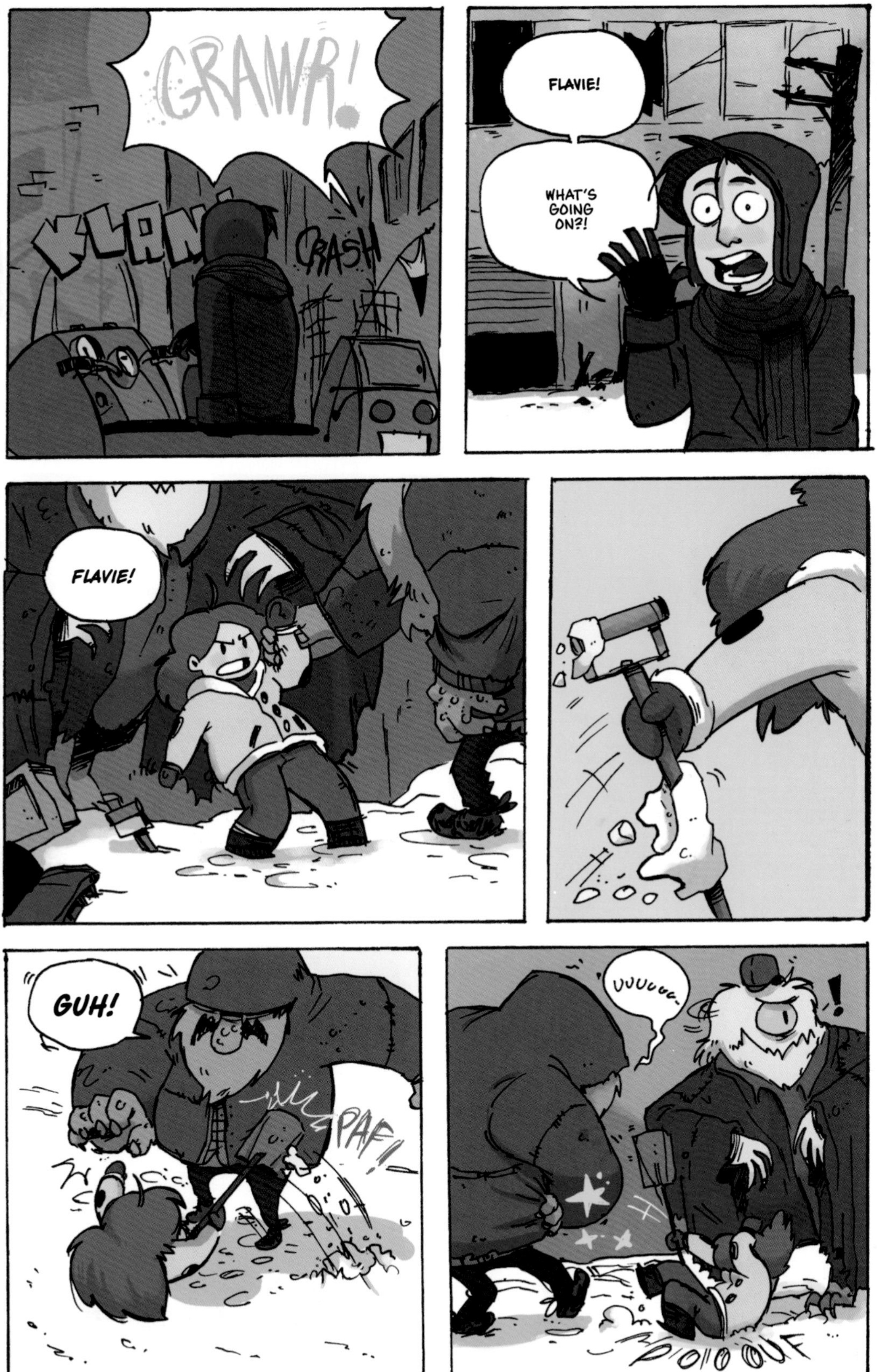

GRAWR!
KLANK
CRASH
FLAVIE!
WHAT'S GOING ON?!
FLAVIE!
GUH!
PAF
UUUUGG..
!
POOOOUF

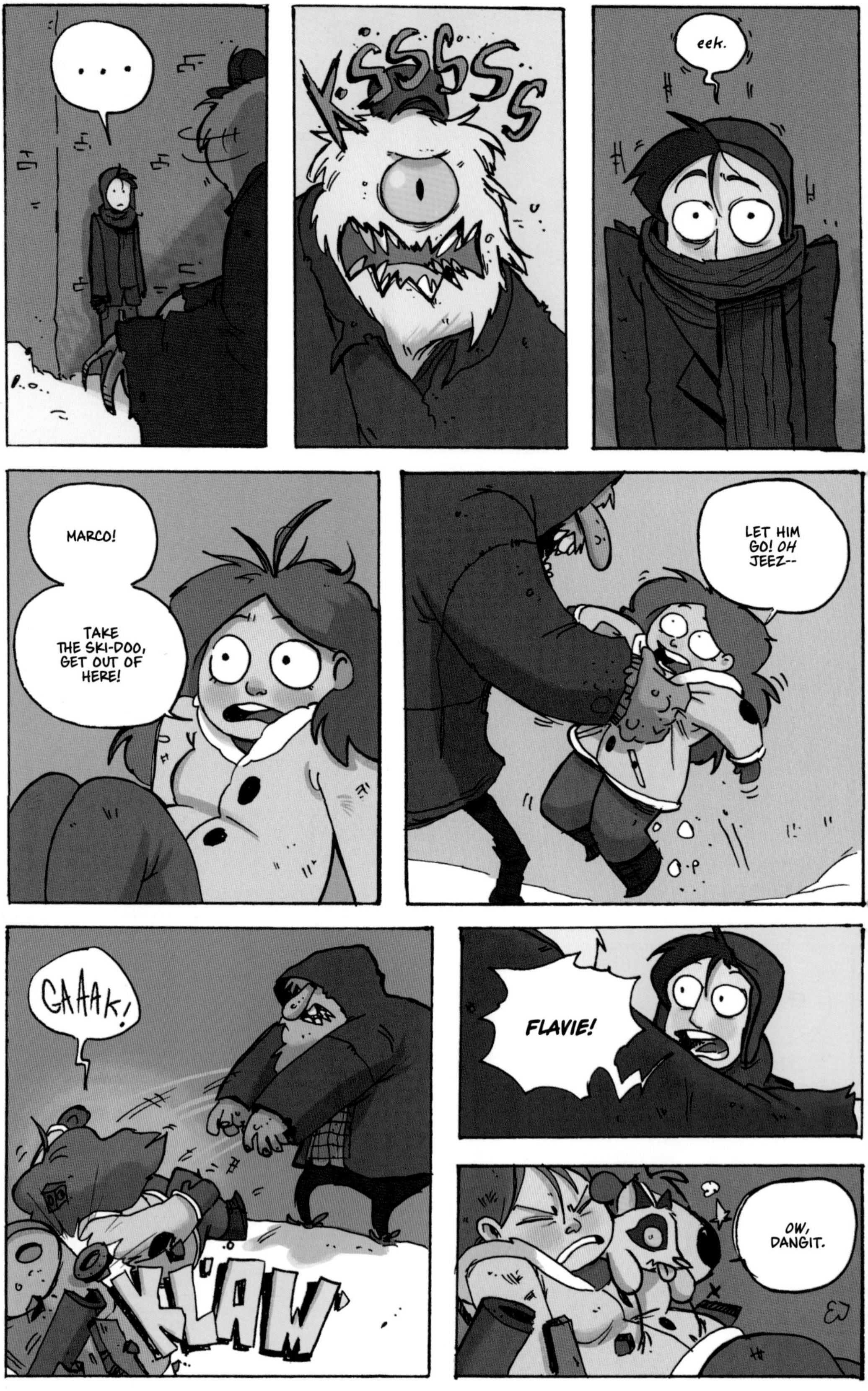
...
KSSSSSS
eek.
MARCO!
TAKE THE SKI-DOO, GET OUT OF HERE!
LET HIM GO! OH JEEZ--
GAAAK!
KLAW
FLAVIE!
OW, DANGIT.

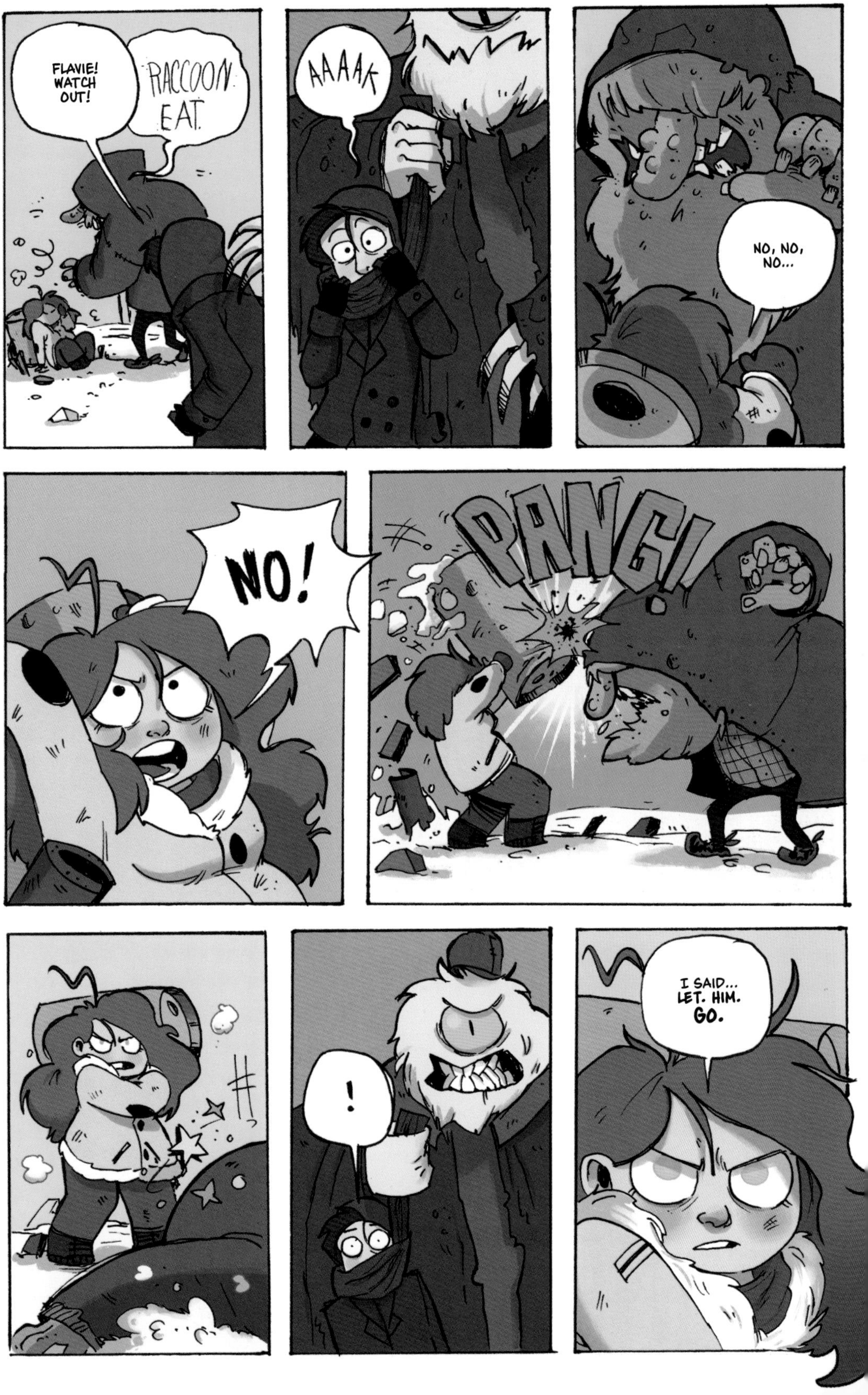
FLAVIE! WATCH OUT!
RACCOON EAT.
AAAAK
NO, NO, NO...
NO!
PANG!
!
I SAID... LET. HIM. GO.

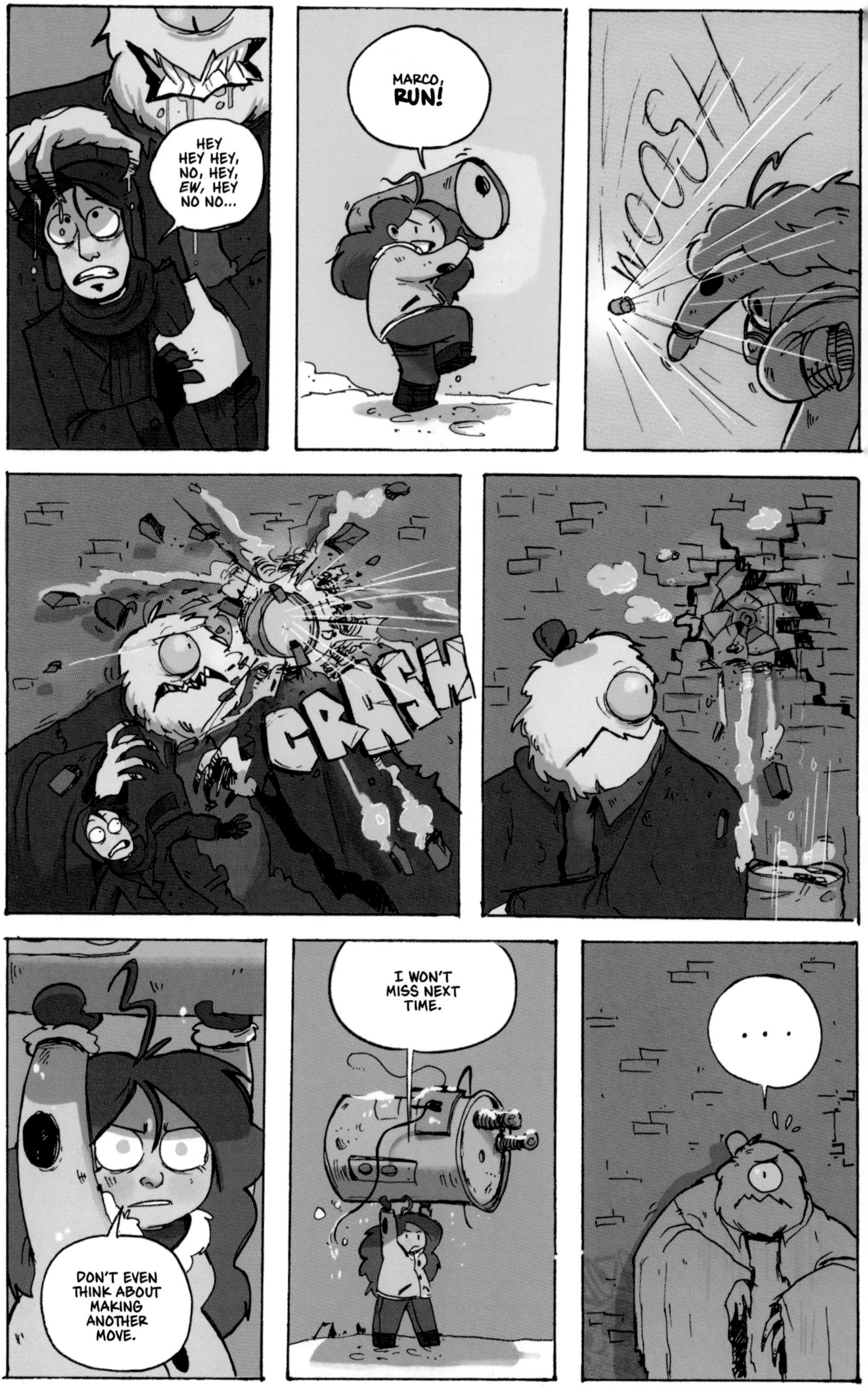
HEY HEY HEY, NO, HEY, EW, HEY NO NO...
MARCO, RUN!
WHOOSH
CRASH
DON'T EVEN THINK ABOUT MAKING ANOTHER MOVE.
I WON'T MISS NEXT TIME.
. . .

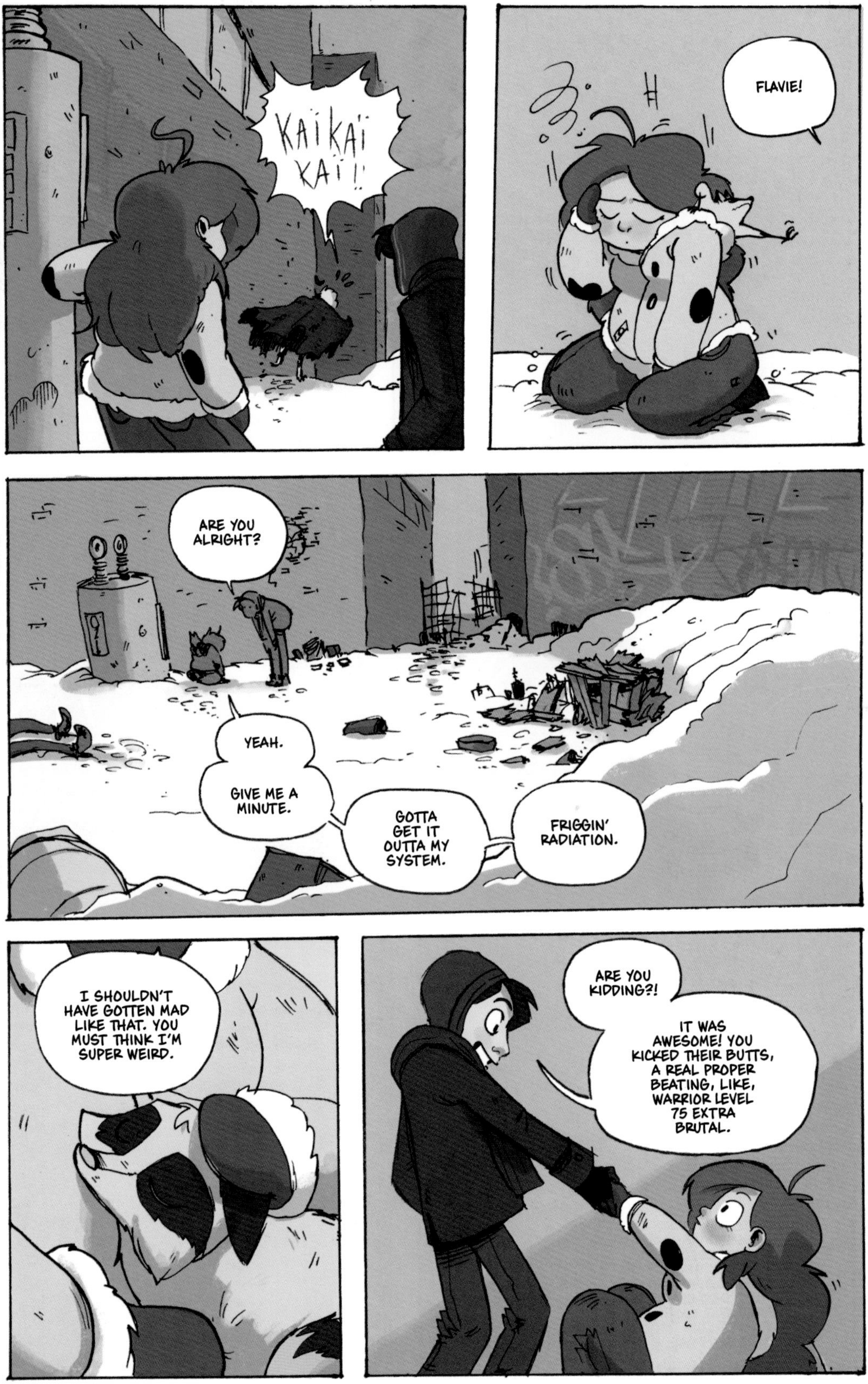
KAI KAI KAI!!
FLAVIE!
ARE YOU ALRIGHT?
YEAH.
GIVE ME A MINUTE.
GOTTA GET IT OUTTA MY SYSTEM.
FRIGGIN' RADIATION.
I SHOULDN'T HAVE GOTTEN MAD LIKE THAT. YOU MUST THINK I'M SUPER WEIRD.
ARE YOU KIDDING?!
IT WAS AWESOME! YOU KICKED THEIR BUTTS, A REAL PROPER BEATING, LIKE, WARRIOR LEVEL 75 EXTRA BRUTAL.

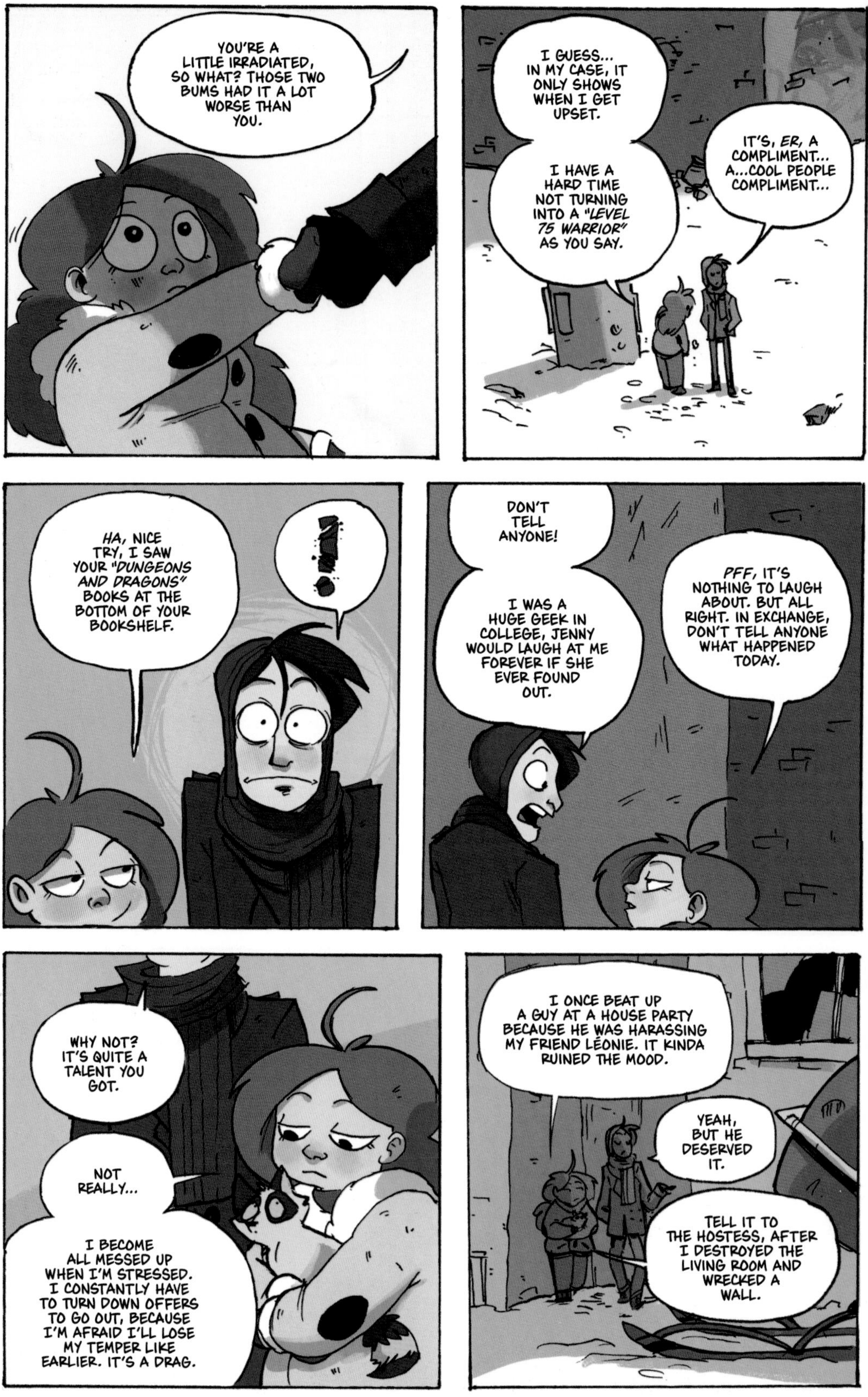
YOU'RE A LITTLE IRRADIATED, SO WHAT? THOSE TWO BUMS HAD IT A LOT WORSE THAN YOU.
I GUESS... IN MY CASE, IT ONLY SHOWS WHEN I GET UPSET.
I HAVE A HARD TIME NOT TURNING INTO A "LEVEL 75 WARRIOR" AS YOU SAY.
IT'S, ER, A COMPLIMENT... A...COOL PEOPLE COMPLIMENT...
HA, NICE TRY, I SAW YOUR "DUNGEONS AND DRAGONS" BOOKS AT THE BOTTOM OF YOUR BOOKSHELF.
!
DON'T TELL ANYONE!
I WAS A HUGE GEEK IN COLLEGE, JENNY WOULD LAUGH AT ME FOREVER IF SHE EVER FOUND OUT.
PFF, IT'S NOTHING TO LAUGH ABOUT. BUT ALL RIGHT. IN EXCHANGE, DON'T TELL ANYONE WHAT HAPPENED TODAY.
WHY NOT? IT'S QUITE A TALENT YOU GOT.
NOT REALLY...
I BECOME ALL MESSED UP WHEN I'M STRESSED. I CONSTANTLY HAVE TO TURN DOWN OFFERS TO GO OUT, BECAUSE I'M AFRAID I'LL LOSE MY TEMPER LIKE EARLIER. IT'S A DRAG.
I ONCE BEAT UP A GUY AT A HOUSE PARTY BECAUSE HE WAS HARASSING MY FRIEND LÉONIE. IT KINDA RUINED THE MOOD.
YEAH, BUT HE DESERVED IT.
TELL IT TO THE HOSTESS, AFTER I DESTROYED THE LIVING ROOM AND WRECKED A WALL.

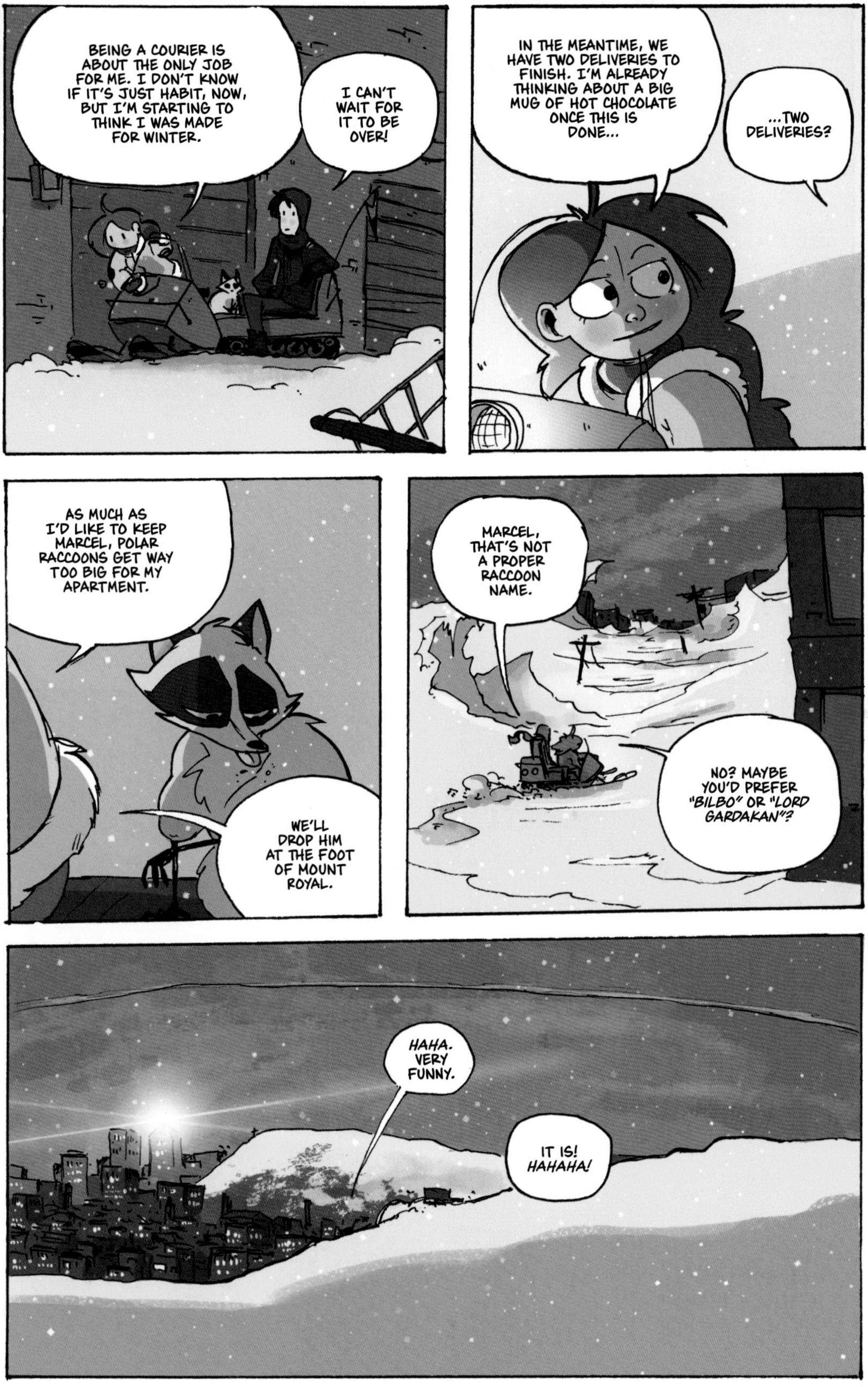
BEING A COURIER IS ABOUT THE ONLY JOB FOR ME. I DON'T KNOW IF IT'S JUST HABIT, NOW, BUT I'M STARTING TO THINK I WAS MADE FOR WINTER.
I CAN'T WAIT FOR IT TO BE OVER!
IN THE MEANTIME, WE HAVE TWO DELIVERIES TO FINISH. I'M ALREADY THINKING ABOUT A BIG MUG OF HOT CHOCOLATE ONCE THIS IS DONE...
...TWO DELIVERIES?
AS MUCH AS I'D LIKE TO KEEP MARCEL, POLAR RACCOONS GET WAY TOO BIG FOR MY APARTMENT.
WE'LL DROP HIM AT THE FOOT OF MOUNT ROYAL.
MARCEL, THAT'S NOT A PROPER RACCOON NAME.
NO? MAYBE YOU'D PREFER "BILBO" OR "LORD GARDAKAN"?
HAHA. VERY FUNNY.
IT IS! HAHAHA!

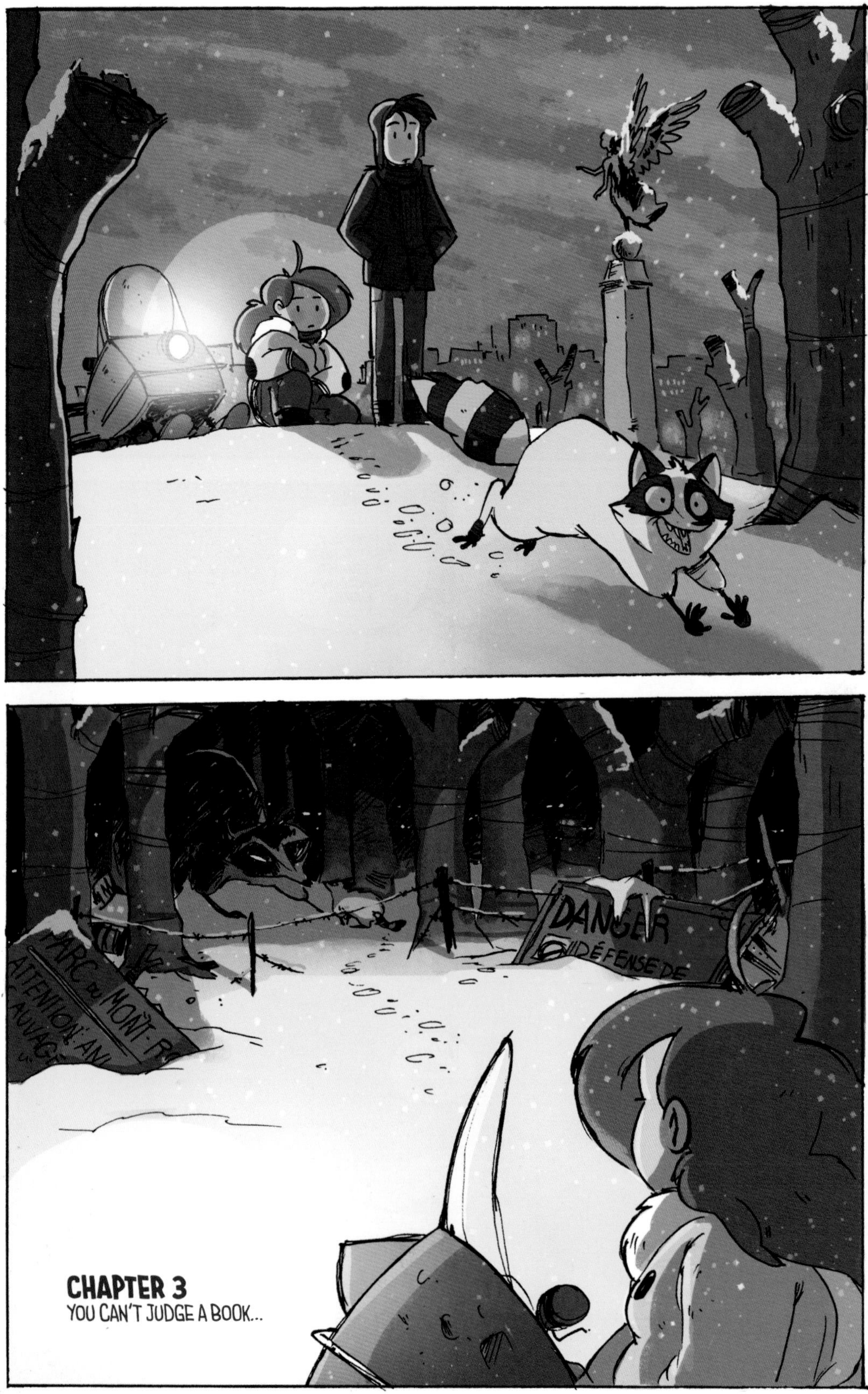
DANGER
DÉFENSE DE

CHAPTER 3
YOU CAN'T JUDGE A BOOK...

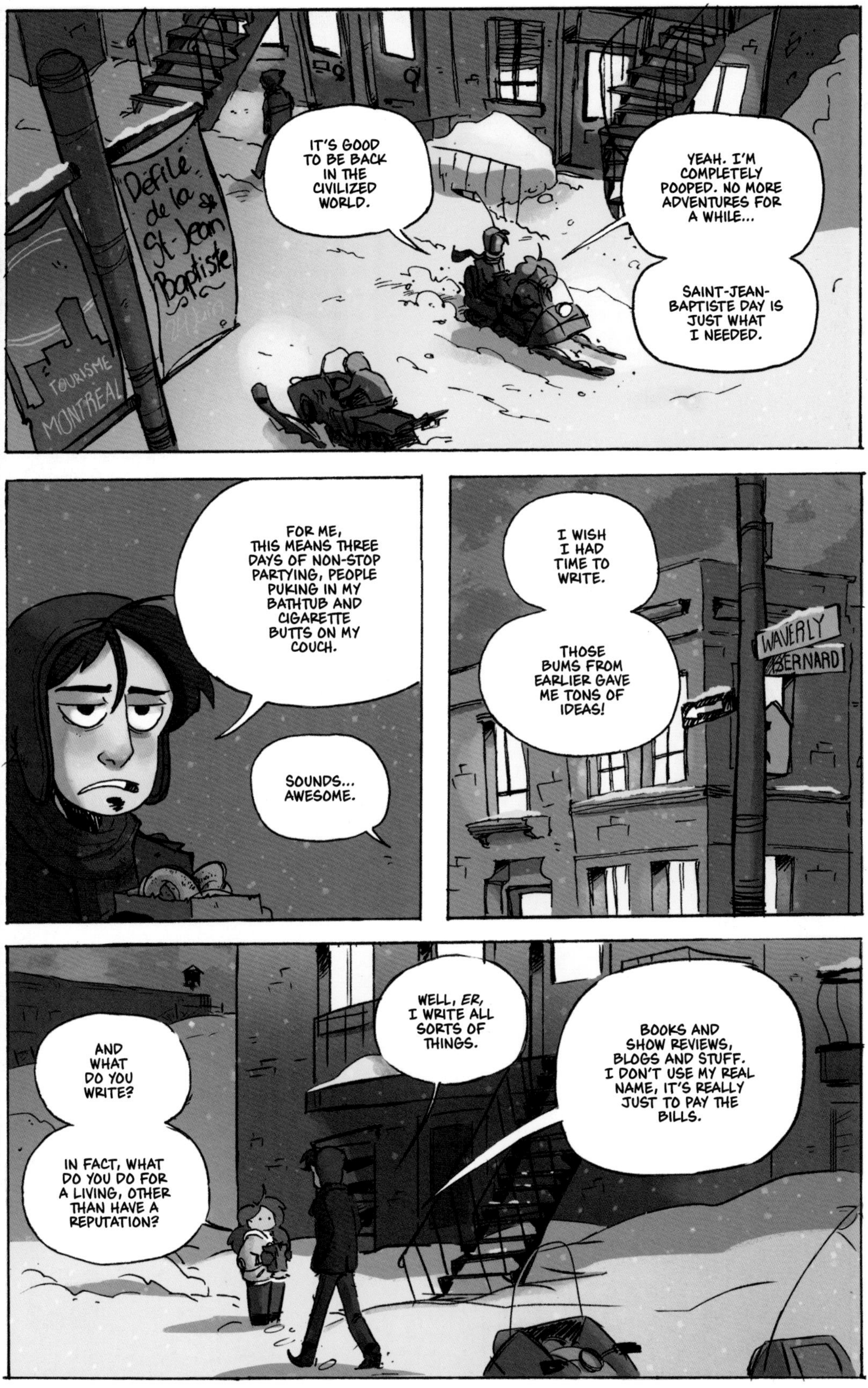
Défilé de la St-Jean Baptiste
24 juin
TOURISME MONTREAL
IT'S GOOD TO BE BACK IN THE CIVILIZED WORLD.
YEAH. I'M COMPLETELY POOPED. NO MORE ADVENTURES FOR A WHILE...
SAINT-JEAN-BAPTISTE DAY IS JUST WHAT I NEEDED.
FOR ME, THIS MEANS THREE DAYS OF NON-STOP PARTYING, PEOPLE PUKING IN MY BATHTUB AND CIGARETTE BUTTS ON MY COUCH.
SOUNDS... AWESOME.
I WISH I HAD TIME TO WRITE.
THOSE BUMS FROM EARLIER GAVE ME TONS OF IDEAS!
WAVERLY
BERNARD
AND WHAT DO YOU WRITE?
IN FACT, WHAT DO YOU DO FOR A LIVING, OTHER THAN HAVE A REPUTATION?
WELL, *ER*, I WRITE ALL SORTS OF THINGS.
BOOKS AND SHOW REVIEWS, BLOGS AND STUFF. I DON'T USE MY REAL NAME, IT'S REALLY JUST TO PAY THE BILLS.

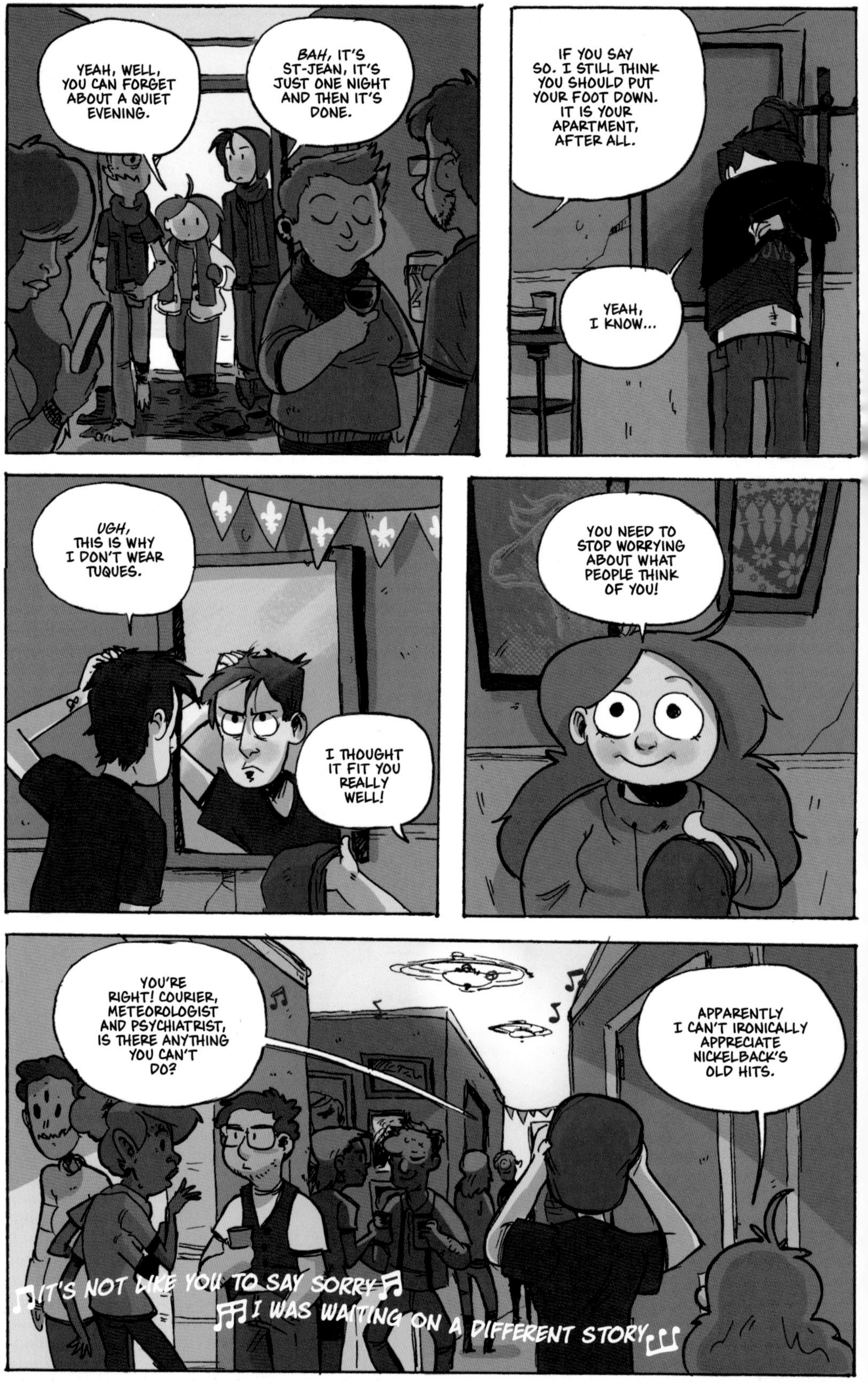
YEAH, WELL, YOU CAN FORGET ABOUT A QUIET EVENING.
BAH, IT'S ST-JEAN, IT'S JUST ONE NIGHT AND THEN IT'S DONE.
IF YOU SAY SO. I STILL THINK YOU SHOULD PUT YOUR FOOT DOWN. IT IS YOUR APARTMENT, AFTER ALL.
YEAH, I KNOW...
UGH, THIS IS WHY I DON'T WEAR TUQUES.
I THOUGHT IT FIT YOU REALLY WELL!
YOU NEED TO STOP WORRYING ABOUT WHAT PEOPLE THINK OF YOU!
YOU'RE RIGHT! COURIER, METEOROLOGIST AND PSYCHIATRIST, IS THERE ANYTHING YOU CAN'T DO?
APPARENTLY I CAN'T IRONICALLY APPRECIATE NICKELBACK'S OLD HITS.
♫ IT'S NOT LIKE YOU TO SAY SORRY ♫
♫ I WAS WAITING ON A DIFFERENT STORY ♫

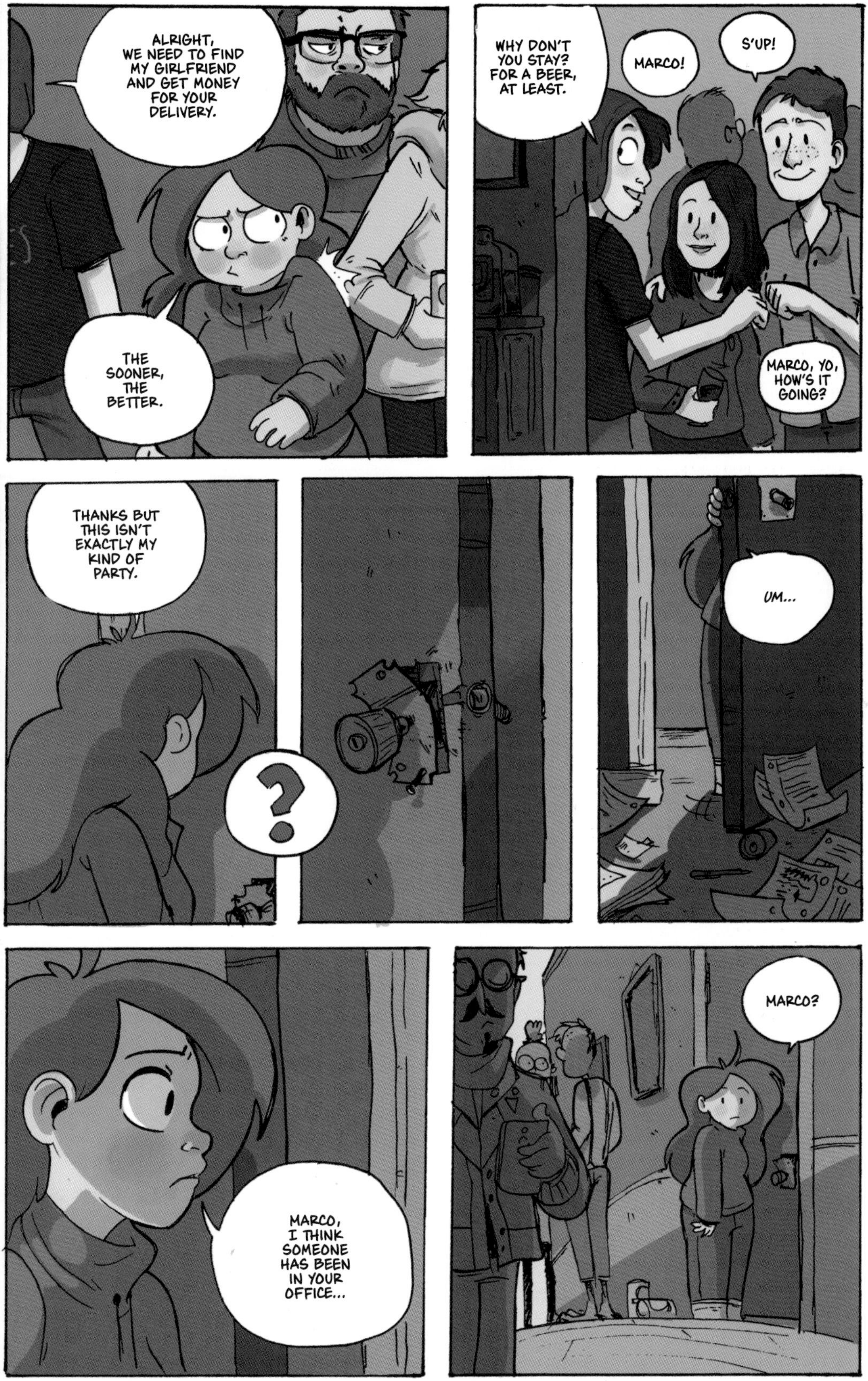
ALRIGHT, WE NEED TO FIND MY GIRLFRIEND AND GET MONEY FOR YOUR DELIVERY.
THE SOONER, THE BETTER.
WHY DON'T YOU STAY? FOR A BEER, AT LEAST.
MARCO!
S'UP!
MARCO, YO, HOW'S IT GOING?
THANKS BUT THIS ISN'T EXACTLY MY KIND OF PARTY.
?
UM...
MARCO, I THINK SOMEONE HAS BEEN IN YOUR OFFICE...
MARCO?

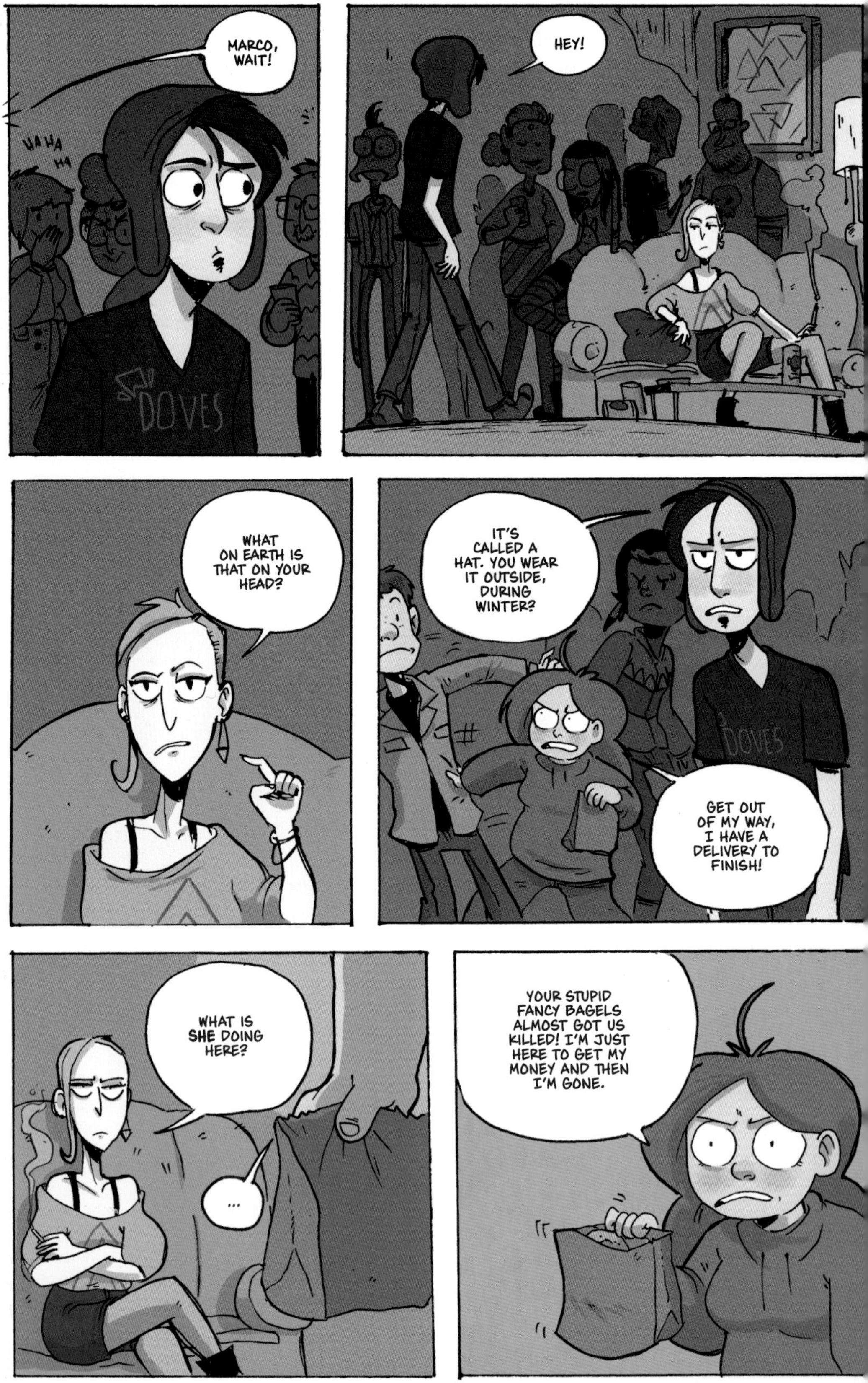
MARCO, WAIT!
HA HA HA
DOVES
HEY!
WHAT ON EARTH IS THAT ON YOUR HEAD?
IT'S CALLED A HAT. YOU WEAR IT OUTSIDE, DURING WINTER?
DOVES
GET OUT OF MY WAY, I HAVE A DELIVERY TO FINISH!
WHAT IS SHE DOING HERE?
...
YOUR STUPID FANCY BAGELS ALMOST GOT US KILLED! I'M JUST HERE TO GET MY MONEY AND THEN I'M GONE.

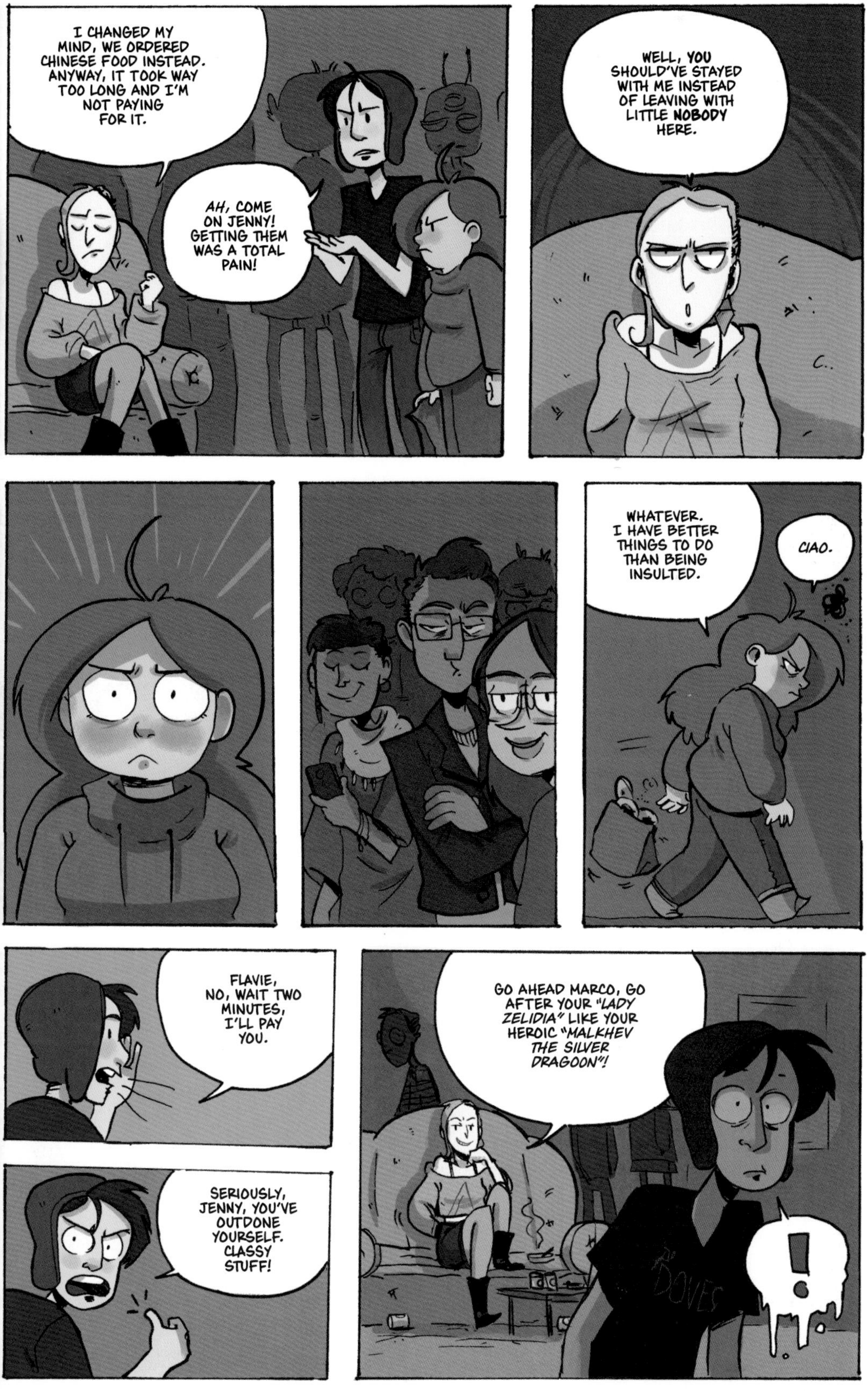
I CHANGED MY MIND, WE ORDERED CHINESE FOOD INSTEAD. ANYWAY, IT TOOK WAY TOO LONG AND I'M NOT PAYING FOR IT.
AH, COME ON JENNY! GETTING THEM WAS A TOTAL PAIN!
WELL, YOU SHOULD'VE STAYED WITH ME INSTEAD OF LEAVING WITH LITTLE NOBODY HERE.
WHATEVER. I HAVE BETTER THINGS TO DO THAN BEING INSULTED.
CIAO.
FLAVIE, NO, WAIT TWO MINUTES, I'LL PAY YOU.
SERIOUSLY, JENNY, YOU'VE OUTDONE YOURSELF. CLASSY STUFF!
GO AHEAD MARCO, GO AFTER YOUR "LADY ZELIDIA" LIKE YOUR HEROIC "MALKHEV THE SILVER DRAGOON"!
!
DOVES

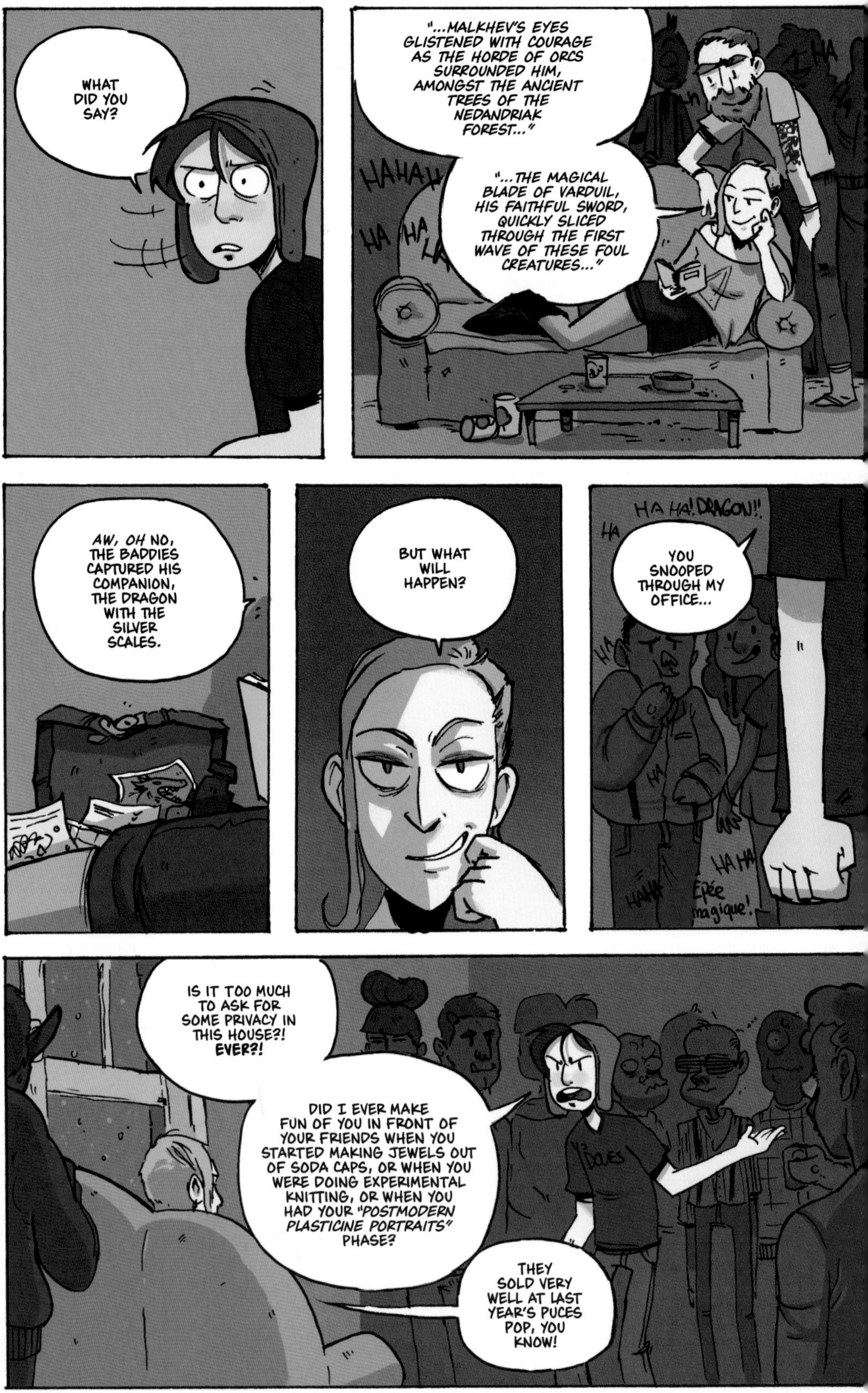
WHAT DID YOU SAY?
"...MALKHEV'S EYES GLISTENED WITH COURAGE AS THE HORDE OF ORCS SURROUNDED HIM, AMONGST THE ANCIENT TREES OF THE NEDANDRIAK FOREST..."
HAHAH
HA HA
"...THE MAGICAL BLADE OF VARDUIL, HIS FAITHFUL SWORD, QUICKLY SLICED THROUGH THE FIRST WAVE OF THESE FOUL CREATURES..."
AW, OH NO, THE BADDIES CAPTURED HIS COMPANION, THE DRAGON WITH THE SILVER SCALES.
BUT WHAT WILL HAPPEN?
HA HA! DRAGON!!
HA
YOU SNOOPED THROUGH MY OFFICE...
HA HA
HAHA
Épée magique!
IS IT TOO MUCH TO ASK FOR SOME PRIVACY IN THIS HOUSE?! EVER?!
DID I EVER MAKE FUN OF YOU IN FRONT OF YOUR FRIENDS WHEN YOU STARTED MAKING JEWELS OUT OF SODA CAPS, OR WHEN YOU WERE DOING EXPERIMENTAL KNITTING, OR WHEN YOU HAD YOUR "POSTMODERN PLASTICINE PORTRAITS" PHASE?
THEY SOLD VERY WELL AT LAST YEAR'S PUCES POP, YOU KNOW!

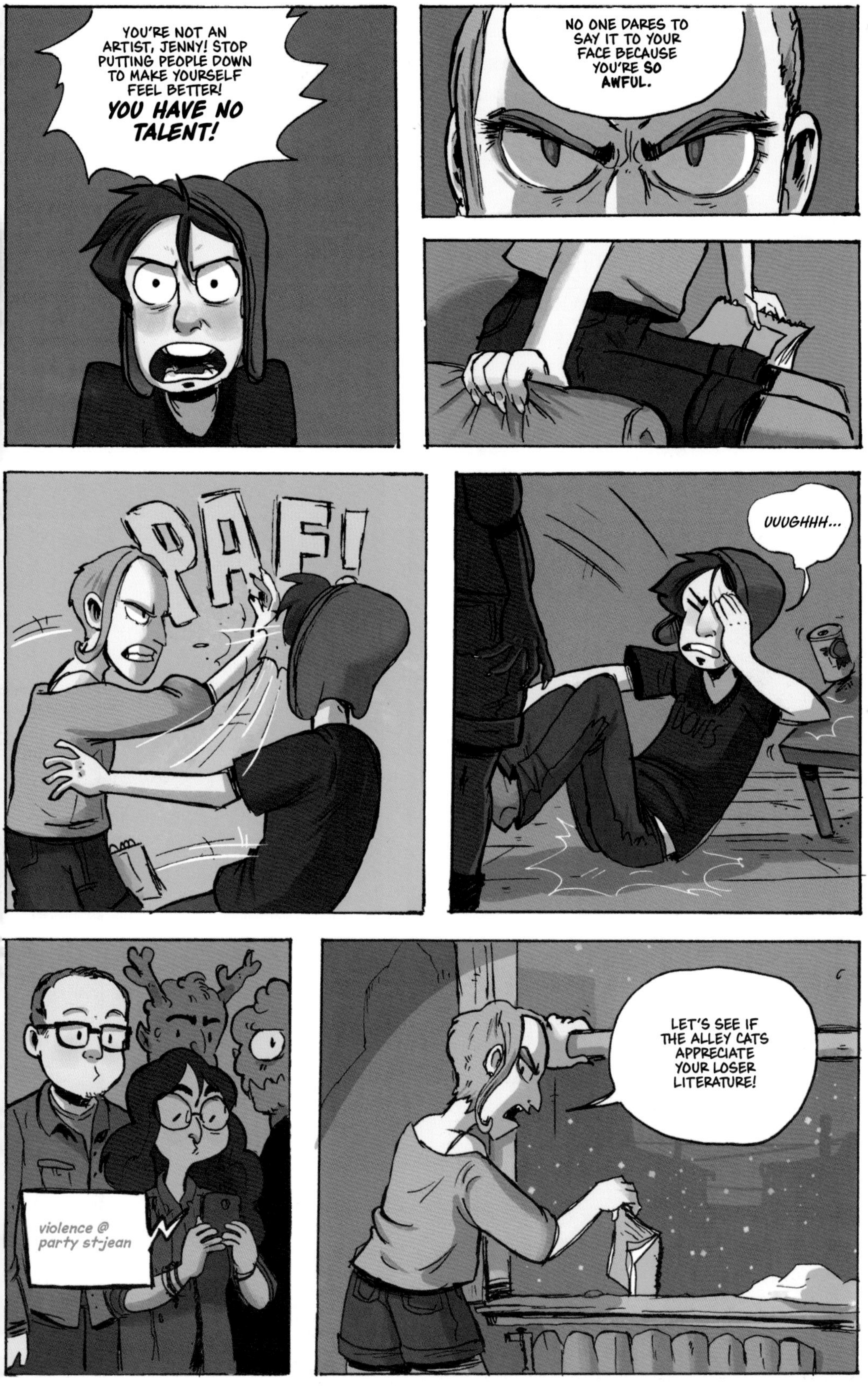

YOU'RE NOT AN ARTIST, JENNY! STOP PUTTING PEOPLE DOWN TO MAKE YOURSELF FEEL BETTER! YOU HAVE NO TALENT!
NO ONE DARES TO SAY IT TO YOUR FACE BECAUSE YOU'RE SO AWFUL.
PAF!
UUUGHHH...
DOVES
violence @ party st-jean
LET'S SEE IF THE ALLEY CATS APPRECIATE YOUR LOSER LITERATURE!

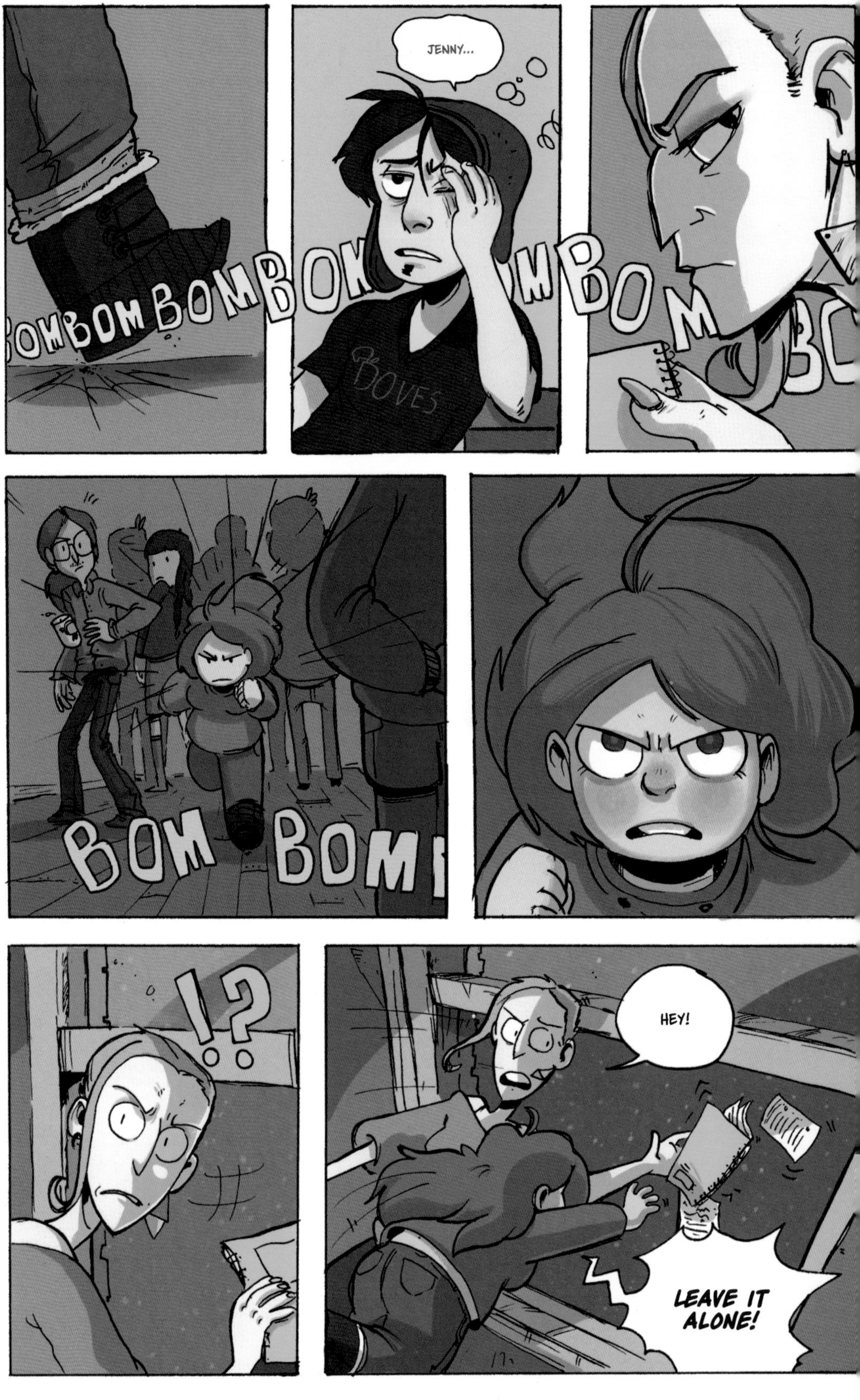
BOMBOMBOMBOMBOMBOMBOM
JENNY...
BOVES
BOM BOM
!?
HEY!
LEAVE IT ALONE!

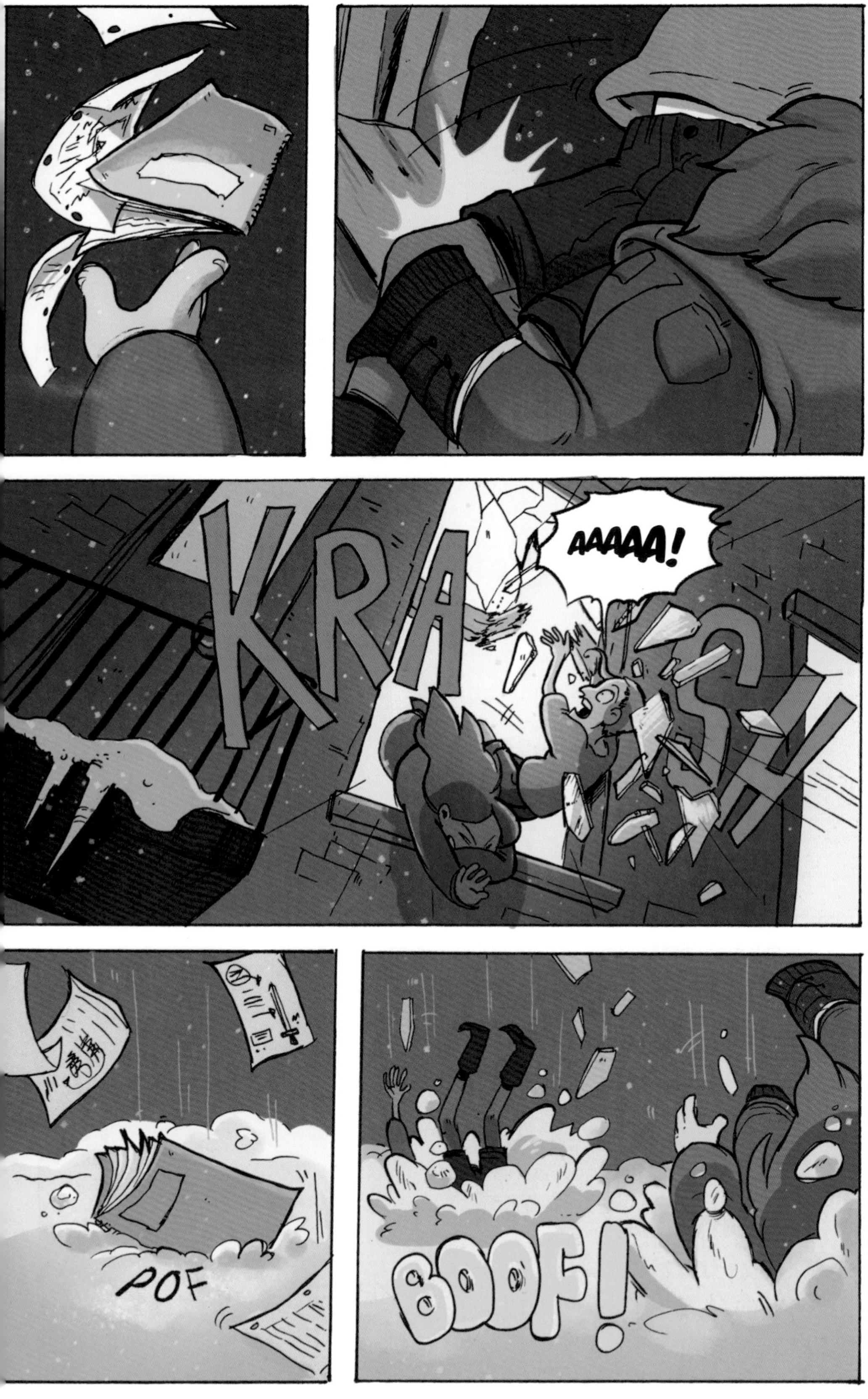
KRA
AAAAA!
CH
POF
BOOF!

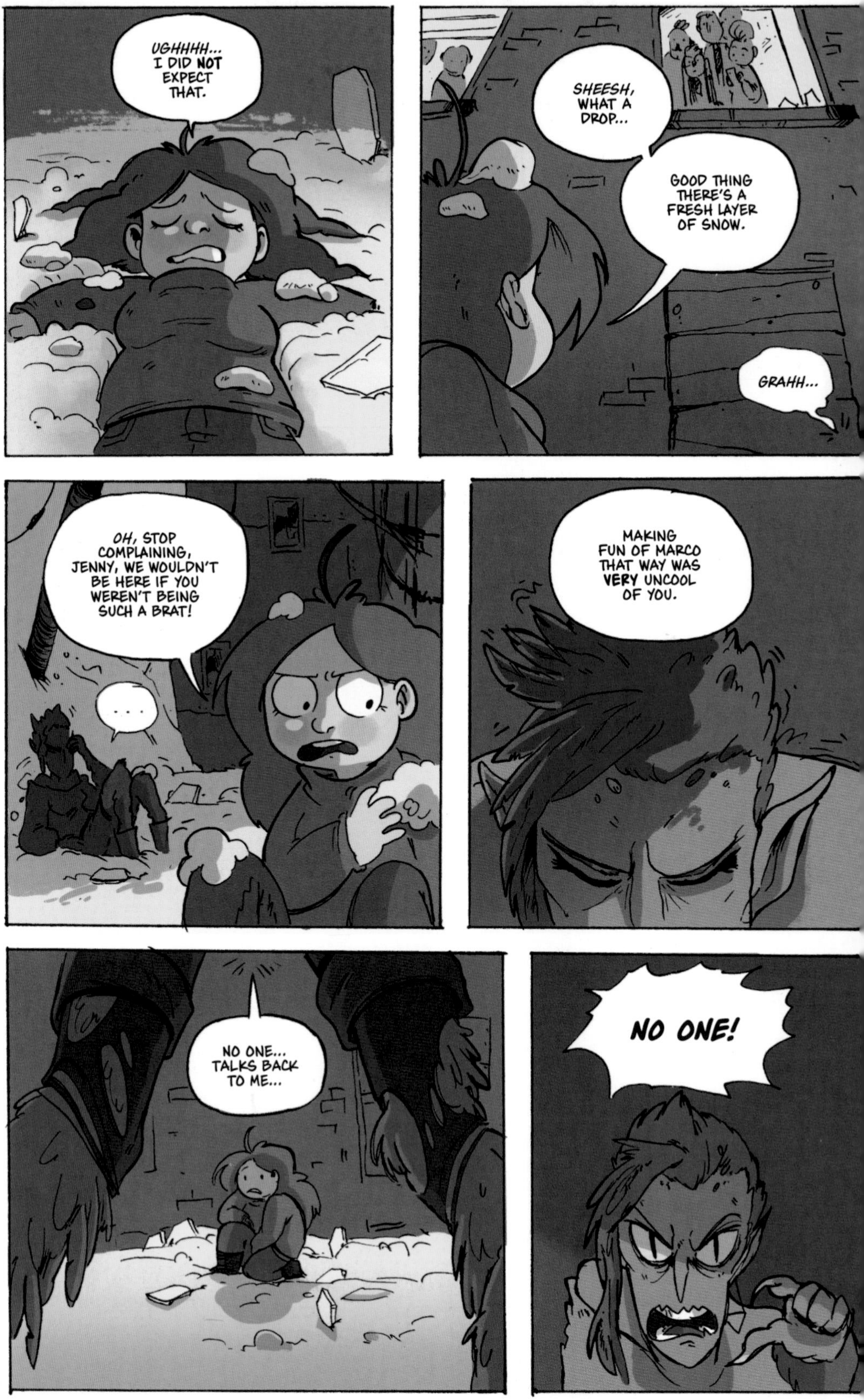
UGHHHH... I DID NOT EXPECT THAT.
SHEESH, WHAT A DROP...
GOOD THING THERE'S A FRESH LAYER OF SNOW.
GRAHH...
OH, STOP COMPLAINING, JENNY, WE WOULDN'T BE HERE IF YOU WEREN'T BEING SUCH A BRAT!
...
MAKING FUN OF MARCO THAT WAY WAS VERY UNCOOL OF YOU.
NO ONE... TALKS BACK TO ME...
NO ONE!

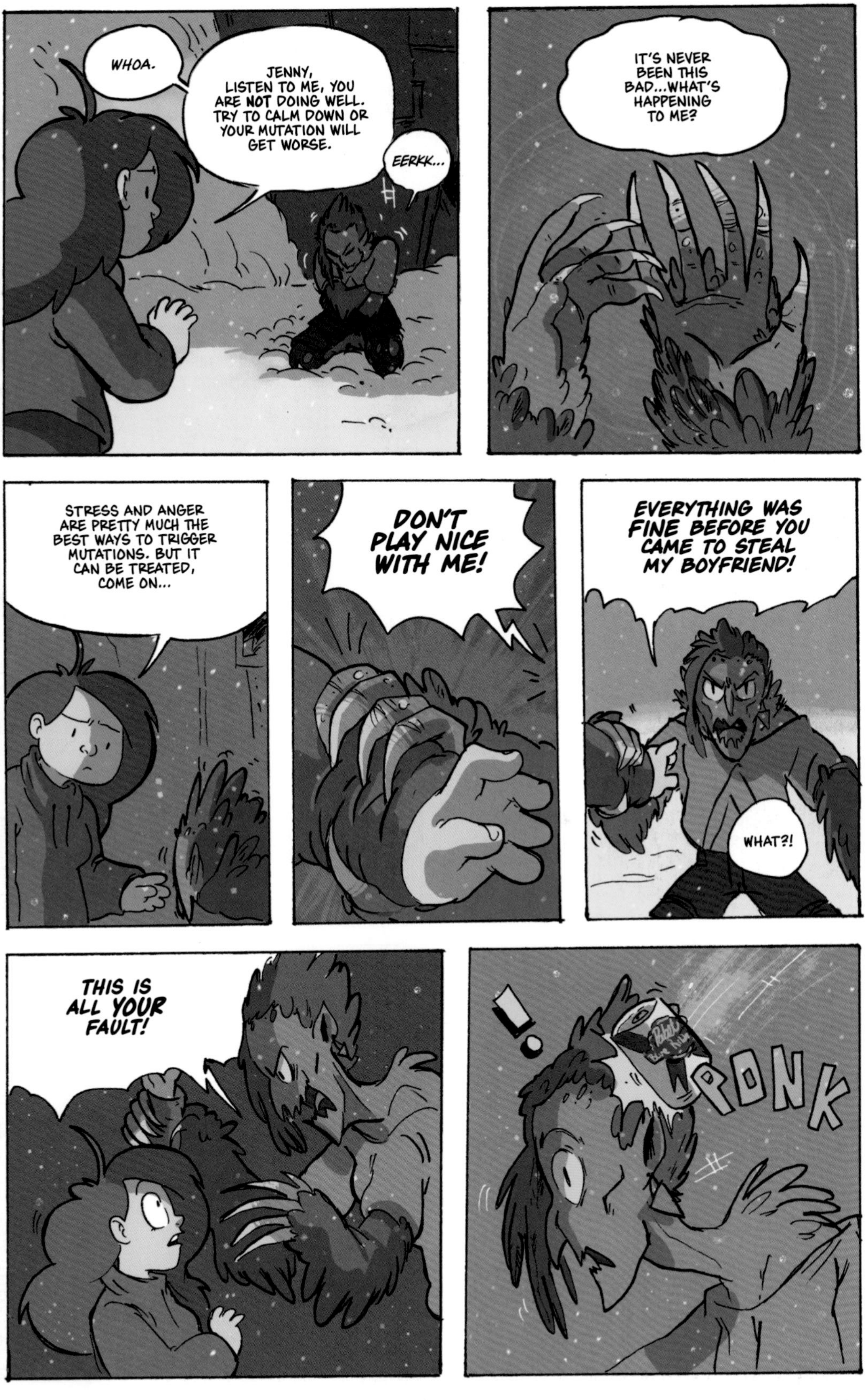
WHOA.
JENNY, LISTEN TO ME, YOU ARE NOT DOING WELL. TRY TO CALM DOWN OR YOUR MUTATION WILL GET WORSE.
EERKK...
IT'S NEVER BEEN THIS BAD...WHAT'S HAPPENING TO ME?
STRESS AND ANGER ARE PRETTY MUCH THE BEST WAYS TO TRIGGER MUTATIONS. BUT IT CAN BE TREATED, COME ON...
DON'T PLAY NICE WITH ME!
EVERYTHING WAS FINE BEFORE YOU CAME TO STEAL MY BOYFRIEND!
WHAT?!
THIS IS ALL YOUR FAULT!
!
PONK

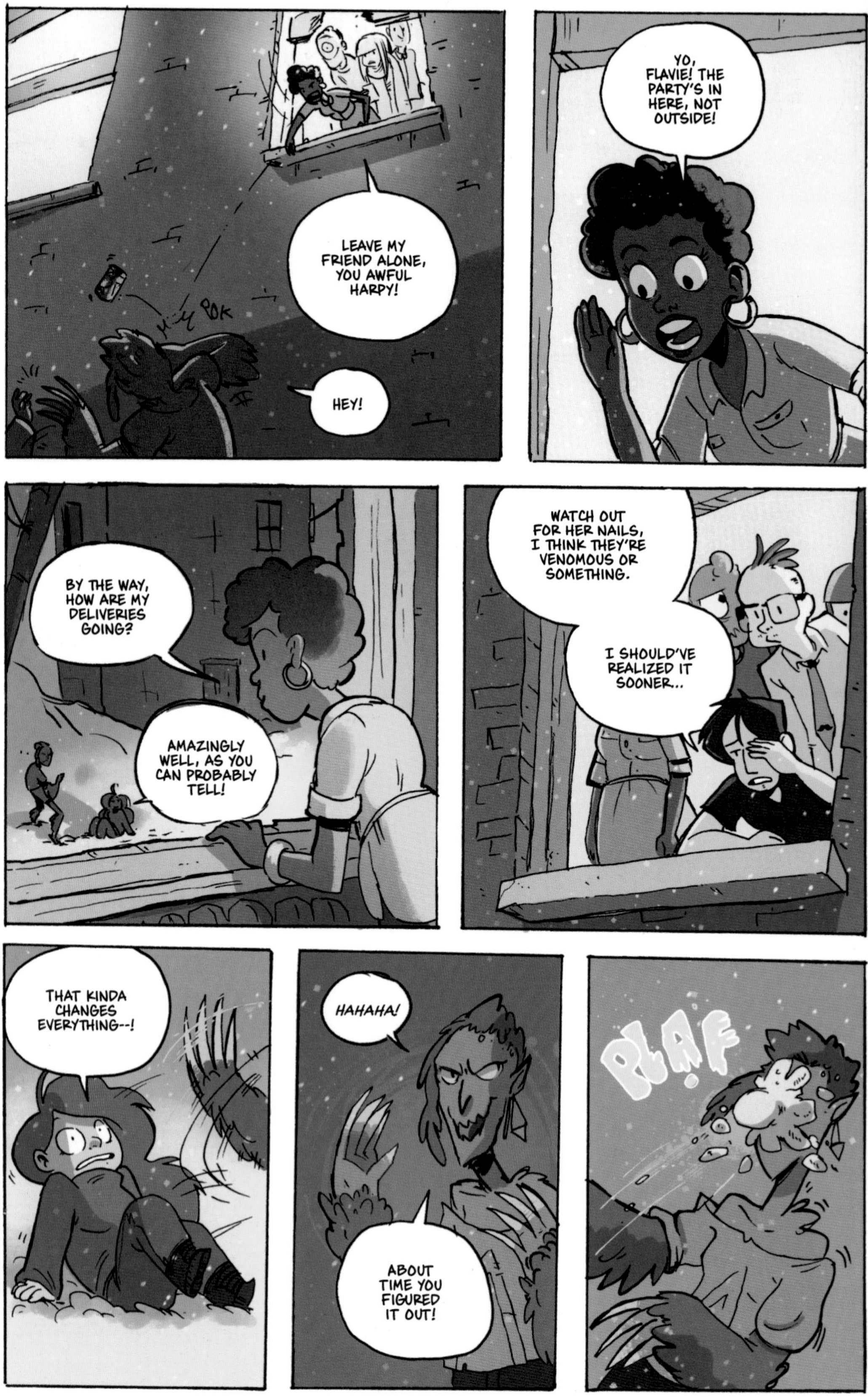

LEAVE MY FRIEND ALONE, YOU AWFUL HARPY!
POK
HEY!
YO, FLAVIE! THE PARTY'S IN HERE, NOT OUTSIDE!
BY THE WAY, HOW ARE MY DELIVERIES GOING?
AMAZINGLY WELL, AS YOU CAN PROBABLY TELL!
WATCH OUT FOR HER NAILS, I THINK THEY'RE VENOMOUS OR SOMETHING.
I SHOULD'VE REALIZED IT SOONER...
THAT KINDA CHANGES EVERYTHING--!
HAHAHA!
ABOUT TIME YOU FIGURED IT OUT!
PLAF

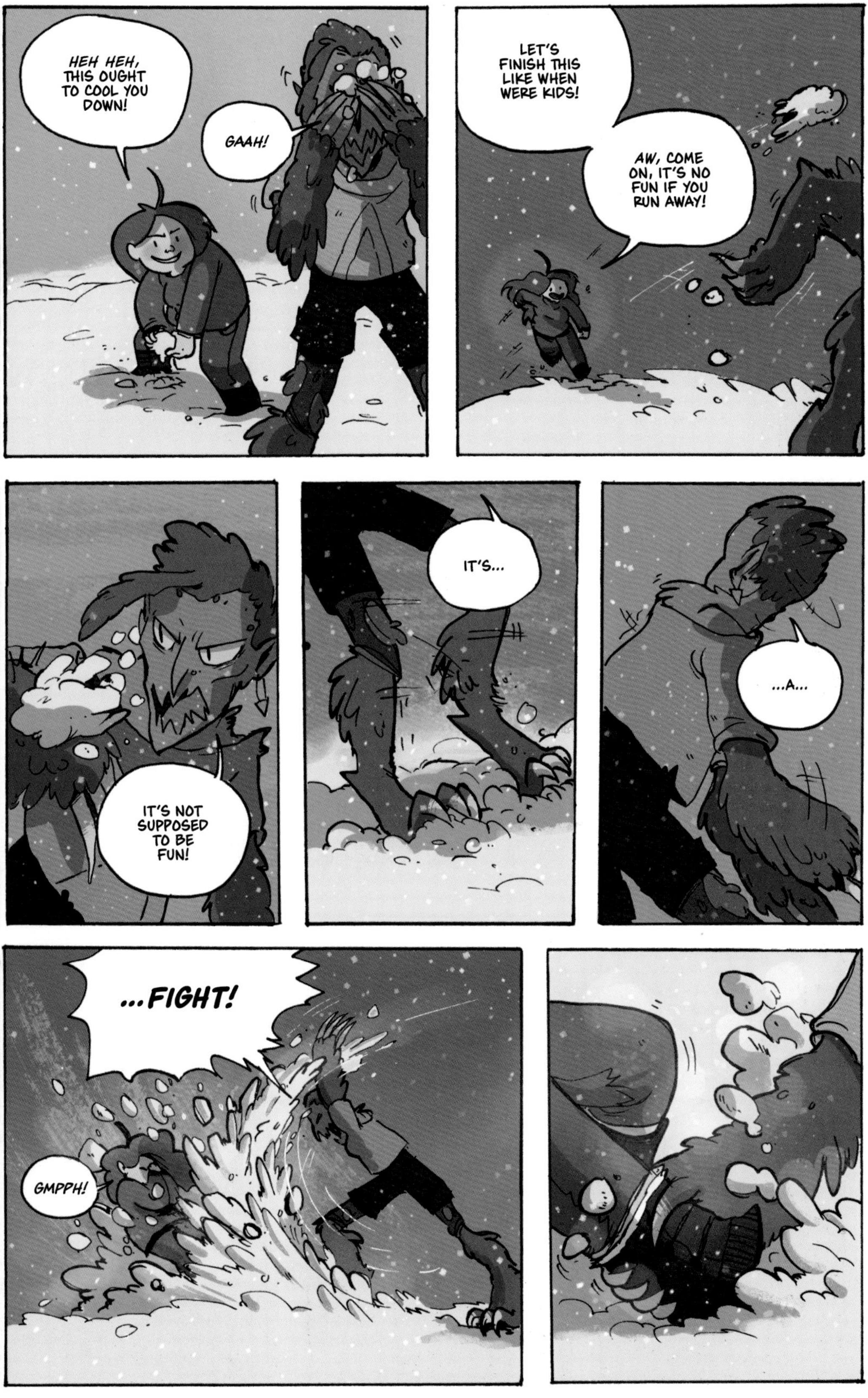
HEH HEH, THIS OUGHT TO COOL YOU DOWN!
GAAH!
LET'S FINISH THIS LIKE WHEN WERE KIDS!
AW, COME ON, IT'S NO FUN IF YOU RUN AWAY!
IT'S NOT SUPPOSED TO BE FUN!
IT'S...
...A...
...FIGHT!
GMPPH!

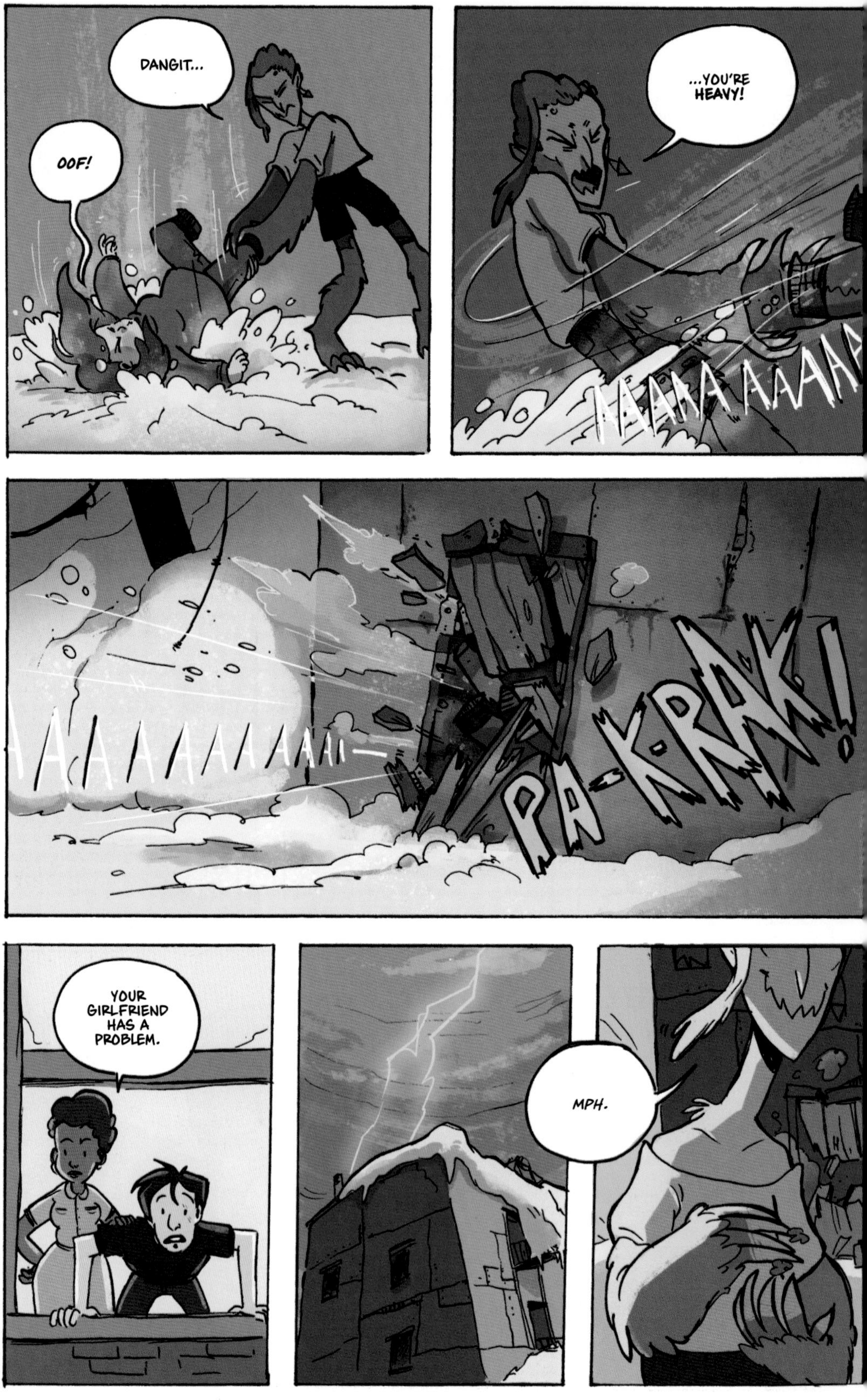
DANGIT...
OOF!
...YOU'RE HEAVY!
AAAAAAAAAA
AAAAAAAAAAA—
PA-KRAK!
YOUR GIRLFRIEND HAS A PROBLEM.
MPH.

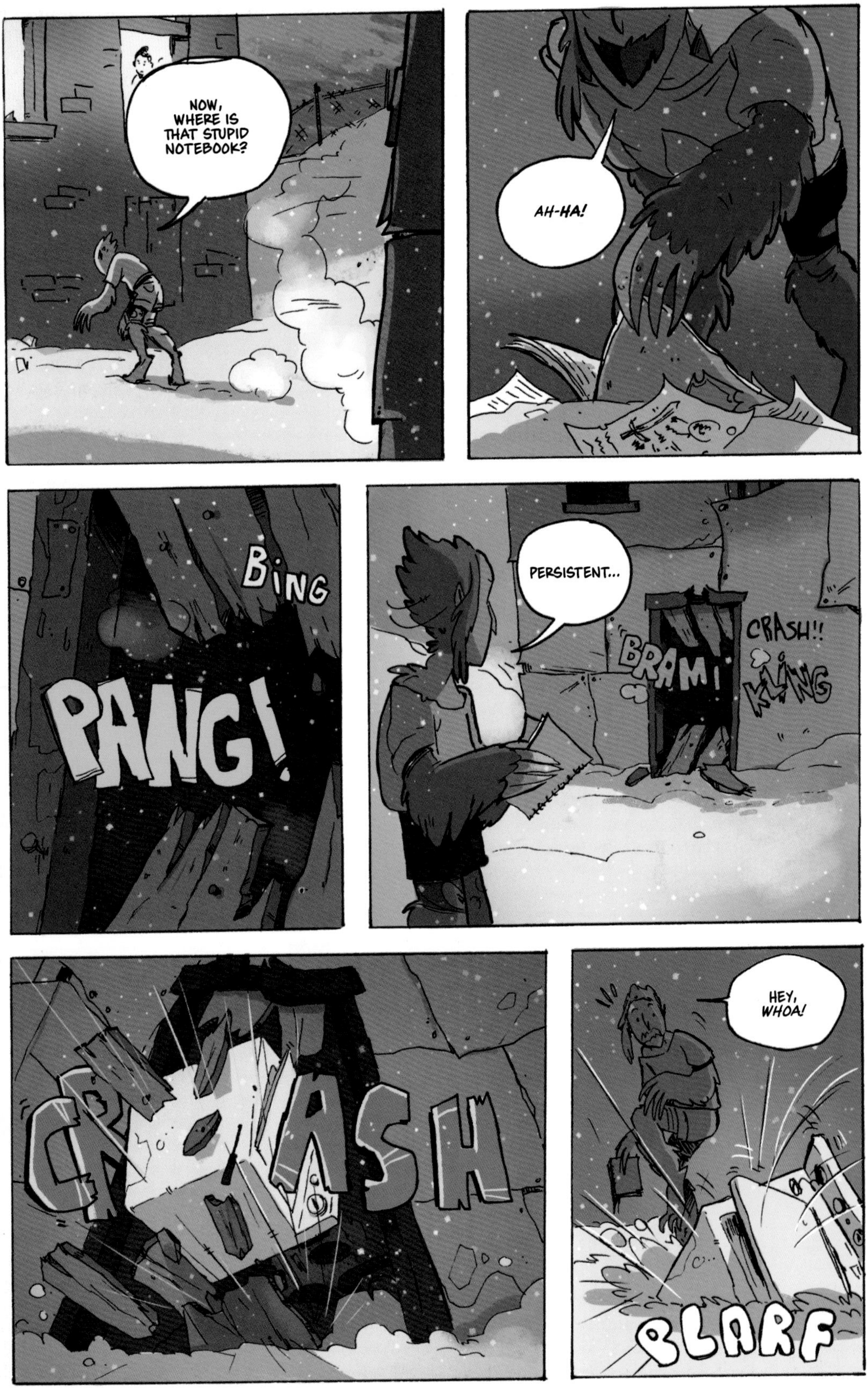
NOW, WHERE IS THAT STUPID NOTEBOOK?
AH-HA!
BING
PANG!
PERSISTENT...
BRAM!
CRASH!!
KLING
CRASH
HEY, WHOA!
BLARF

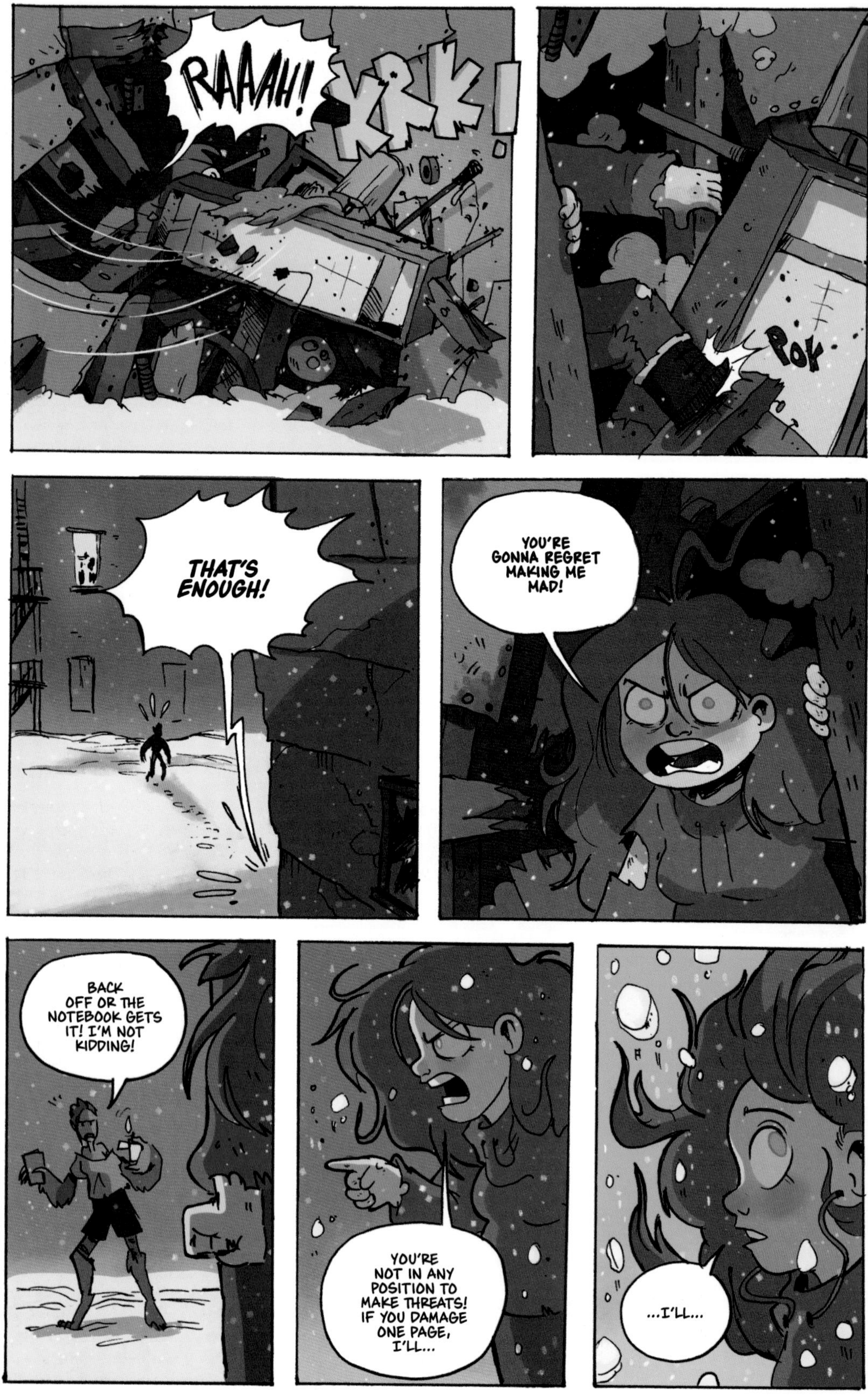
RAAAH!
KRK!
POK
THAT'S ENOUGH!
YOU'RE GONNA REGRET MAKING ME MAD!
BACK OFF OR THE NOTEBOOK GETS IT! I'M NOT KIDDING!
YOU'RE NOT IN ANY POSITION TO MAKE THREATS! IF YOU DAMAGE ONE PAGE, I'LL...
...I'LL...

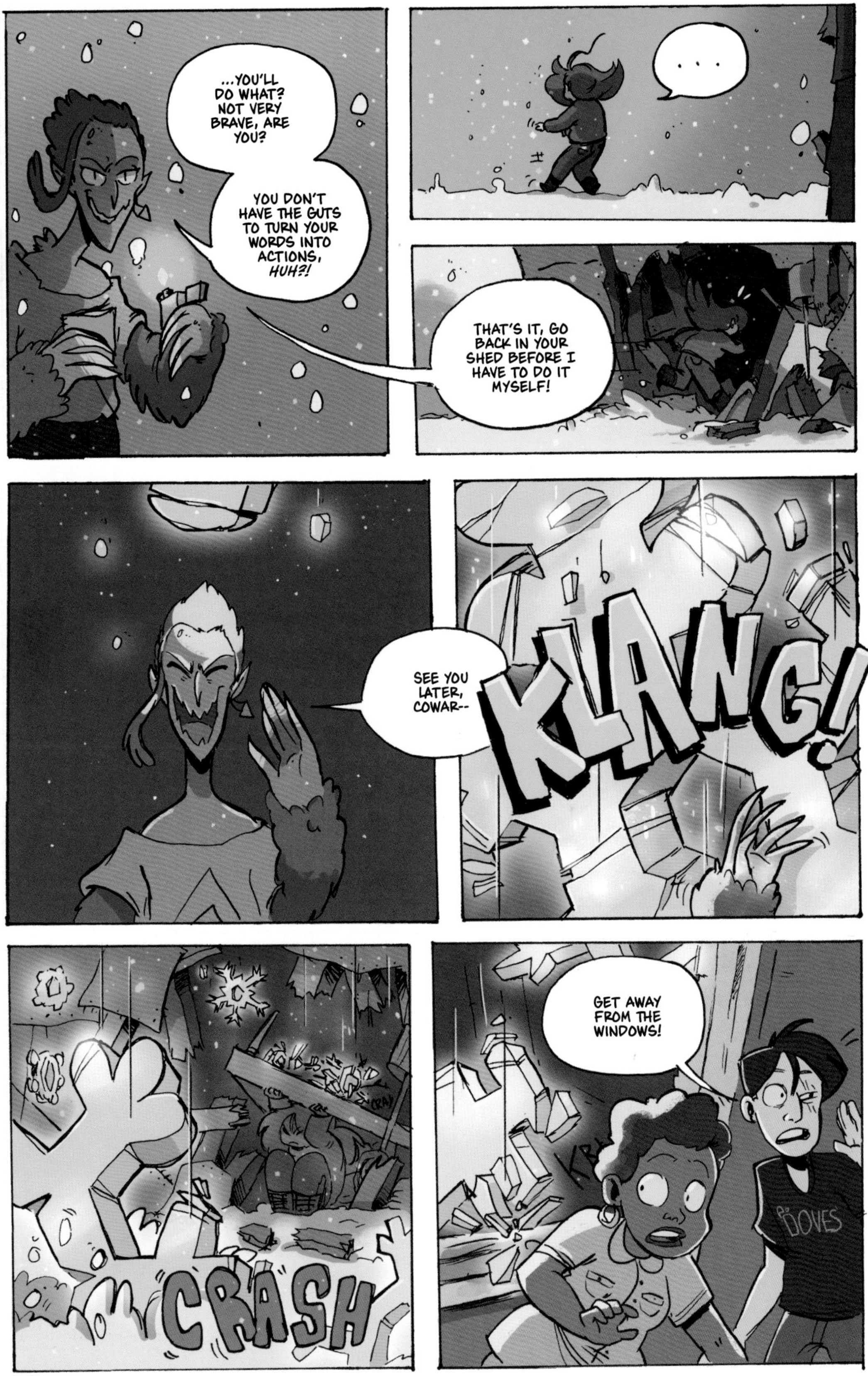

...YOU'LL DO WHAT? NOT VERY BRAVE, ARE YOU?
YOU DON'T HAVE THE GUTS TO TURN YOUR WORDS INTO ACTIONS, *HUH?!*
...
THAT'S IT, GO BACK IN YOUR SHED BEFORE I HAVE TO DO IT MYSELF!
SEE YOU LATER, COWAR--
KLANG!
CRASH
GET AWAY FROM THE WINDOWS!
DOVES

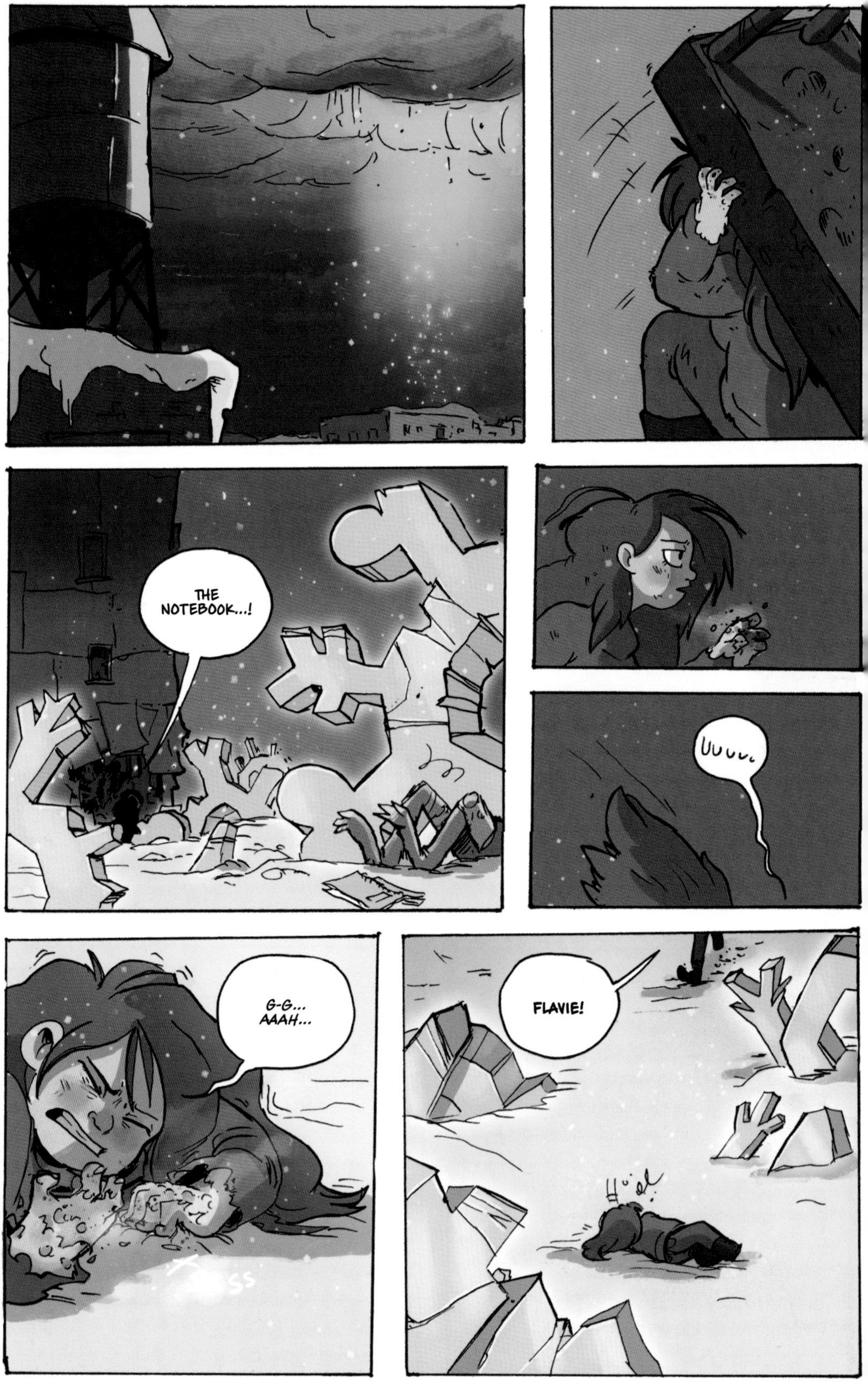
THE NOTEBOOK...!
G-G... AAAH...
FLAVIE!

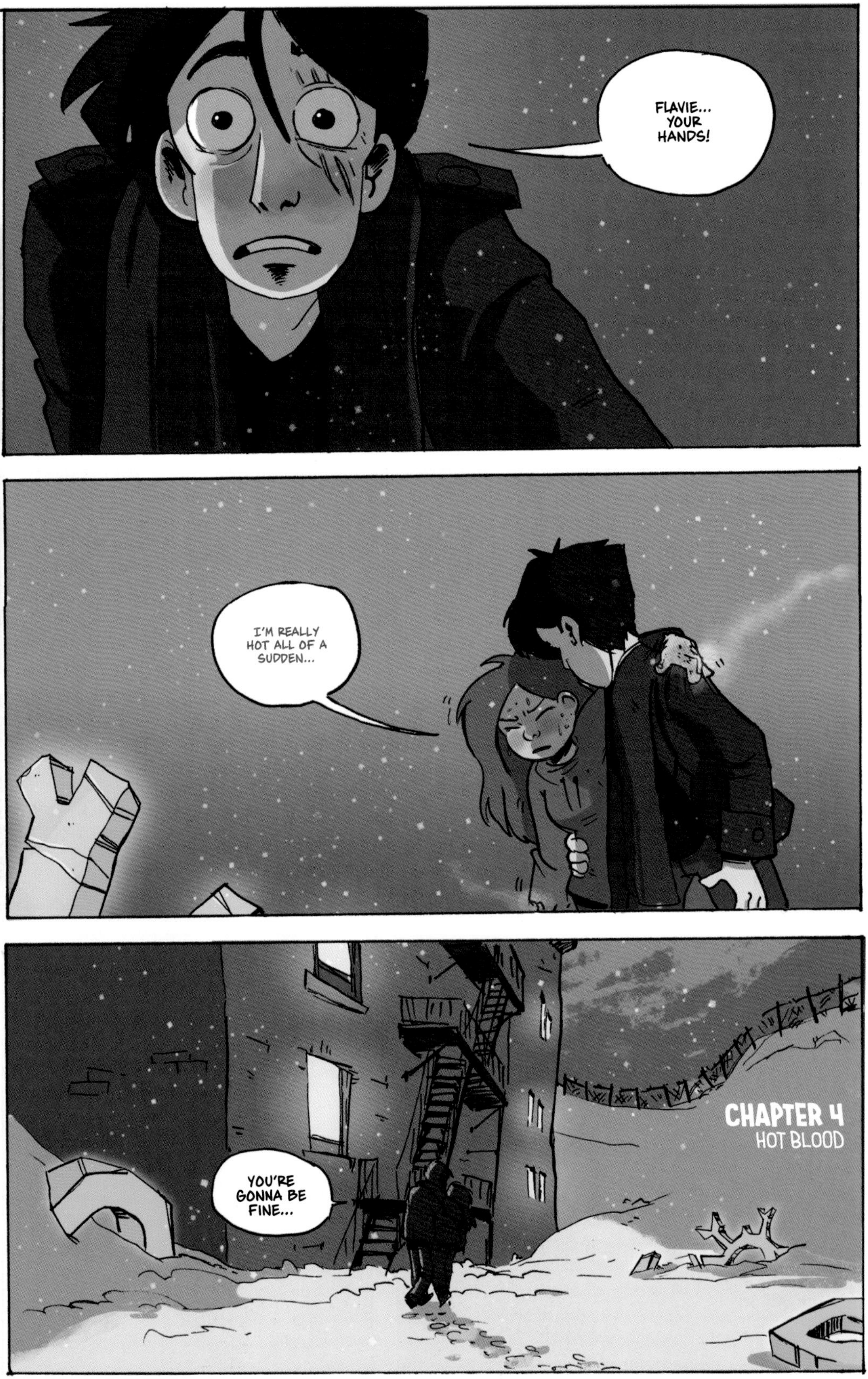
FLAVIE... YOUR HANDS!
I'M REALLY HOT ALL OF A SUDDEN...
YOU'RE GONNA BE FINE...
CHAPTER 4
HOT BLOOD

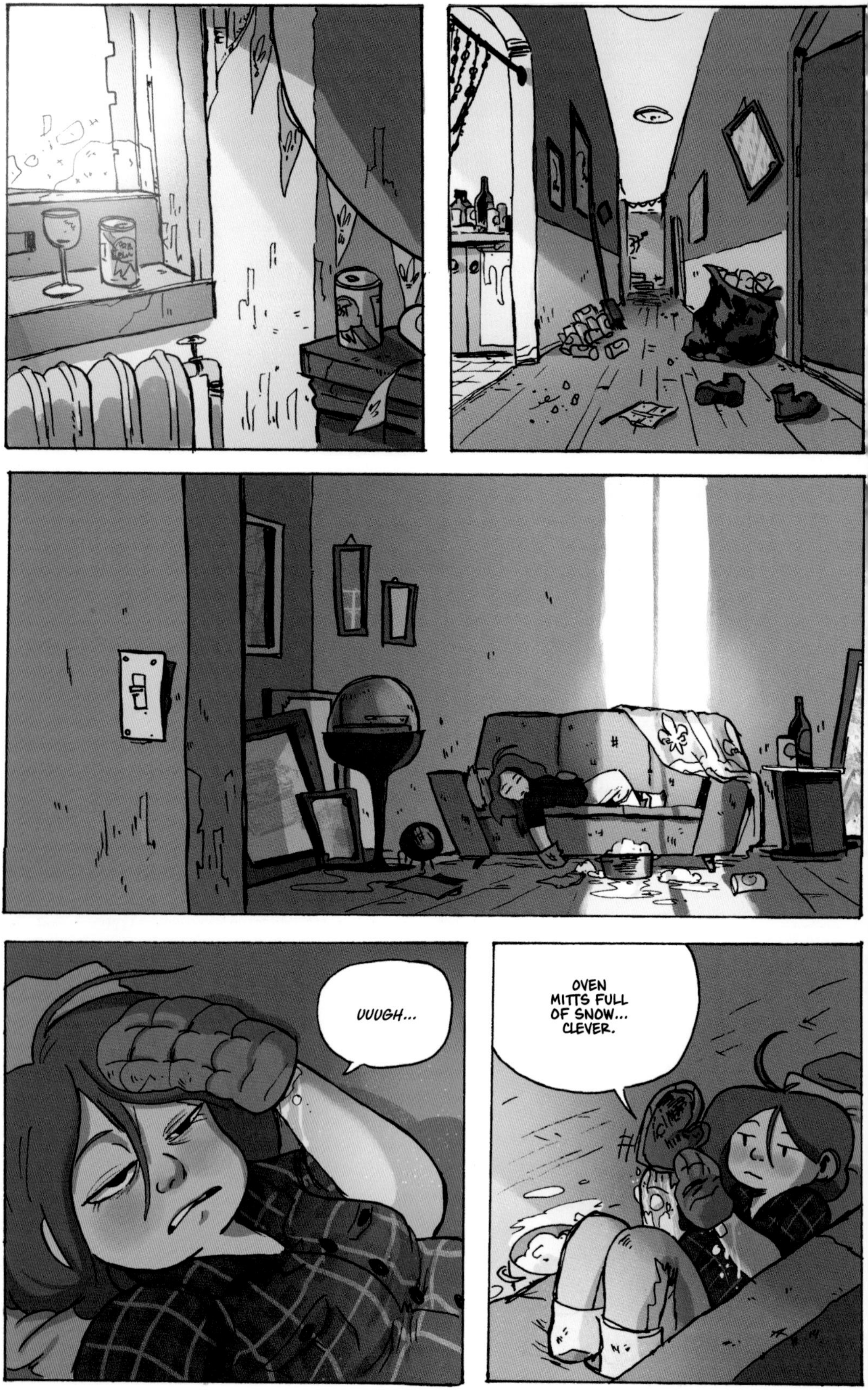
UUUGH...
OVEN MITTS FULL OF SNOW... CLEVER.

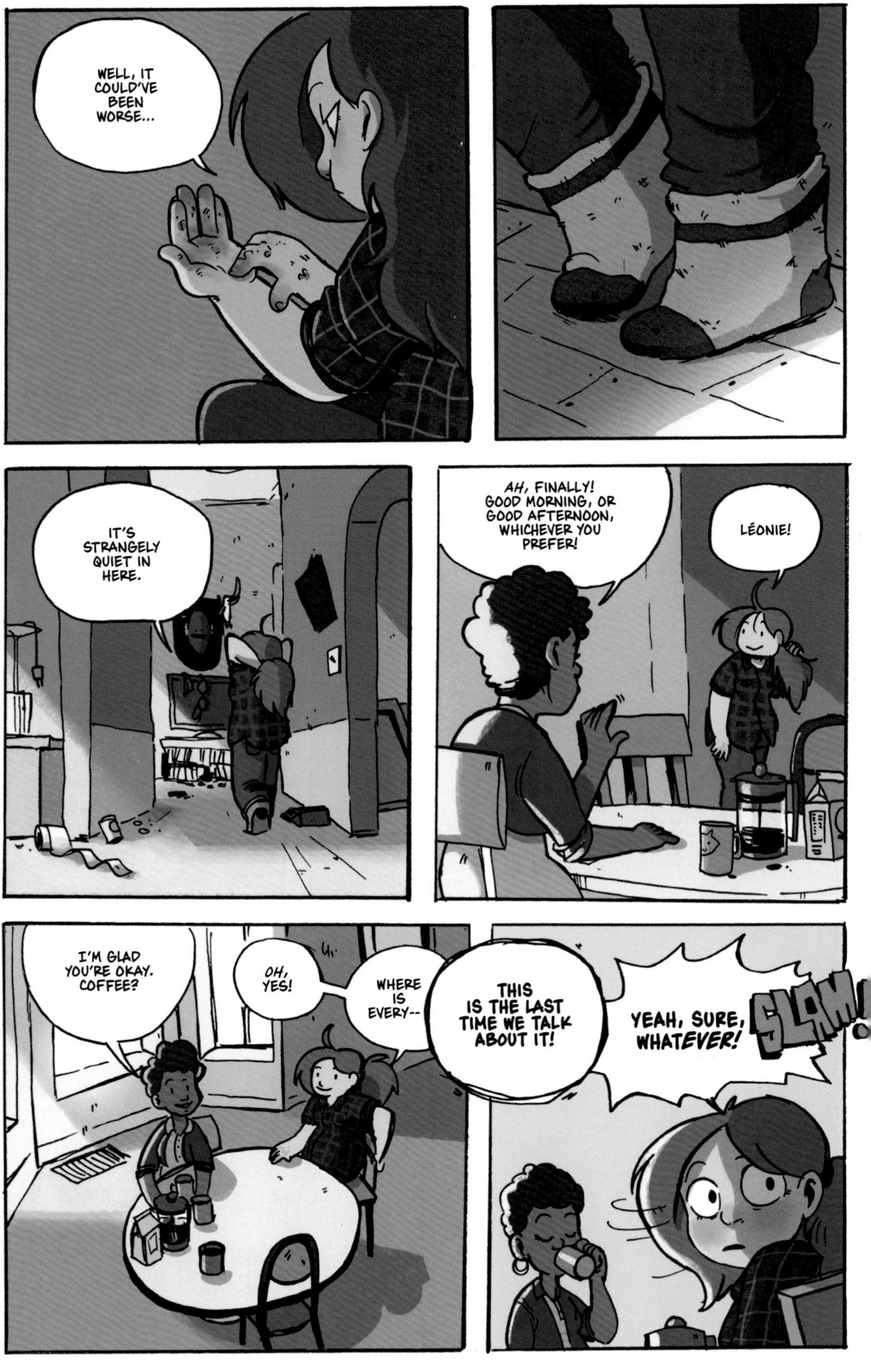
WELL, IT COULD'VE BEEN WORSE...
IT'S STRANGELY QUIET IN HERE.
AH, FINALLY! GOOD MORNING, OR GOOD AFTERNOON, WHICHEVER YOU PREFER!
LÉONIE!
I'M GLAD YOU'RE OKAY. COFFEE?
OH, YES!
WHERE IS EVERY--
THIS IS THE LAST TIME WE TALK ABOUT IT!
YEAH, SURE, WHATEVER!
SLAM!

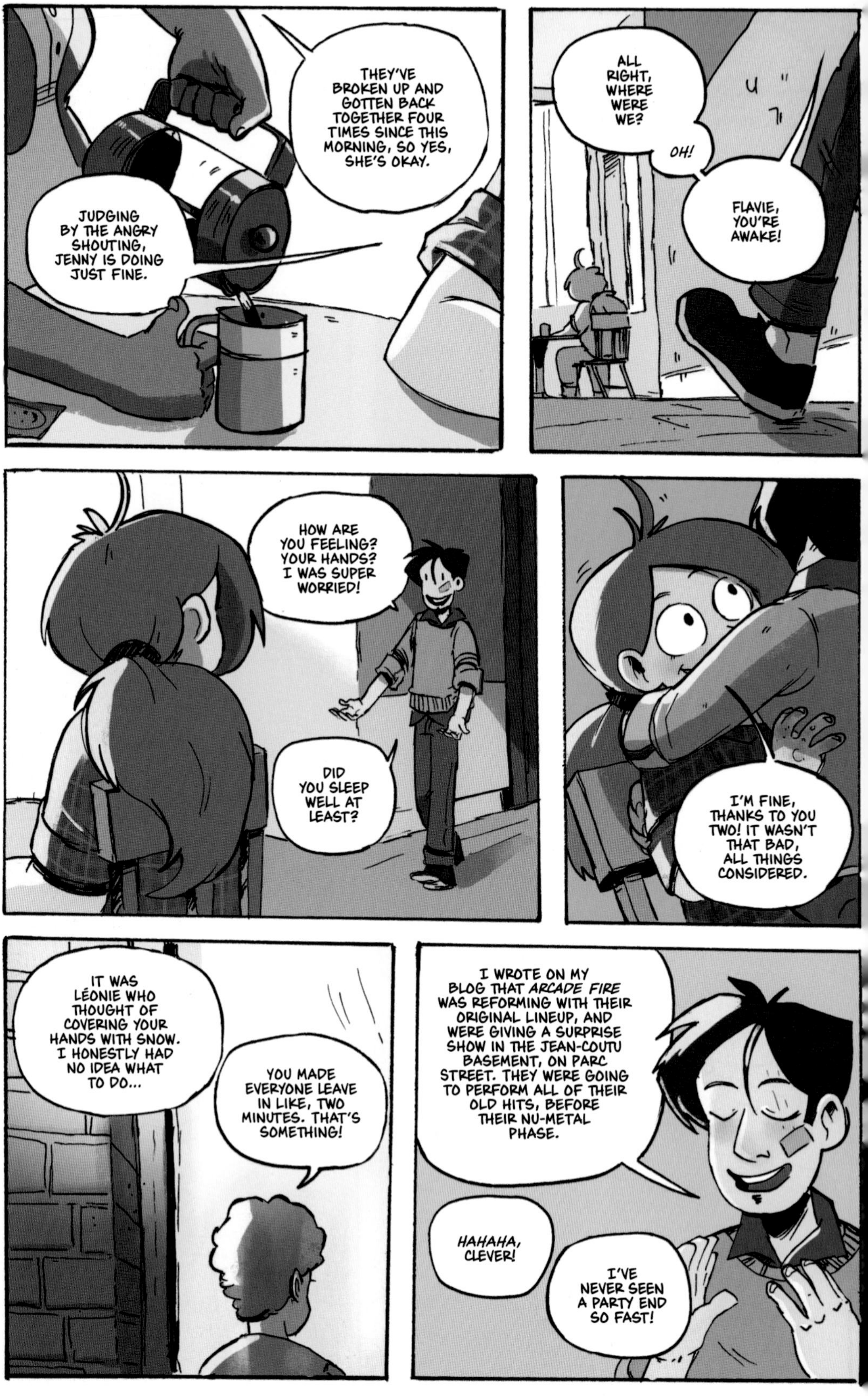

THEY'VE BROKEN UP AND GOTTEN BACK TOGETHER FOUR TIMES SINCE THIS MORNING, SO YES, SHE'S OKAY.
JUDGING BY THE ANGRY SHOUTING, JENNY IS DOING JUST FINE.
ALL RIGHT, WHERE WERE WE?
OH!
FLAVIE, YOU'RE AWAKE!
HOW ARE YOU FEELING? YOUR HANDS? I WAS SUPER WORRIED!
DID YOU SLEEP WELL AT LEAST?
I'M FINE, THANKS TO YOU TWO! IT WASN'T THAT BAD, ALL THINGS CONSIDERED.
IT WAS LÉONIE WHO THOUGHT OF COVERING YOUR HANDS WITH SNOW. I HONESTLY HAD NO IDEA WHAT TO DO...
YOU MADE EVERYONE LEAVE IN LIKE, TWO MINUTES. THAT'S SOMETHING!
I WROTE ON MY BLOG THAT *ARCADE FIRE* WAS REFORMING WITH THEIR ORIGINAL LINEUP, AND WERE GIVING A SURPRISE SHOW IN THE JEAN-COUTU BASEMENT, ON PARC STREET. THEY WERE GOING TO PERFORM ALL OF THEIR OLD HITS, BEFORE THEIR NU-METAL PHASE.
HAHAHA, CLEVER!
I'VE NEVER SEEN A PARTY END SO FAST!

BUT NOW I WANT TO KNOW WHAT HAPPENED TO YOU LAST NIGHT. I'VE MET SOME IRRADIATED PEOPLE, BUT NEVER LIKE THIS.

BAH, IT'S NOTHING. IT DOESN'T EVEN HURT ANYMORE.

STOP ACTING SO TOUGH, FLAVIE BEAUMONT. WE'RE NOT WITH THE MORONS FROM WORK, YOU CAN TELL HIM.

YOU KEEP AVOIDING THE SUBJECT, YOU REFUSE TO SEE A DOCTOR, NO WONDER YOU'RE GETTING WORSE. LAST NIGHT WAS REALLY BAD.

MPH...

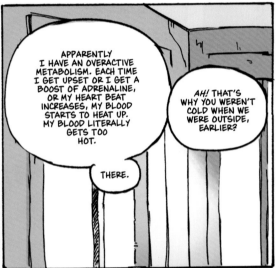

APPARENTLY I HAVE AN OVERACTIVE METABOLISM. EACH TIME I GET UPSET OR I GET A BOOST OF ADRENALINE, OR MY HEART BEAT INCREASES, MY BLOOD STARTS TO HEAT UP. MY BLOOD LITERALLY GETS TOO HOT.

THERE.

AH! THAT'S WHY YOU WEREN'T COLD WHEN WE WERE OUTSIDE, EARLIER?

YEAH. BUT I CAN NEVER PREDICT WHEN IT GETS OUT OF CONTROL, LIKE YESTERDAY.

THAT'S WHY I AVOID STRESSFUL SITUATIONS, PARTIES, BARS... AND PEOPLE IN GENERAL.

YOU WERE NEVER KNOWN FOR YOUR INFINITE PATIENCE TO BEGIN WITH, HUH?

HEY.

IT'S NOT THAT BAD.

HAHAHA!

WE CAN'T BLAME YOU FOR GETTING MAD AT JENNY. SHE HAS A SPECIAL TALENT FOR RUBBING PEOPLE THE WRONG WAY.

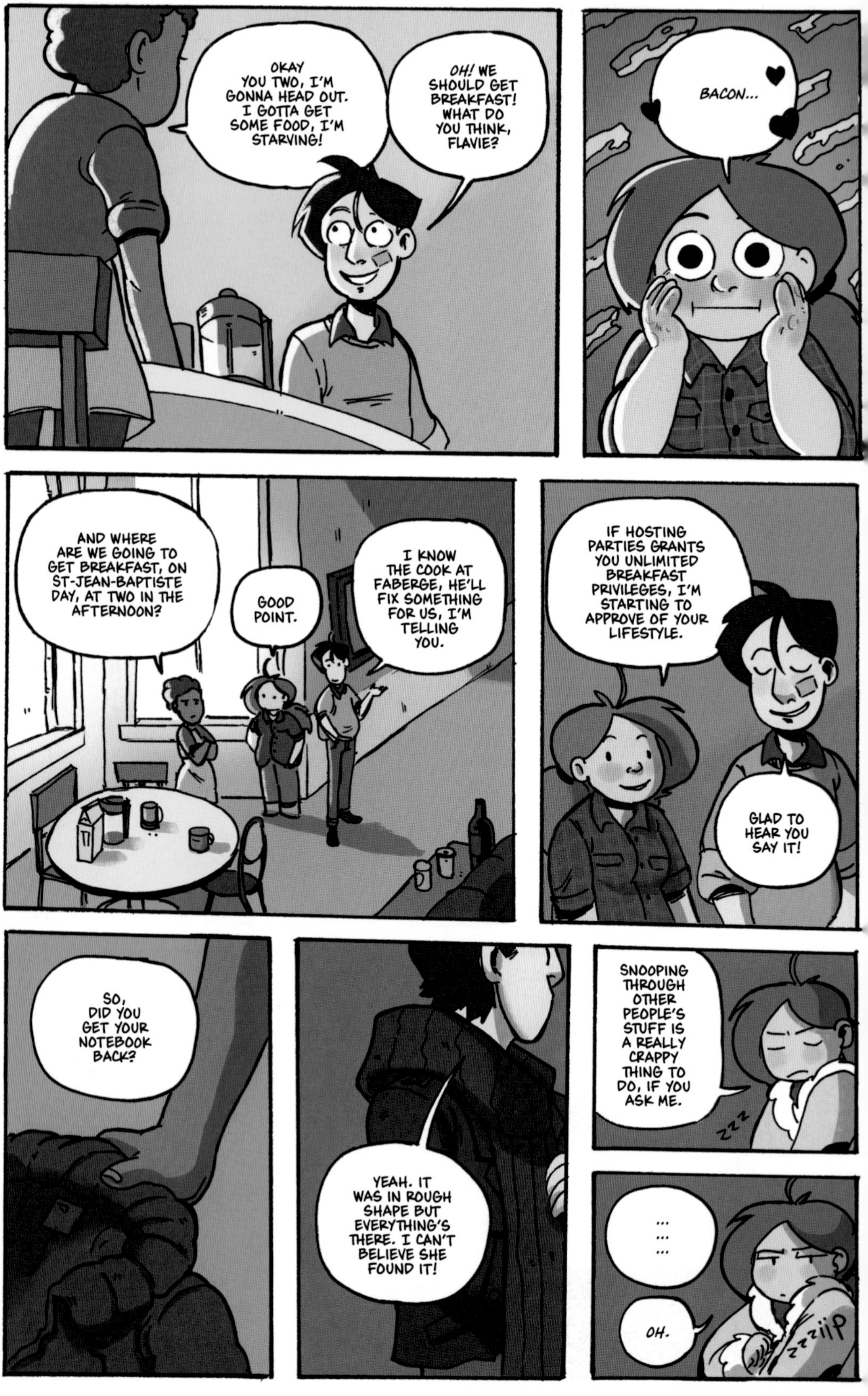
OKAY YOU TWO, I'M GONNA HEAD OUT. I GOTTA GET SOME FOOD, I'M STARVING!
OH! WE SHOULD GET BREAKFAST! WHAT DO YOU THINK, FLAVIE?
BACON...
AND WHERE ARE WE GOING TO GET BREAKFAST, ON ST-JEAN-BAPTISTE DAY, AT TWO IN THE AFTERNOON?
GOOD POINT.
I KNOW THE COOK AT FABERGE, HE'LL FIX SOMETHING FOR US, I'M TELLING YOU.
IF HOSTING PARTIES GRANTS YOU UNLIMITED BREAKFAST PRIVILEGES, I'M STARTING TO APPROVE OF YOUR LIFESTYLE.
GLAD TO HEAR YOU SAY IT!
SO, DID YOU GET YOUR NOTEBOOK BACK?
YEAH. IT WAS IN ROUGH SHAPE BUT EVERYTHING'S THERE. I CAN'T BELIEVE SHE FOUND IT!
SNOOPING THROUGH OTHER PEOPLE'S STUFF IS A REALLY CRAPPY THING TO DO, IF YOU ASK ME.
ZZZ
...
...
...
OH.
ZZZ

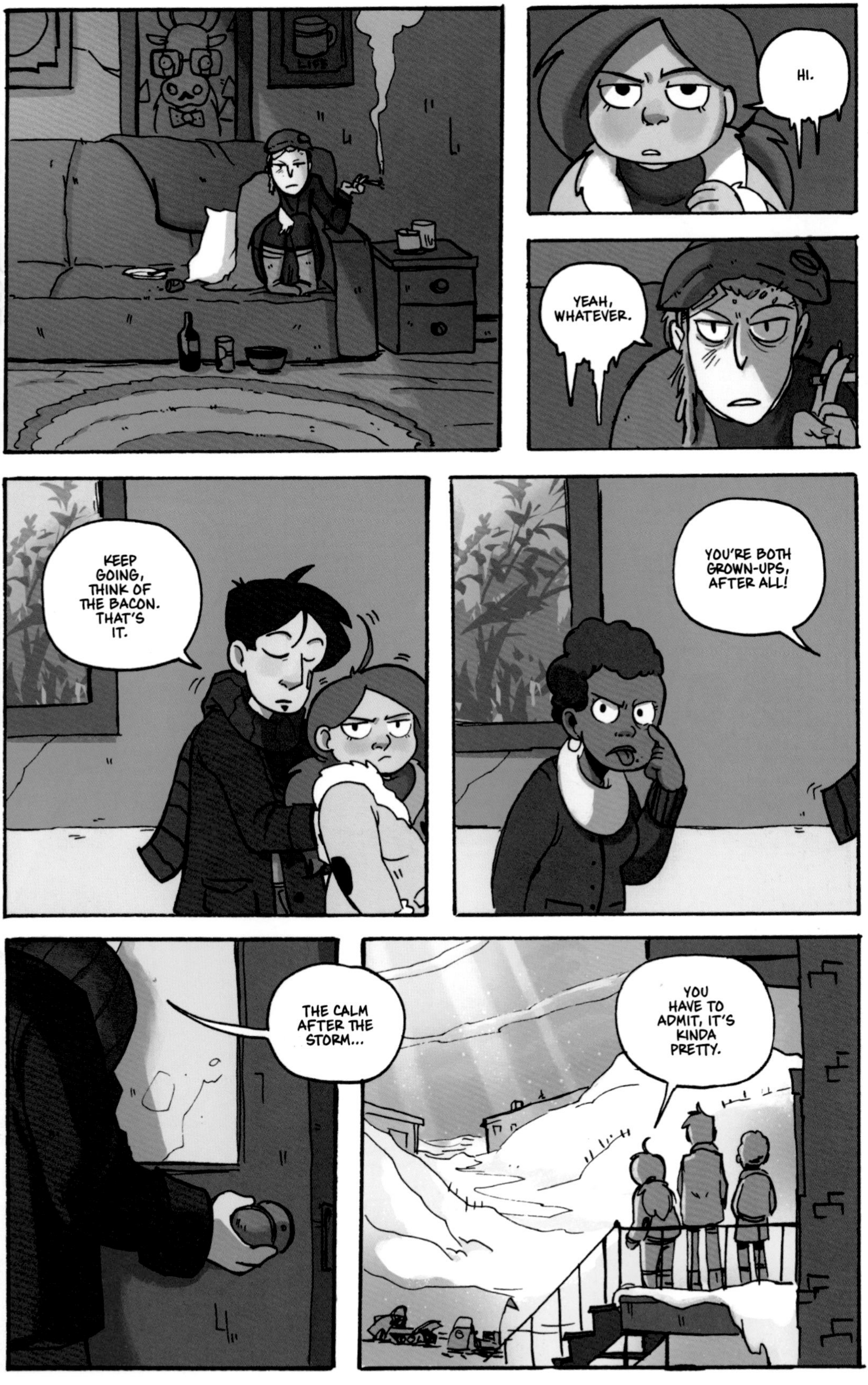
HI.
YEAH, WHATEVER.
KEEP GOING, THINK OF THE BACON. THAT'S IT.
YOU'RE BOTH GROWN-UPS, AFTER ALL!
THE CALM AFTER THE STORM...
YOU HAVE TO ADMIT, IT'S KINDA PRETTY.

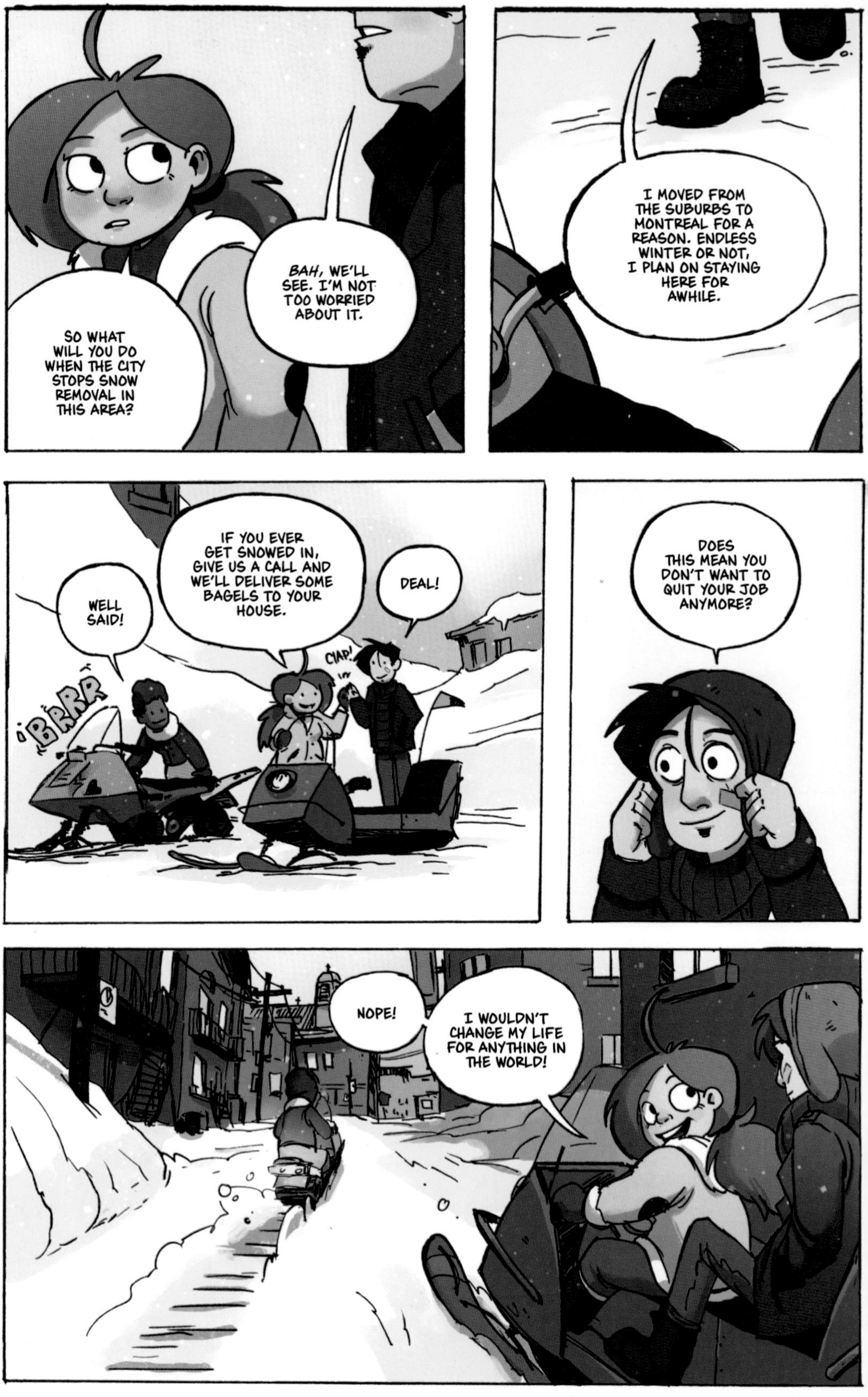
SO WHAT WILL YOU DO WHEN THE CITY STOPS SNOW REMOVAL IN THIS AREA?
BAH, WE'LL SEE. I'M NOT TOO WORRIED ABOUT IT.
I MOVED FROM THE SUBURBS TO MONTREAL FOR A REASON. ENDLESS WINTER OR NOT, I PLAN ON STAYING HERE FOR AWHILE.
WELL SAID!
IF YOU EVER GET SNOWED IN, GIVE US A CALL AND WE'LL DELIVER SOME BAGELS TO YOUR HOUSE.
DEAL!
¡BRRR
CLAP!
DOES THIS MEAN YOU DON'T WANT TO QUIT YOUR JOB ANYMORE?
NOPE!
I WOULDN'T CHANGE MY LIFE FOR ANYTHING IN THE WORLD!

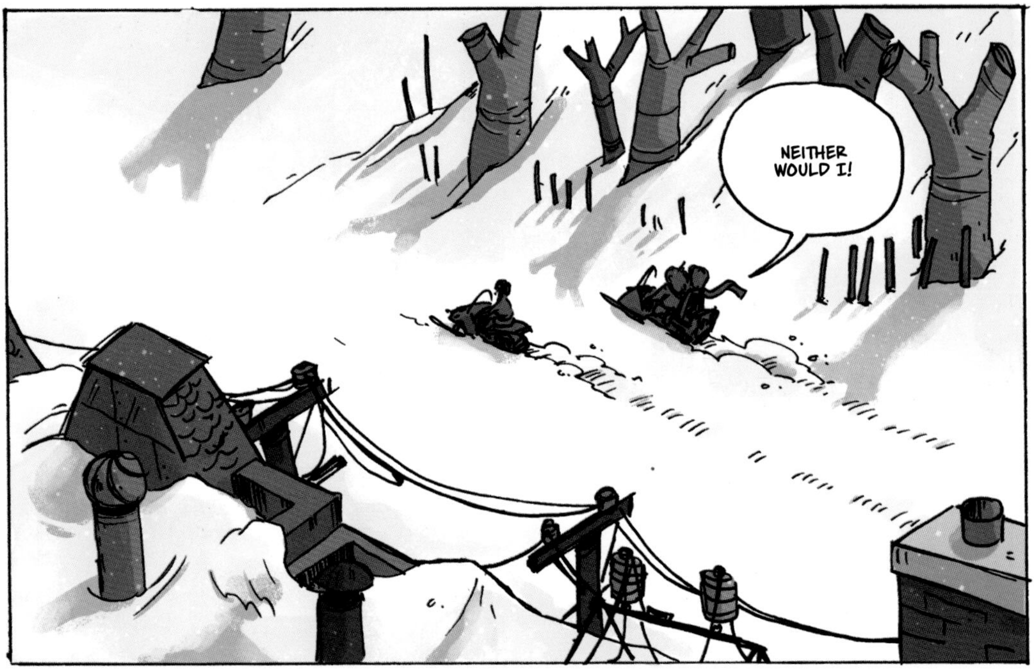
NEITHER WOULD I!

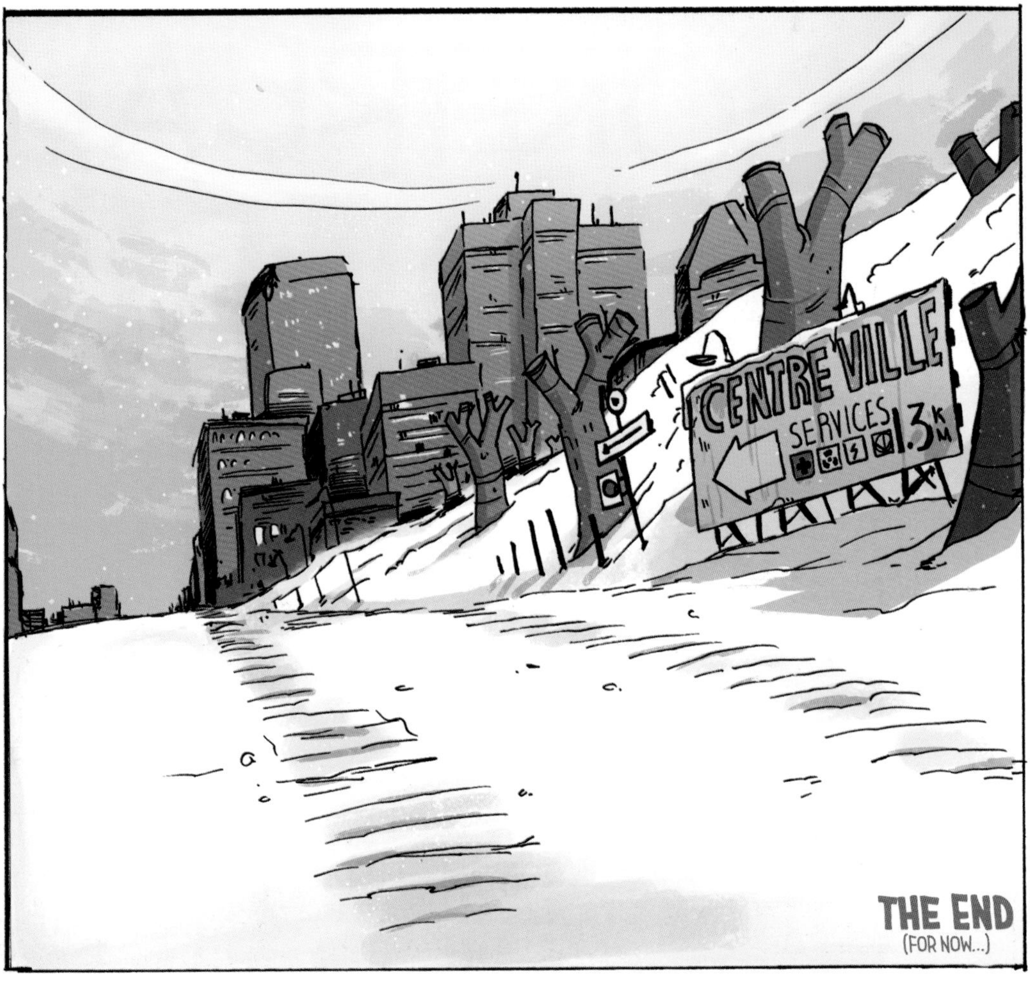
CENTRE VILLE
SERVICES
1.3 KM
THE END
(FOR NOW...)

MONTREAL WILDLIFE

✩ ✦ ✦

An Amateur Illustrated Guide
and Other Observations

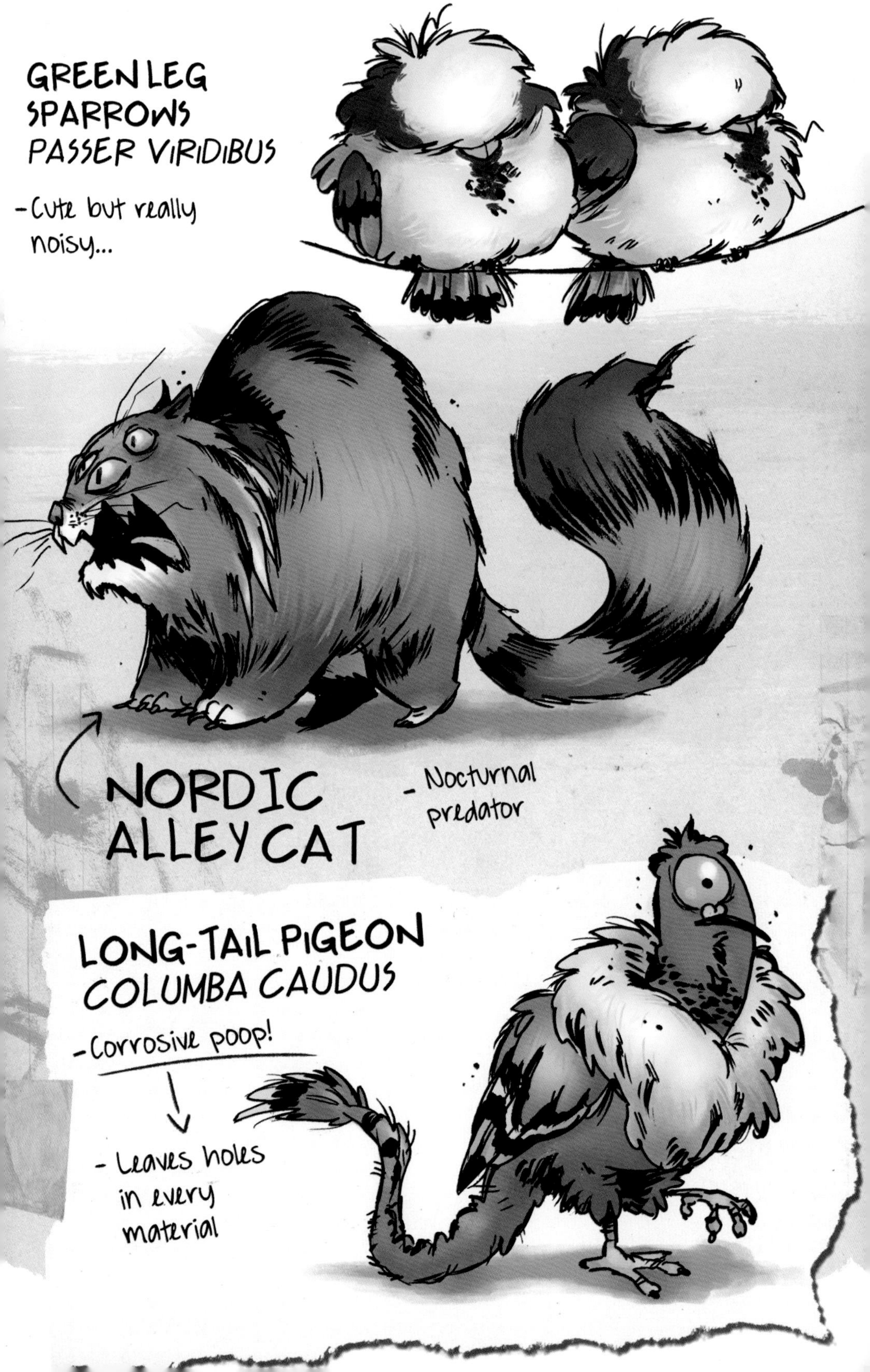
GREEN LEG SPARROWS
PASSER VIRIDIBUS
-Cute but really noisy...
NORDIC ALLEY CAT
- Nocturnal predator
LONG-TAIL PIGEON
COLUMBA CAUDUS
-Corrosive poop!
- Leaves holes in every material

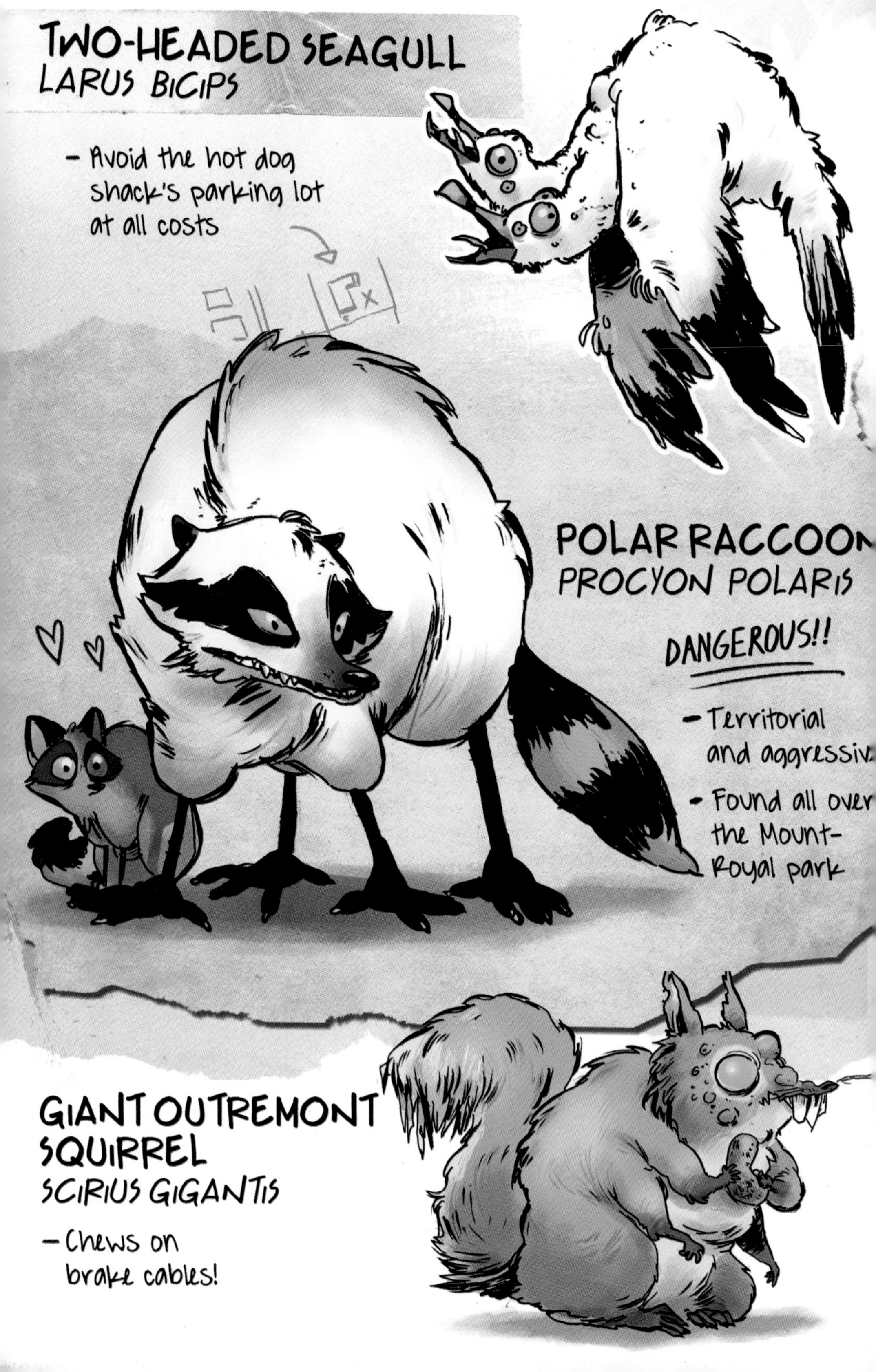

TWO-HEADED SEAGULL
LARUS BICIPS
- Avoid the hot dog shack's parking lot at all costs
POLAR RACCOON
PROCYON POLARIS
DANGEROUS!!
- Territorial and aggressiv
- Found all over the Mount-Royal park
GIANT OUTREMONT SQUIRREL
SCIRIUS GIGANTIS
- Chews on brake cables!

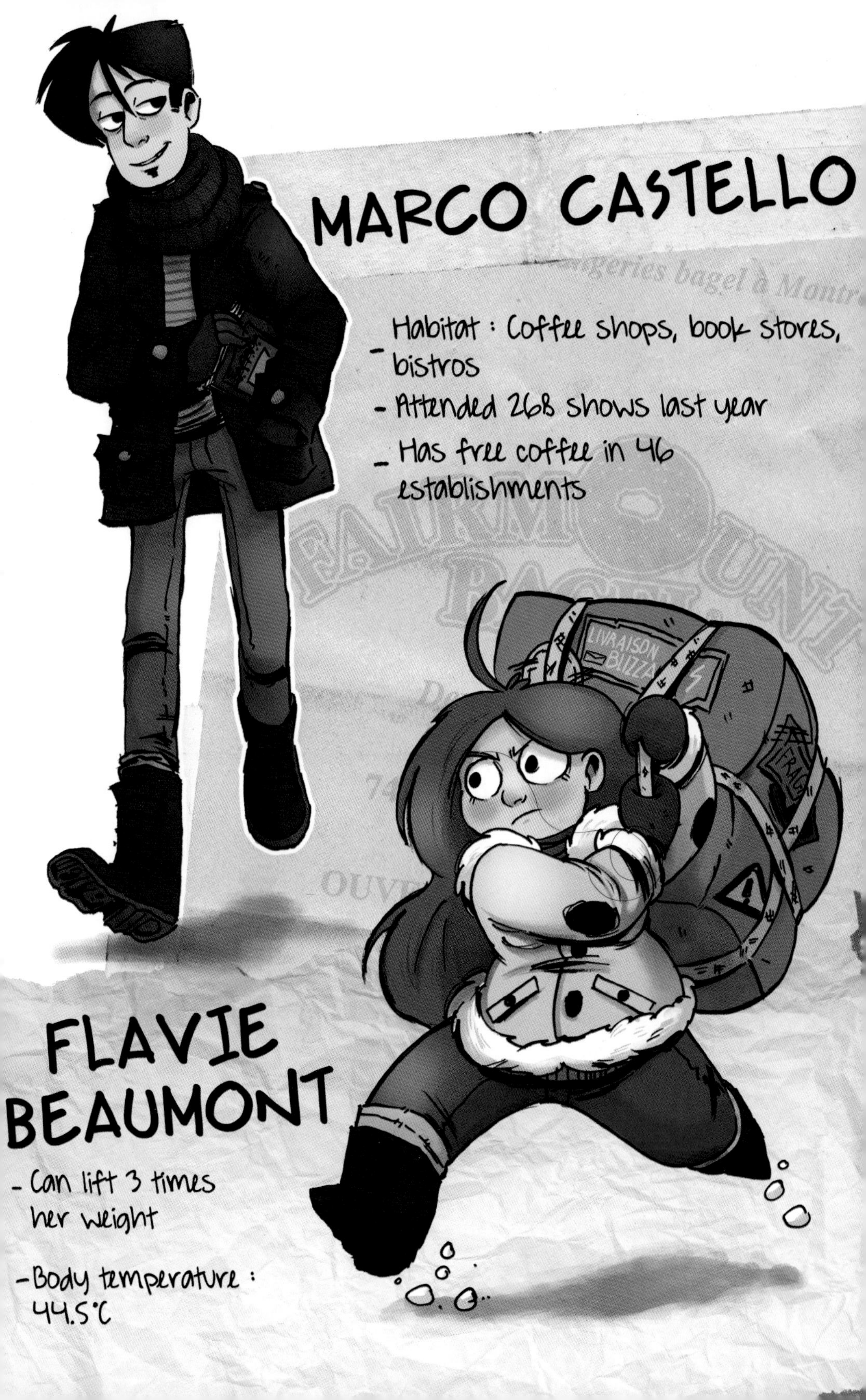
MARCO CASTELLO
- Habitat : Coffee shops, book stores, bistros
- Attended 268 shows last year
- Has free coffee in 46 establishments
LIVRAISON BLIZZA
FLAVIE BEAUMONT
- Can lift 3 times her weight
- Body temperature : 44.5°C

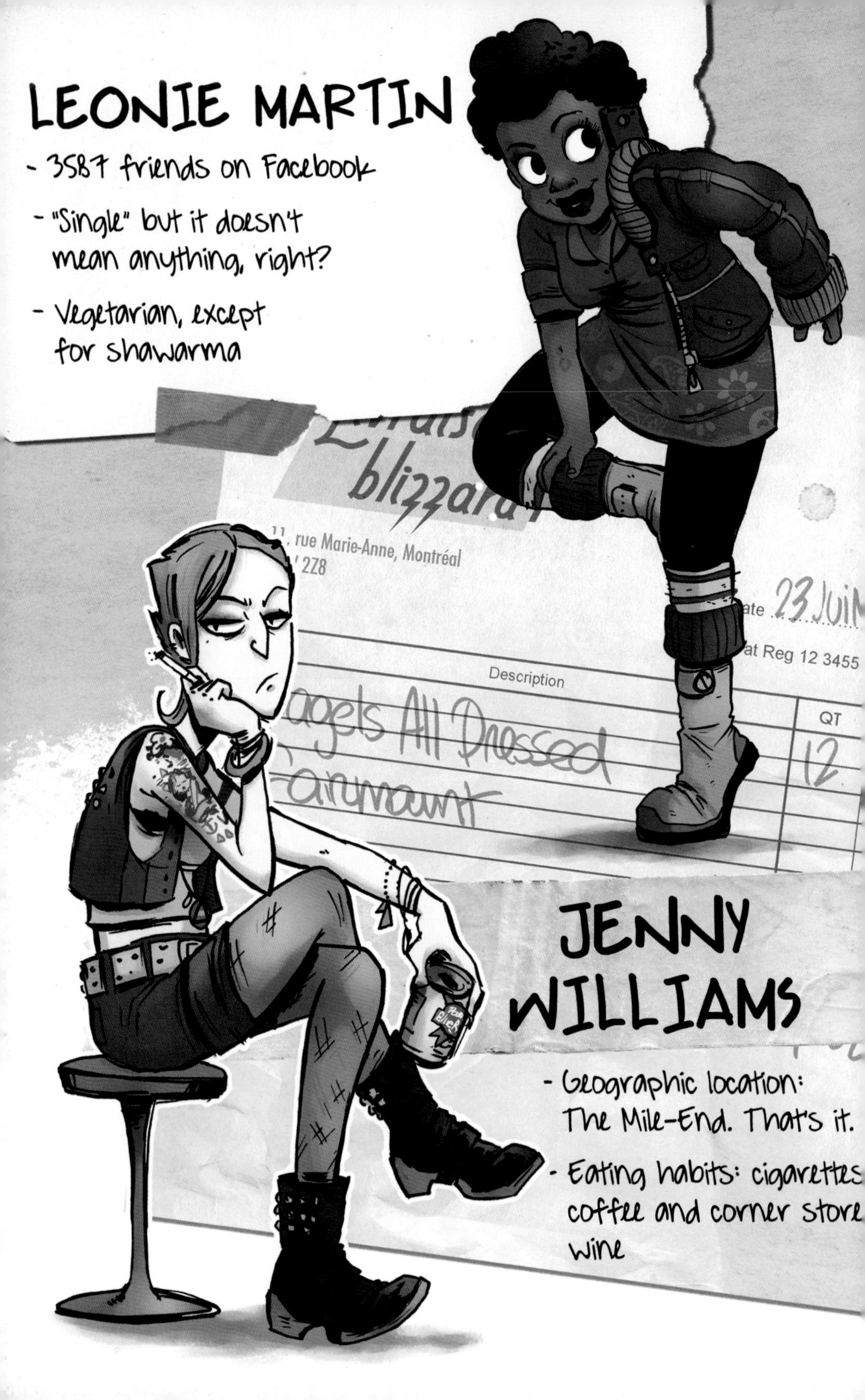
LEONIE MARTIN
- 3587 friends on Facebook
- "Single" but it doesn't mean anything, right?
- Vegetarian, except for shawarma
rue Marie-Anne, Montréal
Description
QT
12
JENNY WILLIAMS
- Geographic location: The Mile-End. That's it.
- Eating habits: cigarettes, coffee and corner store wine

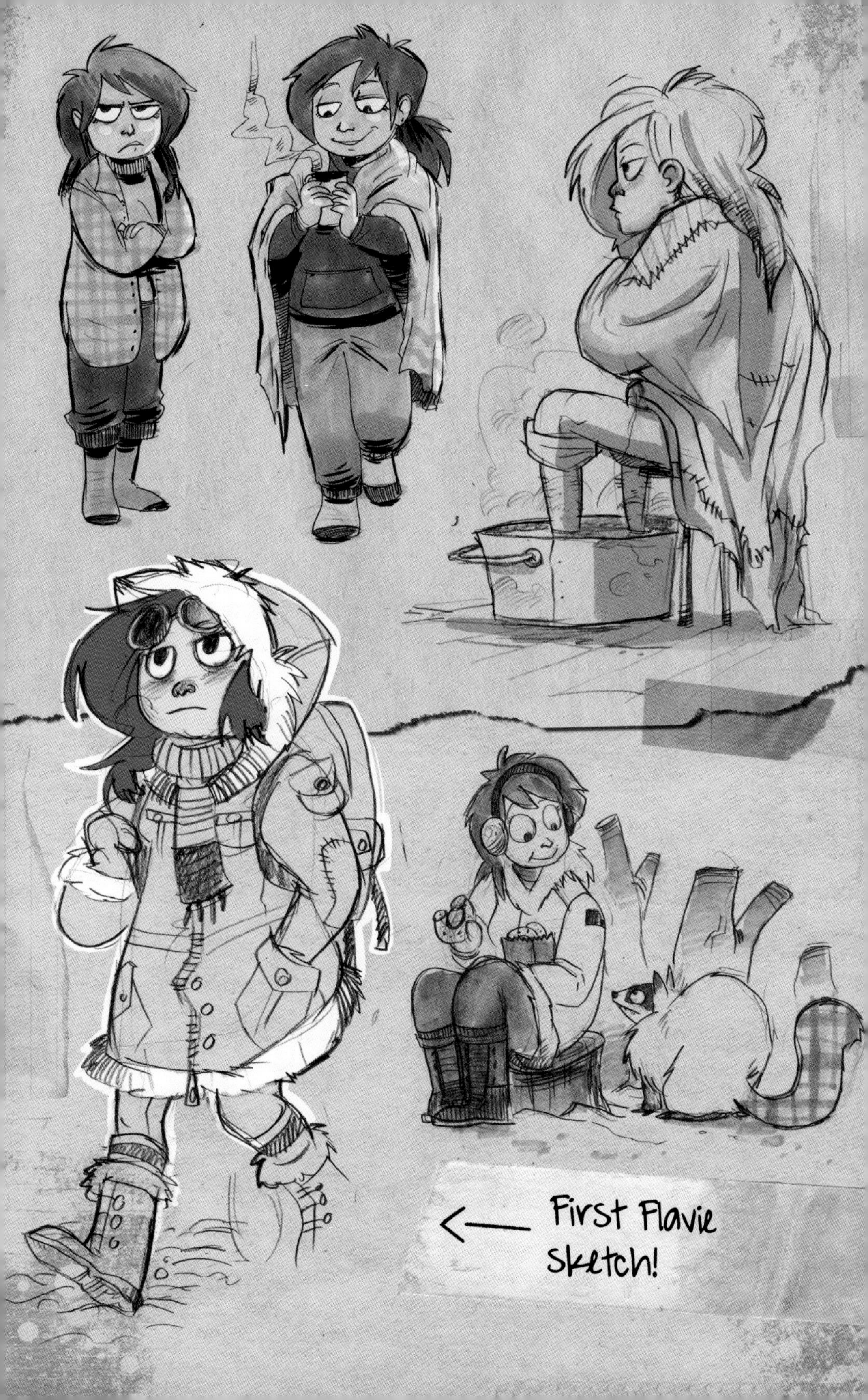
← First Flavie sketch!

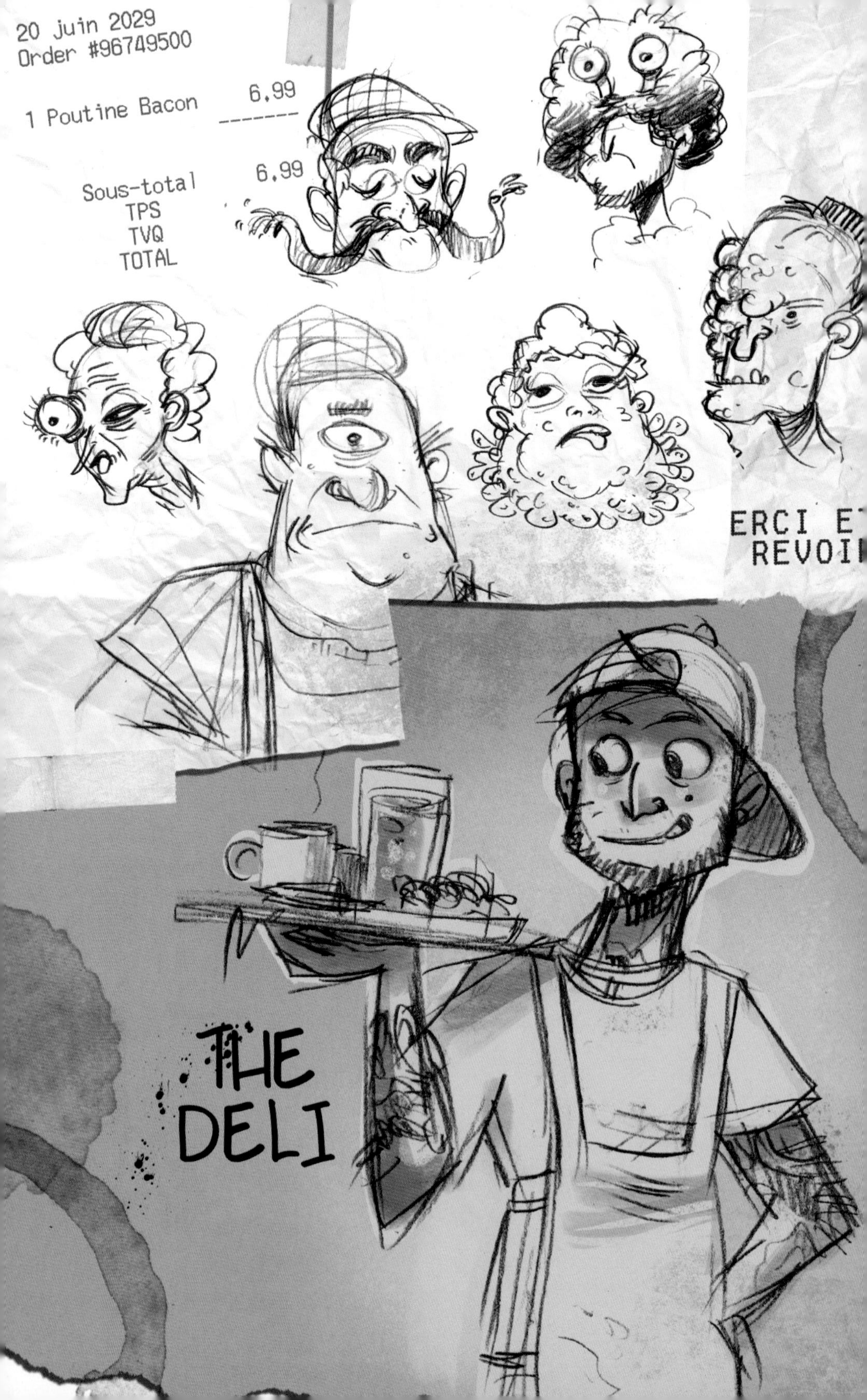

20 juin 2029
Order #96749500
1 Poutine Bacon 6,99
Sous-total 6,99
TPS
TVQ
TOTAL
ERCI ET
REVOI
THE DELI

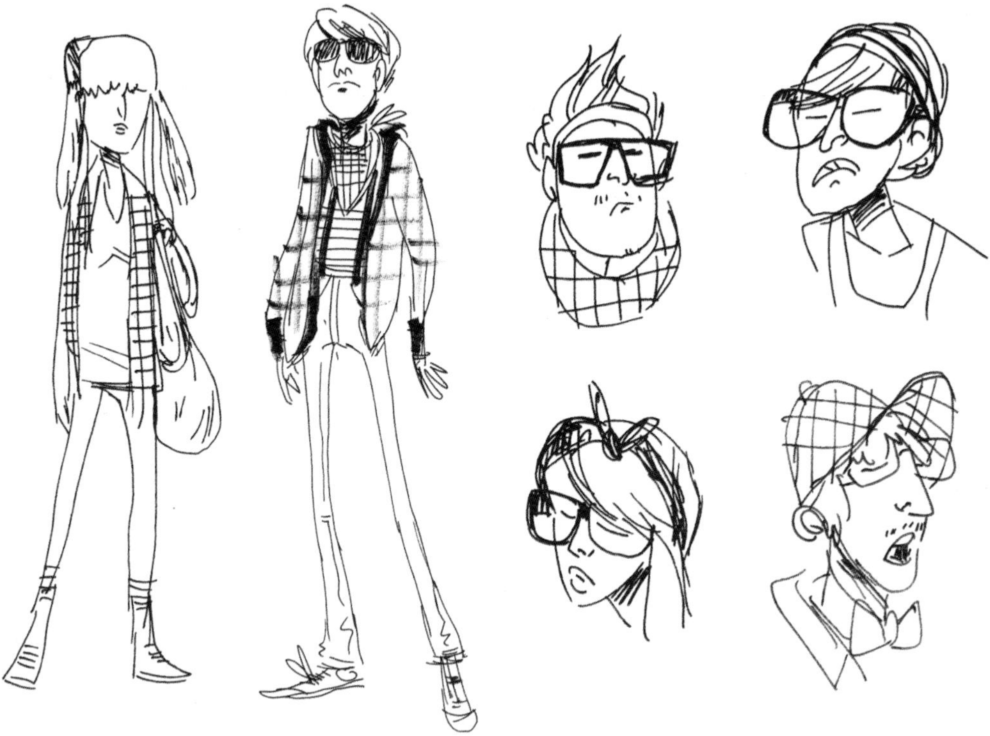

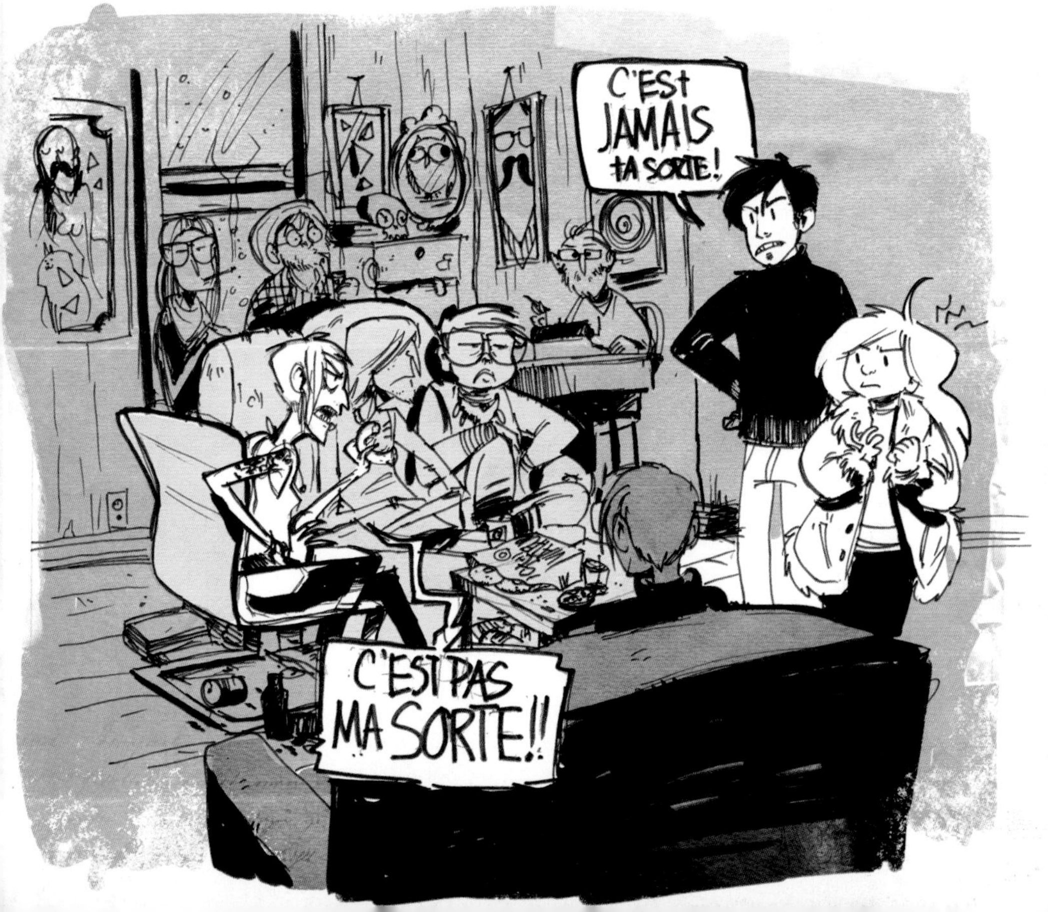
C'Est JAMAIS tA SORTE!
C'EST PAS MA SORTE!!

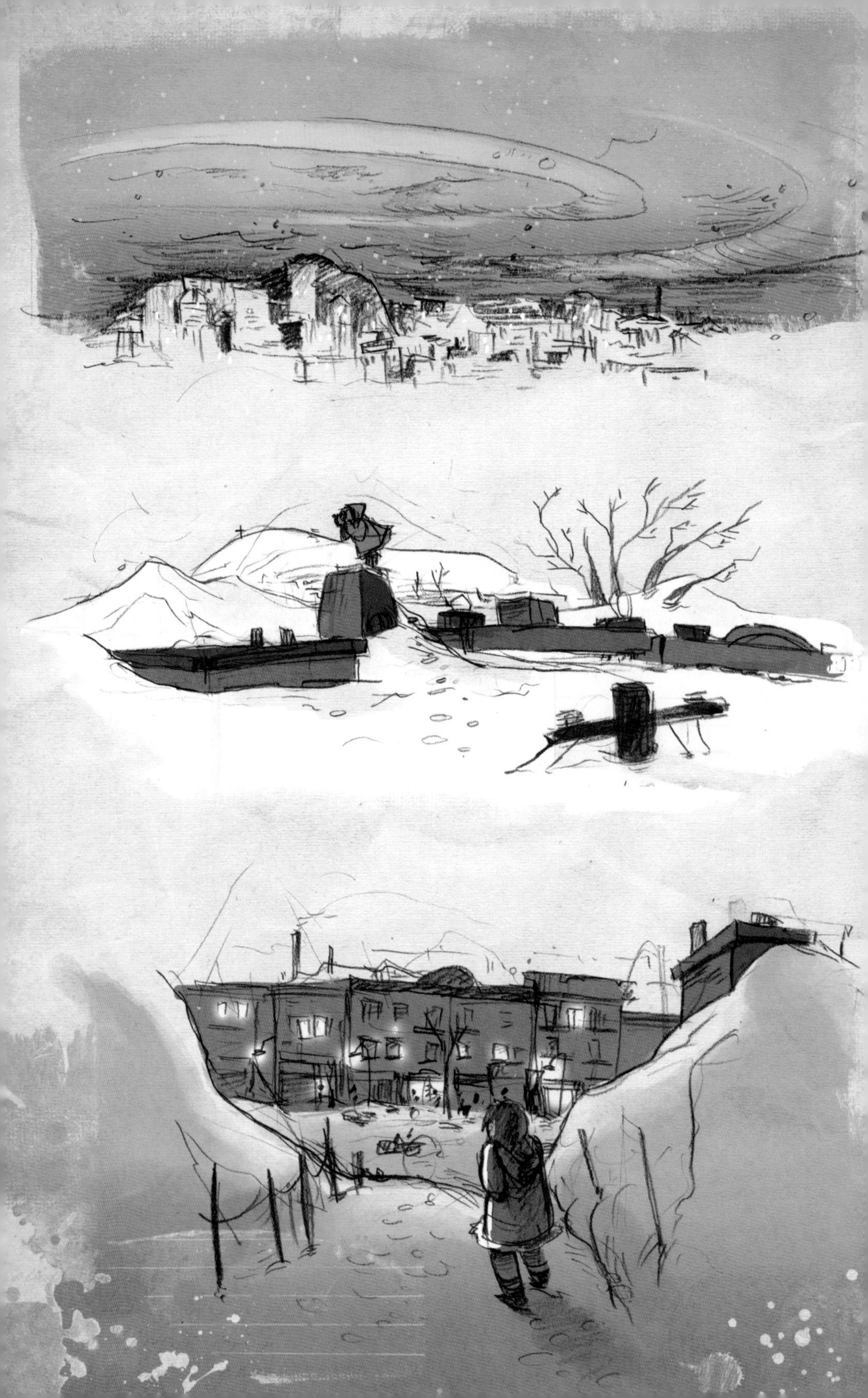

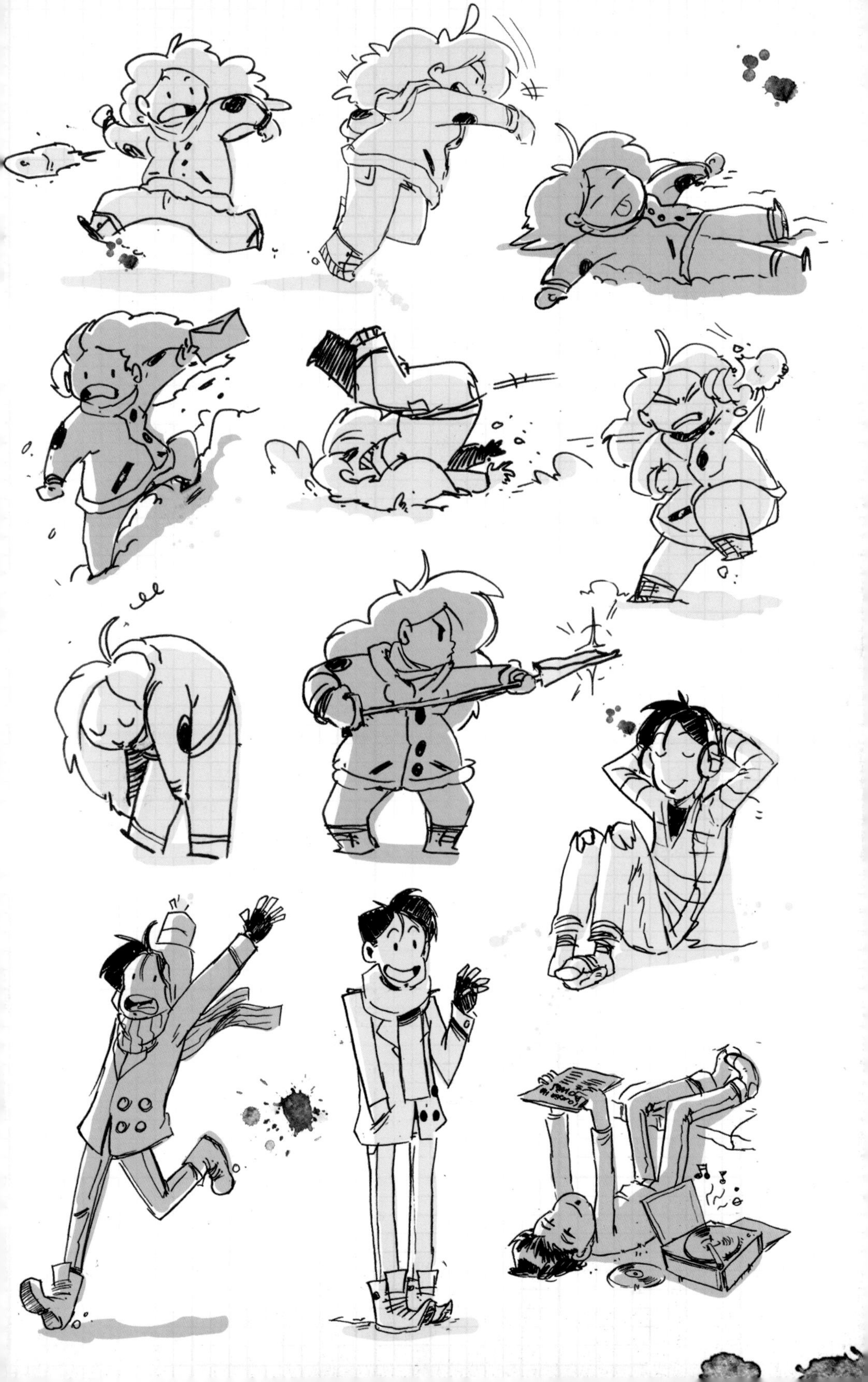

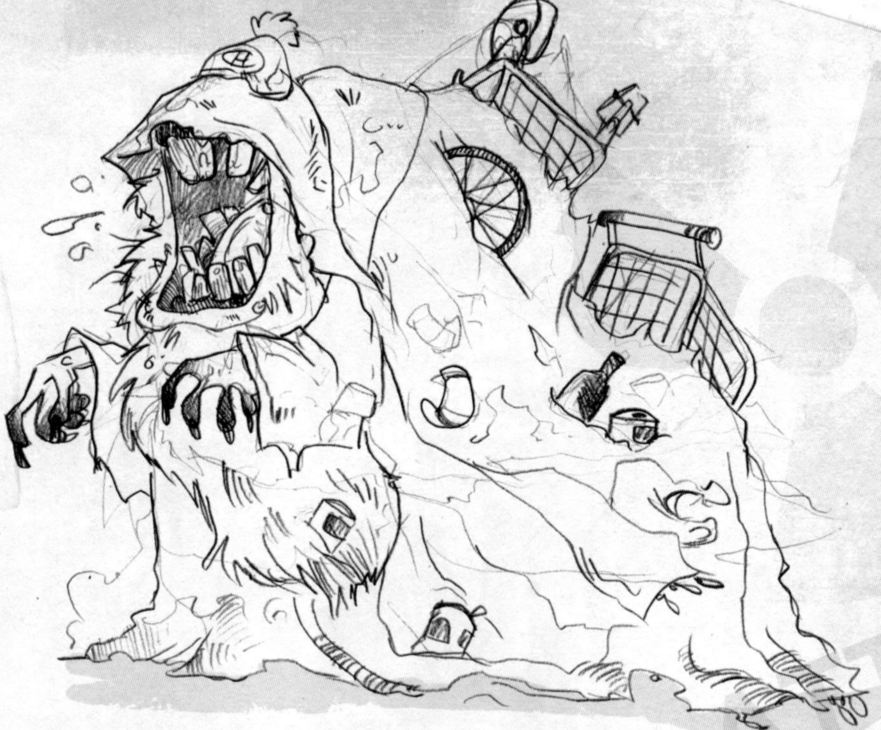

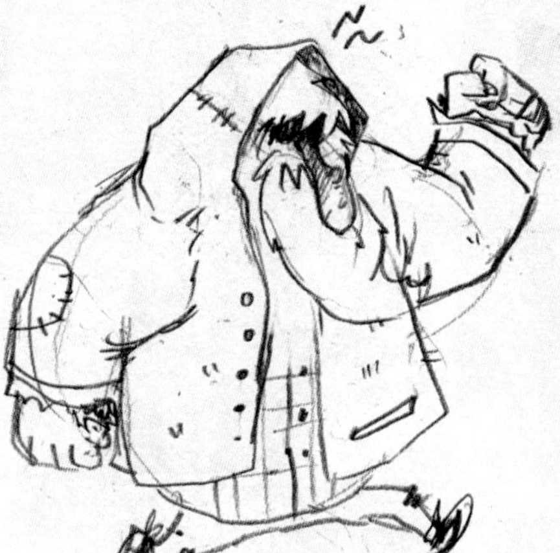

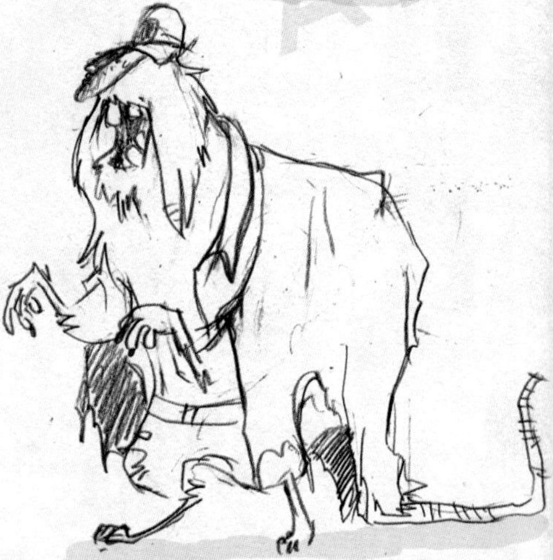

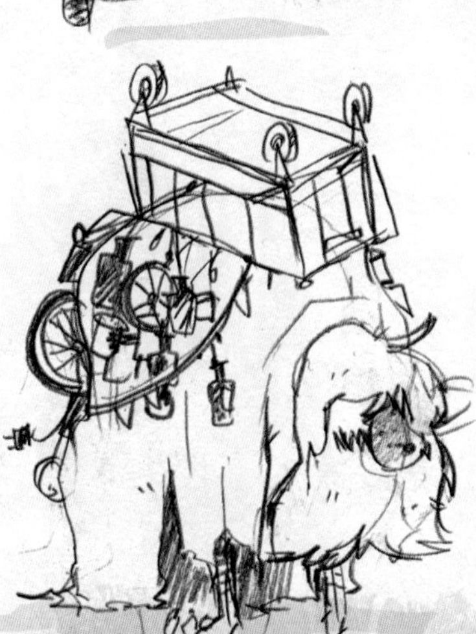

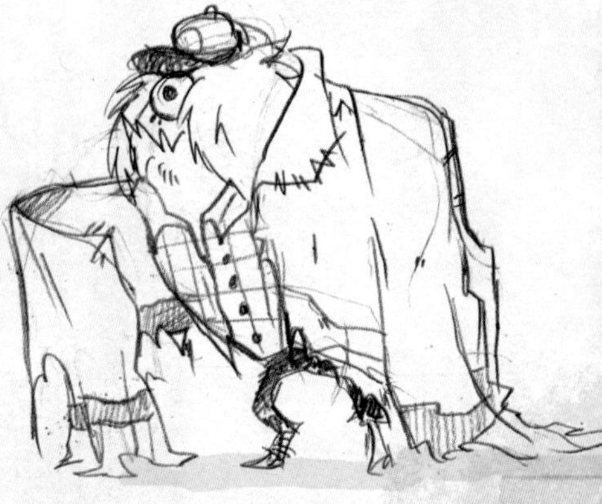

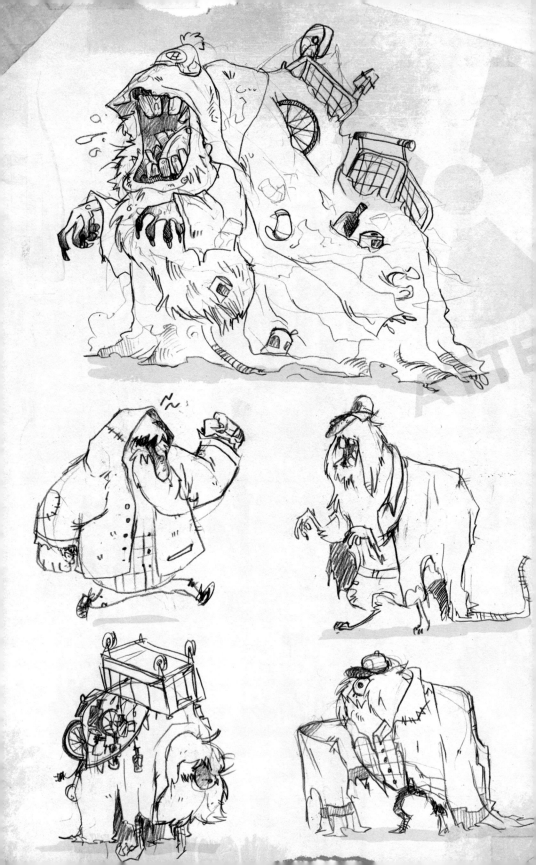

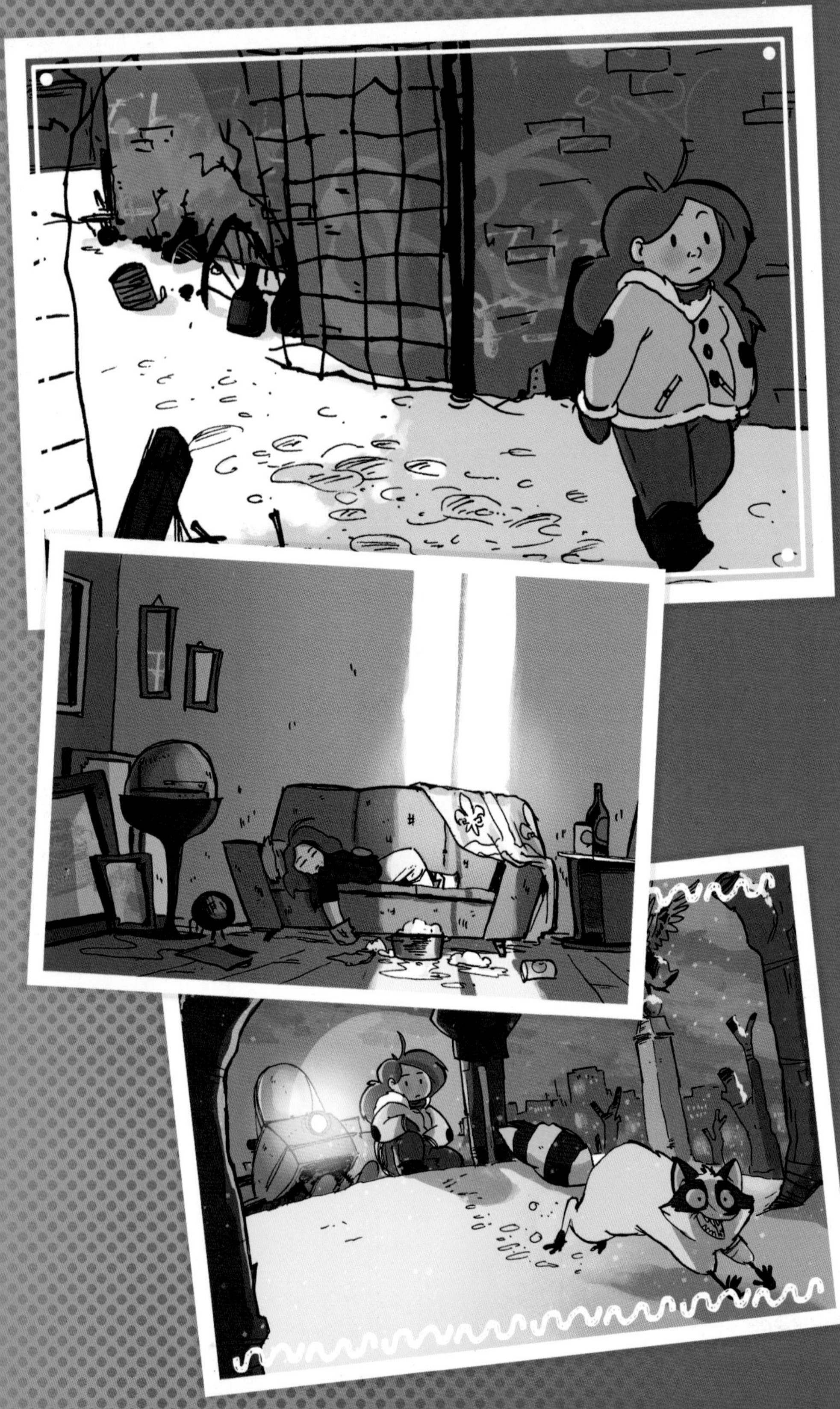

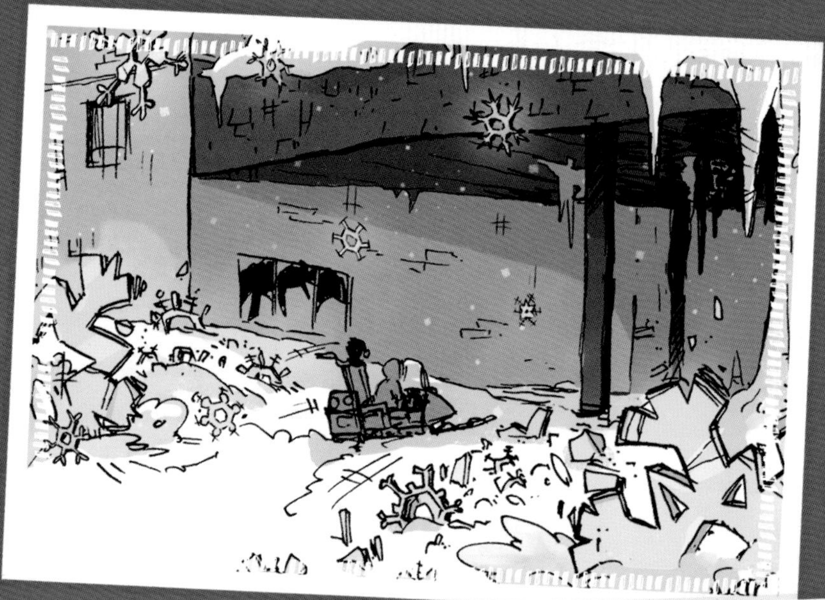

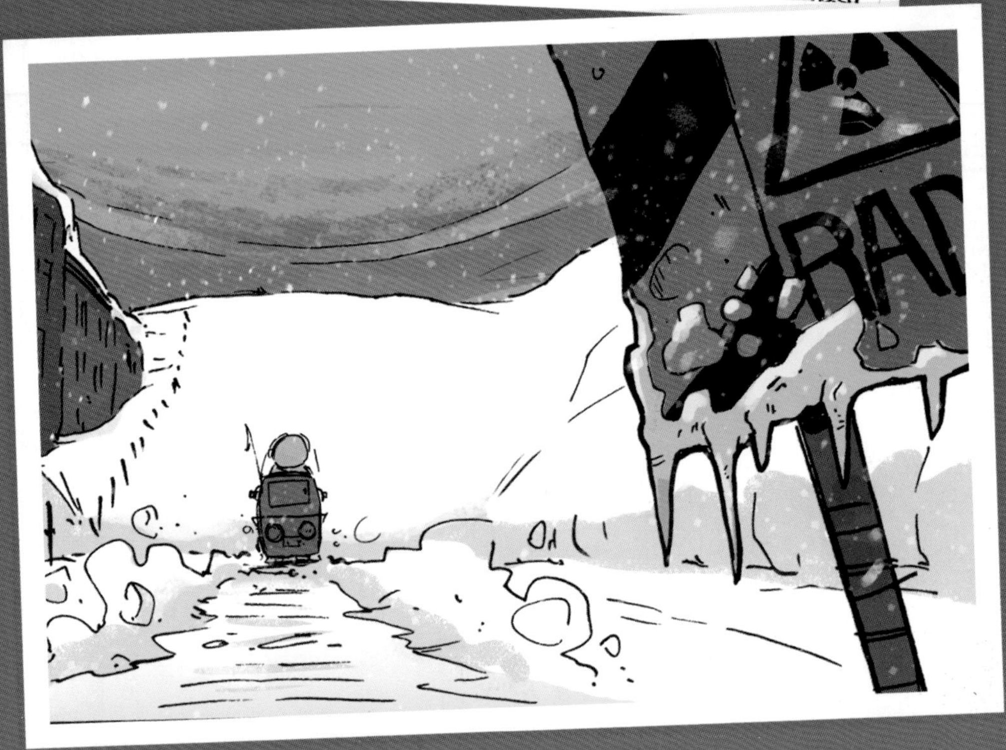

SEE YOU IN VOLUME TWO!

DISCOVER
ALL THE HITS

STEVENSON • ELLIS • WATTERS • ALLEN
LUMBERJANES
BEWARE THE KITTEN HOLY
NEW YORK TIMES BESTSELLING SERIES

Allison + Treiman + Cogar
GIANT DAYS
VOLUME ONE

From a writer of Disney's Moana
RIBON • FISH • PEER
SLAM!
VOLUME ONE

Hope Larson • Brittney Williams • Sarah Stern
GOLDIE VANCE
"Scoot over Nancy Drew..."
—Los Angeles Times
Volume One

THE BACKSTAGERS

TYSON HESSE'S
DIESEL
IGNITION

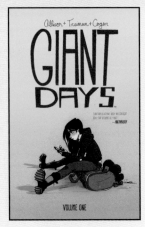

Lumberjanes
Noelle Stevenson, Shannon Watters, Grace Ellis, Brooke Allen, and Others
Volume 1: Beware the Kitten Holy
ISBN: 978-1-60886-687-8 | $14.99 US
Volume 2: Friendship to the Max
ISBN: 978-1-60886-737-0 | $14.99 US
Volume 3: A Terrible Plan
ISBN: 978-1-60886-803-2 | $14.99 US
Volume 4: Out of Time
ISBN: 978-1-60886-860-5 | $14.99 US
Volume 5: Band Together
ISBN: 978-1-60886-919-0 | $14.99 US

Giant Days
John Allison, Lissa Treiman, Max Sarin
Volume 1
ISBN: 978-1-60886-789-9 | $9.99 US
Volume 2
ISBN: 978-1-60886-804-9 | $14.99 US
Volume 3
ISBN: 978-1-60886-851-3 | $14.99 US

Jonesy
Sam Humphries, Caitlin Rose Boyle
Volume 1
ISBN: 978-1-60886-883-4 | $9.99 US
Volume 2
ISBN: 978-1-60886-999-2 | $14.99 US

Slam!
Pamela Ribon, Veronica Fish, Brittany Peer
Volume 1
ISBN: 978-1-68415-004-5 | $14.99 US

Goldie Vance
Hope Larson, Brittney Williams
Volume 1
ISBN: 978-1-60886-898-8 | $9.99 US
Volume 2
ISBN: 978-1-60886-974-9 | $14.99 US

The Backstagers
James Tynion IV, Rian Sygh
Volume 1
ISBN: 978-1-60886-993-0 | $14.99 US

Tyson Hesse's Diesel: Ignition
Tyson Hesse
ISBN: 978-1-60886-907-7 | $14.99 US

Coady & The Creepies
Liz Prince, Amanda Kirk, Hannah Fisher
ISBN: 978-1-68415-029-8 | $14.99 US

BOOM! BOX

AVAILABLE AT YOUR LOCAL COMICS SHOP AND BOOKSTORE
To find a comics shop in your area, call 1-888-266-4226
WWW.**BOOM-STUDIOS**.COM